THE
TRAIL WALKING
HANDBOOK

THE
TRAIL WALKING
HANDBOOK

CLIVE TULLY

BROCKHAMPTON PRESS
LONDON

First Published 1994 by
Blandford
Wellington House
125 Strand
LONDON
WC2R 0BB

A Cassell Imprint
Copyright © Clive Tully 1994 and 1995

ISBN 1 86019 8627

Printed at Oriental Press, Dubai, U.A.E.

This edition published 1998 by Brockhampton Press,
a member of Hodder Headline PLC Group

Acknowledgements

MANY OF THE PHOTOGRAPHS come from my own wildly
disorganized collection, but the breadth of picture subjects is
down to the assistance of the following, many of whom
provided photographs at extremely short notice.

CLIVE TULLY

BERGHAUS LTD.
BRASHER BOOT COMPANY
BURTON MCCALL LTD.
CASCADE DESIGNS
CEBE
CRAGHOPPERS LTD.
EPPIK
EUROPA SPORT
FIELD & TREK PLC
FIRST ASCENT
GIFFARD NEWTON LTD.
ALAN HINKES
KARRIMOR INTERNATIONAL LTD.
LINE 7
ALLCORD LTD.
LOWE ALPINE
MICROWRITER LTD.
ADE MILLER
TOBY MOLINS
MORRIS NICHOLSON CARTWRIGHT LTD.
MOUNTAIN EQUIPMENT
MSR
NIKON UK LTD.
DAVID OSWIN
PHOENIX MOUNTAINEERING LTD.
PRE-MAC (KENT) LTD.
RISOL LTD.
ROHAN DESIGNS PLC
SILVA (UK) LTD.
SPRAYWAY LTD.
THE NORTH FACE
JOHN TAYLOR
RAY WOOD
W. L. GORE AND ASSOCIATES LTD.
JACK WOLFSKIN ADVENTURE EQUIPMENT LTD.

Contents

CHAPTER 1

Introduction to Trailwalking

by Clive Tully

WALKING is the most popular leisure activity in the UK. You might not think so if you looked at the amount of money that's spent on facilities for walkers, compared with, say, the amount the government pumps into the arts. Even compared to the second most popular sporting leisure pastime, swimming, the funding available to promote walking, and to protect those areas where walking is popular, is pretty thin.

In places, the popularity of walking has outstripped the available resources for keeping paths in good order. But despite all that, millions happily wander along quiet footpaths, enjoying fresh air, good views and healthy exercise.

Of course, walking is something which comes naturally to most of us – after all, we've been doing it since we were toddlers! For many, the first attempt at something which doesn't involve tarmac or concrete underfoot might be a nature trail. Way-marked trails abound in forests, on nature reserves, in National Parks. But how do you graduate? How do you become more proficient? If your sense of adventure starts leading you to more challenging walks, in wilder country where you don't have the immediate cop-out of a road within half a mile, you're already on your way.

This, if anything, is the difference between the recreational walker happy to stroll along undemanding footpaths, and you – the Trail Walker. An important step in the progression is learning how to use a map and compass. Once you can safely navigate your way through bad weather and featureless terrain, you're no longer bound by signposts, cairns and the like – which can often be more confusing than helpful. Not that you're likely to go off-track all that much more. But at least you learn to appreciate what taking a different route can

mean and, at the very least, you can still find your way when the route marked on the map as a distinct line disappears before your eyes!

I discovered the pleasure of walking at an early age. I lived at the very edge of a town called Baden, in Switzerland. My brother and I were able to cross the road from our apartment block, and head straight into a network of tracks taking us for miles across forested hills. We'd wander endlessly in the summer, tramping up and down forestry tracks. And in winter, wrapped up warm and shod in wellington boots, we'd drag our Davos sledge on endless expeditions, towing it on the uphill stretches and letting gravity take over on the downhill ones. But after I returned to England it was a good 15 years before I rediscovered the fun of walking in wild country. It's a pity I didn't rediscover it earlier – but better late than never!

These days, I spend much of my time walking in different countries worldwide, sampling some of the incredible variety that's on offer. But while I'm always interested in seeking out new horizons, I'm as happy tramping around the Peak District, or the Yorkshire Dales, where I did much of my early walking before my career as an outdoors and travel writer took off. And I wouldn't dream of criticizing those people I've met who are quite happy to restrict their walking to one or two areas of the UK. They've got to know the intimate details of the landscape in a way I can never expect to match.

But if my opening words to this introduction sounded a touch harsh, rather than immediately leaping into the boundless joys of walking, it's because of the following facts. The last ten years or so have seen walking become respectable, partly because of the heightened interest in all things promoting better health. And you can't ignore the fact that many may well be attracted to walking as a sport now that technology has well and truly established itself in clothing and equipment. The stereotype of a bearded walker with tartan shirt, tweed

Trekking amidst dramatic mountains – the dream of any trail walker.

breeches and Mars bar is well and truly at the bottom of the wardrobe.

It's become a good hook for attracting tourism, too. While people have been enjoying walking holidays for years, there's an increasing number of companies offering walking and trekking holidays, from undemanding strolls along waymarked trails to major mountain treks requiring not just proficiency but stamina as well.

And all of this does make me worry slightly. I have friends in the travel industry who fondly remember Torremolinos, when it was an attractive

Readjust your lacing if need be to maintain optimum foot comfort.

little village, before the developers moved in. And if you think of the mess that some popular walking spots are in, you may understand my anxiety. Some people seem to have this urge to 'tame' the wilderness, and they're the ones I'd rather see lying cooking on a beach on the Costa del Sol.

I'm sometimes asked whether you need any special attributes to enjoy walking or whether there are any special exercises to get you in trim for it. The short answer is that provided you recognize your limits, and don't push yourself too far, any erect biped can do it! And as for keeping in trim for it, all you have to do is go out and walk. I used to go running, but I found it doing nasty things to my knees. You get no such problems with walking.

Having said that, you might want to increase your fitness for a trekking holiday – certainly a good idea if you want to get the most out of it. The first thing I did after giving up a 'real' job to become a writer was go on a 300-mile (480km) walk from coast to coast across the Scottish Highlands. It was a big progression from the shorter backpacking trips I was used to, and the one thing which stood me in good stead – before I left the office job – was to run up and down the stairs in the six-storey office building several times every day!

The aim of *The Trail Walking Handbook* is to provide you with everything you need to know to set you off in the right direction. It covers everything from the basic details of navigating with a map and compass, and first aid, to the clothing and equipment which add to both enjoyment and safety. A summer stroll along a footpath not far from the car park might not demand much in the way of clothing or equipment. But change the season, the altitude, or simply move further away from civilization, and you have a different story altogether.

Since its first issue in July 1990, *Trail Walker* magazine has been a continuing success story, and I am indeed fortunate to have been able to call on so many of the magazine's regular contributors to put together *The Trail Walking Handbook*.

Dr. Christine Fenn is a nutritionist who works as consultant to the British Olympic cross-country and biathlon ski teams, the European Space Agency, and the British Antarctic Survey. She was adviser to the British 40th anniversary Everest expedition, trekking with the climbers to base camp.

Paddy Dillon's knowledge of the trails in the UK and Ireland is unrivalled. If there's a path in these countries – Paddy's walked it!

Steve Cooling is a teacher who, with his wife Trish, took a year off work to walk round the world. Well, walk in different parts around the world, to be more precise.

Getting the correct fit is essential for walking comfort.

Roland Smith is information officer for the Peak National Park. But with a distinguished background in journalism, Roly still turns out books and writes regularly for the outdoors press.

Terry Storry spent ten years as an outdoors instructor at Plas y Brenin, the Sports Council's National Centre for Mountain Sports in Snowdonia. He is a qualified mountain and canoe guide.

Bill O'Connor contributed Chapter 8 on scrambling. An accomplished climber and photographer, Bill's photographs grace many an upmarket equipment manufacturer's brochures.

Now at *Trail Walker* magazine, **Graham Thompson** worked for several years as a Youth Hostel warden in the Lake District, taking advantage of every spare moment to walk and backpack in the Lakeland mountains.

Hugh Westacott is well known as an author of walking books and guides. He also runs a company called Rucksack Holidays, which brings Americans to Britain for walking holidays.

Alan Hinkes has all the qualifications to be a mountaineering legend. He's made numerous ascents in the Alps, and taken part in over 20 expeditions to the Himalaya. And he's reached more 26 000-ft (8000-m) summits than any other climber in the UK. He's a qualified British mountain guide, so if you want someone to guide you up Everest, Alan's your man.

And finally, there's me. I've been writing about walking equipment since 1979 and I've plodded a fair few trails in different parts of the world. There are still plenty more for me to discover and, if *The Trail Walking Handbook* inspires you to seek out a few for yourself, who knows – we might just bump into each other somewhere. But then again – in the nicest possible way – I rather hope we don't!

CHAPTER **2**

Nutrition for Endurance Exercise

What to eat to keep you on the energy trail

by Christine Fenn

WHY IS IT that some people can charge up a hill, burning up the trail, while others struggle to get to the top? Have you ever felt tired and sluggish, your legs like lead . . . and that's at the beginning of the walk? Not enough energy perhaps? You probably do have enough energy, but may be lacking in the right type of energy, which is crucial for strenuous exercise.

The amount of energy (measured in calories) that you need will obviously depend on how active you are. A day in the hills burns up a lot more calories than sitting reading this book or planning your route. The exact amount of energy that you will need depends upon several factors, such as how heavy you are, how heavy your pack is, how much uphill walking you will be doing, and if you will be walking against the wind or in deep snow. Carrying a heavy load on your back is very practical, as it lets you stuff your hands in your pockets when it's cold, but luckily it is also the most energy efficient way of bearing weight. If you carried the contents of your pack in shopping bags, your energy needs would be higher.

CALORIES STORED IN THE BODY

As an average figure, most men need about 3500 calories, and women (who tend to be smaller and have a different body composition compared with men) will need 2500 calories of energy each day. However, we already have a substantial amount of calories stored in the body.

You have 3 energy stores in your body – protein, fat and carbohydrate. There is a huge potential store of protein but only in extreme circumstances, such as starvation, does the body break down its protein store (muscle), to use as an energy source. The choice of fuel to burn to provide energy then comes down to two sources – fat and carbohydrate. You can see from the table that you have a relatively small store of carbohydrate, but a much greater store of fat. Both fat and carbohydrate can be burnt by the body to provide energy, but what determines which fuel is used?

Energy stores in the body

	Mr Average 11 stone (70kg)	Ms Average 9 stone (57kg)
Fat	75 600 calories	102 000 calories
Protein	24 000 calories	16 000 calories
Carbohydrate	1200 calories	850 calories

Different fuels are used to provide energy, depending on the type of activity being undertaken. One of the main factors that determines which fuel is burnt during exercise is the intensity of the exercise (another is how well trained your muscles are). Energy is released from fat relatively slowly, and is therefore used to fuel low intensity activities such as sitting reading this book or strolling along the beach. More strenuous exercise, such as fast walking with a pack or pounding up a hill requires a much faster supply of energy, and this is provided by burning carbohydrate.

You have a limited amount of carbohydrate stored in your body (approximately 1200 calories for men and 850 for women) and, when this has been used up, fatigue sets in and you just have to slow down. That's when your legs feel heavy and it's a real struggle to get to the top.

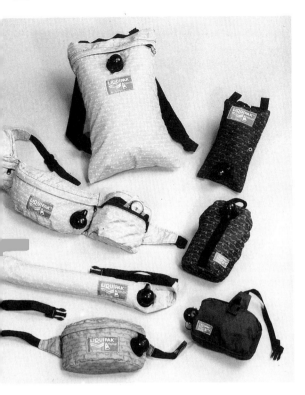

Water carrying has progressed beyond plastic bottles. The Liquipak range of flexible liquid carriers.

There are many causes of fatigue, but running out of carbohydrate is one of them. Carbohydrate can be seen as the jet-fuel in the body which can be ignited to provide a fast supply of energy. But like jet-fuel, it is used up rapidly, and must be replaced in order to maintain speed and performance. Fat is at the other end of the spectrum as the peat-burner, offering a prolonged, steady source of energy, of which there is a good supply to keep things ticking over.

Pounding over the hills with a pack on your back is a jet-fuelled activity. When the jet-fuel runs out you have an alternative supply of energy from the peat-burner to fall back on, but this cannot provide the same type of powerful energy, so, if you want to keep going, you just have to slow down. Carbohydrate is your jet-fuel, and you have to know where to get it at each meal.

As shown in the table, there is a large amount of energy in the body stored as fat. The 75 000 calorie store in men is equivalent to 41 tubs of margarine or butter, while women have the equivalent of 55 tubs! Some of this fat is useful. It insulates and pro-

tects your internal organs, such as your kidneys, from cold and damage. Next time you fall on your rucksack, packed with flask, tins of sardines and other hard lumpy objects, you can be thankful to your fat stores for softening the blow!

CONQUERING FATIGUE – CARBOHYRDRATE CAN!

Most people eat enough energy (in terms of calories), but consuming enough carbohydrate at each meal can help conquer fatigue, and help you recover from a strenuous day in the hills.

Breakfast is the easiest way of getting started on the carbohydrates – and you need it. After eight hours' sleep your brain has used up your carbohydrate stores, so you need to replace this fuel before you head for the hills. If you can't face breakfast, then pack extra scones and sandwiches for mid-morning by which time you will have joined the rest of the human race – your muscles will let you know when they want feeding. But what do you eat during the day to keep up your carbohydrate intake?

Refuelling en Route

Most people think of sugar when their energy levels are falling, and reach for a well-known chocolate bar. Sugar is a type of carbohydrate and will give you a rapid energy fix, but it will also produce a rapid fall in your energy levels because of its effect on insulin. If you fill your rucksack with sweets and chocolate, you will put yourself on a roller-coaster of energy highs and lows. You'll also be packing your false teeth in future, as eating chocolate and toffee is the best way to rot your nashers!

Another problem with sugary foods is that they contain sugar – and not much else. You miss out on essential vitamins and minerals. The B vitamins, such as riboflavin and thiamine, are especially important during strenuous exercise, as they provide the spark to release the energy from carbohydrate. Even if you are stocked full of jet-fuel, if you don't have the B vitamins to act as the ignition key, that fuel will be useless!

Recovery fuel

At the end of the day, and especially if you are walking or backpacking over several days, you must plan your evening meal to refill your carbohydrate stores. The best-quality carbohydrate foods are the starchy ones such as bread, pasta, rice, root vegetables, peas, baked beans and sweetcorn. These are the foods to eat to recover your jet-fuel, ready for the next day's challenge. Masses of pasta or rice, with a small amount of meat or tomato sauce, has lots of carbohydrate and is easy to prepare, especially if the members' kitchen at the Youth Hostel is just about to close, or you are fighting for the last ring on the burner in a bothy.

If you base your diet on these foods, there is an added pay-off. A diet for peak performance is a healthy diet, which will help to protect you from illnesses such as cancer and heart disease.

How high is a high carbohydrate diet? You need to eat at least eat half (50 per cent), of your energy as carbohydrate. This can mean quite a change in your diet, as most people stuff themselves with greasy and fatty foods, and don't have much room for filling carbohydrate! If your energy requirement is 3500 calories each day, then half of this as carbohydrate is 16oz (460g). Check the following list of carbohydrate foods to see how far along the energy trail you are.

CARBOHYDRATE CONTENT OF FOODS

Food	Amount	Ounces (Grams) of carbohydrate	
Brown rice, boiled	1 serving	2	(53)
Deep-pan pizza	1 slice	1	(40)
Hot cross bun	1	1	(38)
Baked potato	1 medium	1	(35)
Spaghetti, boiled	small serving	1	(34)
Malt loaf	2 slices	1	(34)
Weetabix	2 biscuits	1	(31)
Milk, semi-skimmed	1 pint	1	(29)
Wholemeal bread roll	1	1	(27)
Wholemeal fruit scone	1	¾	(24)
Raisins/sultanas	2 handfuls	¾	(23)
Cornflakes	small bowl	¾	(21)
Baked beans in tom. sauce	small can	¾	(21)
Porridge	small bowl	½	(18)
Banana	1	½	(15)
Apple	1	¼	(11)

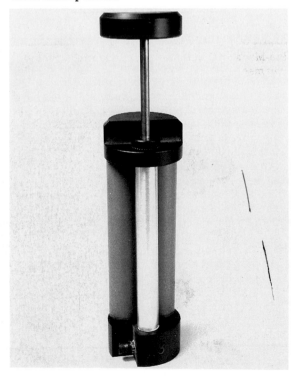

The Pre-Mac Trekker Travel Well, a handy pocket-sized water purifier.

DO'S AND DON'TS FOR YOUR LUNCH-BOX.

Do's

● **Do** take thick slices of bread with small amounts of fatty fillings, such as meat or cheese.
● **Do** take high carbohydrate fillings for your sandwiches: banana and honey, lettuce and Marmite, jam or marmalade are ideal.
● **Do** go easy on the butter: fish paste, meat paste, mayonnaise and tomatoes give moistness without the fat.
● **Do** take hot soup or tea/coffee to warm you up. It's always colder than you think at the highest point on your walk. More food won't warm you up, but hot food will.
● **Do** take high carbohydrate snacks with you. Scones, pancakes, fruit cake, malt loaf, dried apricots and raisins, and muesli fruit bars will satisfy the snack attack.

Don'ts

● **Don't** miss out on breakfast. You need to keep your body topped up with jet-fuel, and breakfast is an easy way to load up on carbohydrates.

- **Don't** walk with someone who has missed breakfast, since they will end up eating the extra food that you brought!
- **Don't** take fatty foods such as pork pies, Cornish pasties, lumps of cheese or chunks of the Sunday roast with you. Fatty foods take hours to digest, and will still be in your stomach when you have returned to civilization and have your feet up in the pub.
- **Don't** take a rucksack full of chocolate and sweets. You will have energy highs and lows all day. Your body can't cope with these energy swings. Enjoy chocolate and biscuits along with starchy carbohydrate foods, not instead of them.

HOW MUCH ENERGY DO YOU NEED?

The energy cost of trail walking

Activity	calories per hour
Brisk walking, 4mph (6kph), on flat ground, no pack	360
Walking, 4mph (6kph), 5% uphill gradient, no pack	540
Walking, 4mph (6kph), 5% uphill gradient, with 44lb (20kg) pack	720
Looking at the scenery/bird watching/photos/ eating a high carbohydrate lunch	120
Walking, 2mph (3kph), on flat ground with a 70lb (32kg) pack	480
Walking downhill, with a 70lb (32kg) pack	300
Walking in deep snow, no pack	540

All figures are based on an average 11 stone (70kg) man. The energy cost for each activity will be less for women and lighter men.

EAT WELL – VEGETARIAN STYLE

Stoking up before a day in the hills can mean tucking into eggs, bacon and sausage for breakfast, and taking a food box stocked with ham sandwiches and pork pies. This combination is not ideal, however, because overall it contains too much fat, and it would, of course, be totally unsuitable for a vegetarian. An increasing number of adults are now leaning towards a vegetarian diet, and maybe you, or your fellow walkers, are giving the outdated 'meat and two veg' meal a body swerve?

Depending on which survey you read, vegetarians account for anything between 3 and 7 per cent of the British population – that's up to 3 million people! As a group in general, vegetarians are more likely to be young than old, female than male, and live in England rather than Wales or Scotland. Another characteristic of vegetarians is that they tend to be health conscious – so the chances are they'll be out there in the hills getting lungfuls of fresh air and keeping fit.

Vegetarianism is a broad term and is used to describe a range of eating patterns with varying degrees of restrictions. A vast number of the world's population exclude certain meats and animal products for religious reasons. There are many other cultural, social, philosophical and economic reasons why individuals choose to restrict their eating, so the term vegetarian tends to cover many different diets for example, semi- or demi-vegetarians simply avoid red meat, while fruitarians (an extreme form of vegetarianism), avoid all foods of animal origin, and also pulses and cereals.

Pre-Mac's PWP water purifier, a robust gravity-fed unit made for extended use.

On the hands, on the face, on the feet. A splash of water revives any walker. Black Forest.

There is some evidence to suggest that vegetarians are more healthy compared with meat eaters, but this may be due to other reasons apart from diet. Vegetarians tend to be non-smokers, take more exercise and be more aware of what they eat. However, a vegetarian diet is not automatically healthy – a meal of fried eggs and chips, apple pie and ice-cream would not score highly in the health stakes if eaten every day. Most adult vegetarians, however, tend to include wholefood, natural and fresh foods in their diet.

Also, a survey carried out in 1990 by the Releat Company, to identify the reasons why people followed a vegetarian diet, showed that health came out tops, followed by financial, taste and moral issues. The survey didn't ask how many were walkers, but there are certainly plenty of foods suitable for vegetarian trail walkers.

As with any pattern of eating, whether or not a vegetarian diet provides the correct balance of nutrients will depend on the range and amounts of foods chosen. A vegetarian diet based on pasta, pulses, rice, potatoes and bread with smaller amounts of cheese, eggs and dairy foods is ideal for heading off into the hills. Dehydrated meals based on textured vegetable protein (TVP) are suitable for vegetarians, easy to prepare in a Youth Hostel, and useful to refuel your carbohydrate energy stores ready for the next day. A new vegetarian protein food called 'Quorn' is now available and is particularly useful if you like the texture of meat chunks.

Breakfast Feast

Winter walking in deep snow can use as much as 540 calories per hour (for an average 11 stone (70kg) man – the energy cost will be less for women and lighter men), and that's without a pack or battling against strong winds! So if you're planning a weekender or day in the hills, you need to have a good meal the night before, and pack in the calories before you go. Start the day with a high carbohydrate breakfast, as carbohydrate helps to prevent fatigue during strenuous exercise. This is where a vegetarian style of eating really scores, as foods such as porridge, muesli, high fibre breakfast cereals, toast, winter fruit salad (dried apricots, apple, prunes and figs), or potato scones will supply the all-important carbohydrate fuel for a day in the hills. This type of feast will benefit everyone, not only vegetarians.

Ideal Breakfast Foods

- Porridge, Weetabix, Shredded Wheat, corn-flakes, bran flakes, grape-nuts, fruit and fibre, home-made muesli. **Beware:** Frosties, Sugar Puffs, Alpen, Country Store and Harvest Crunch have lots of sugar. For health, and the free plastic gift, mix with the low sugar varieties listed above.
- Toast, muffins, crumpets with jam, honey, mar-malade, Marmite, peanut butter.
- Fruit juice, bananas, grapefruit, orange seg-ments, kiwi fruit.

Vegetarian Snacks and Stokers

- For sandwiches, cut the bread thicker, and go easy on the fatty fillings. If you want a change from cheese and pickle or peanut butter, try some of the other nut butters such as three-nut butter, tahini (sesame seed paste) with Marmite, vegetarian pâtés or spreads.
- Take hot thick vegetable, leek and potato, or lentil soup for a treat on top.
- Fruit cake, wholemeal raisin muffins, malt loaf and current buns all travel well in a rucksack, and are ideal high carbohydrate snacks.
- Muesli bars, flapjacks, dried bananas, apricots and raisins are easy to carry in your pocket to eat on the move if the weather is bad.

Vegetarian meals for refuelling

A backpacking weekend may involve staying overnight in a Youth Hostel or bothy. Freeze-dried meals, which can be prepared by adding boiling water and eaten directly from the packet are useful. Look out for Regal Meals produced by Raven Foods, Peak '90 and Outdoor Cuisine, as some of these (vegetable stew, vegetarian stroganoff and goulash, for example) are suitable for vegetarians – although the choice of main meals is quite limited compared with the selection offered for meat eaters.

If you avoid tea and coffee, try herb and fruit teas or mulled apple juice instead. Dilute concentrated apple juice (from health foods shops) with boiling water, and add a few cloves and a stick of cinnamon to the brew. Why not make it in your flask for the next day's hillwalking and savour the warm, spicy aroma when you reach top?

Are you a vegetarian?

Semi- or Demi-Veg: Eat poultry, fish, eggs and dairy products, but not red meat or meat prod-ucts.

Lacto-ovo-vegetarian: Avoid all meat, fish and poultry, but eat eggs, milk, yogurt, cheese, butter etc.

Lacto-vegetarian: Eat milk, yogurt, cheese etc., but no meat, fish, poultry or eggs.

Vegan: Avoid all foods of animal origin. Eat only vegetables, vegetable oils, cereals, nuts, fruit and seeds.

Fruitarian: A stricter form of veganism. No cereals and pulses, diet based on raw and dried fruit, nuts, honey and olive oil.

CHAPTER 3

Kitting Up

Clothing and equipment for day walking

by Clive Tully

DO YOU REALLY need any special clothing or equipment for walking? There's one diehard school of opinion which reckons you can do it without spending any money, let alone cashing in the life insurance. But the fact is that, like any other sport or activity, you may be able to make do, but you'll do a lot better, more comfortably and safely too, if you use kit designed for the job. As with so many things, you get what you pay for. If you're on a limited budget, the best course of action is to spend most of it on decent boots, spending less on waterproofs and rucksack.

If money isn't exactly a problem, you'll happily be able to dispose of £500 on the very best walking boots (£100–£150), waterproofs (jackets alone can be over £200) and midwear garments (some fleece tops can top £100!)

LAYERING

What you wear when you're outdoors probably contributes more to your enjoyment of whatever you're doing than anything else. But the funny thing is, if your clothing does its job properly, you won't notice it. If it's less than adequate, however, it's a pretty safe bet you'll soon start to feel uncomfortable. And that goes across the board, whether you're talking about socks, thermal underwear, insulated anoraks or waterproofs.

The human body relies on its own temperature control system. It makes you perspire when warm, so that evaporative cooling can take place. And when it's cold, it progressively shuts down the circulation to the extremities of the body, to conserve body heat in the vital inner core. In fact, at around 70°F (21°C), a naked human body can be in perfect equilibrium. In our climate, overheating may not seem much of a danger, but it can happen in the height of summer, particularly if you exert yourself. But for practical purposes, our main concern is with the effects of the wind, cold and wet. Separately, they are uncomfortable nuisances – together, they are potential killers.

Keeping that equilibrium is best done by using clothing in layers – with each layer designed to do a specific job. So what's new about layering? Unless we're baking in Mediterranean heatwaves, it's something we do with our clothing as a matter of course. And walkers have been talking about it for years, even when a cotton T-shirt, woollen check shirt and knitted wool pullover were the norm. But with the profusion of new fabrics with all manner of properties, layering has taken on a new meaning.

At its most basic level, layering is simply the most efficient way of controlling your temperature. It's most efficient on your rucksack, too, because the things you aren't wearing are less likely to take up as much space packed away as bulkier items of clothing. From the insulation angle, several thin layers will always work better than one thick one, and it provides the flexibility for intermediate control which you wouldn't get with a single, bulkier item of warmwear which is either on you, or in the rucksack. And while it's obviously very effective for walkers, where levels of exertion can vary throughout a walk, I find it is also the best philosophy when it comes to travelling.

If you're trekking among big mountains, for example, it's possible to be in air temperatures close to freezing, but while you're in the sun, it feels warm enough to walk in shorts and T-shirt. Move into the shade, though, and you suddenly realize how chilly it really is. It's conditions like this where the flexibility that layered clothing offers comes into its own. In the UK, the biggest factor affecting the apparent temperature is the wind, so it's important that one layer can keep that at bay and, for the sake of lightness, a polycotton or micro-fibre shirt or jacket is your best bet.

When it really gets cold . . . You can't beat a pair of long johns for extra warmth.

In the world of modern outdoors clothing, the layering concept has worked itself into three distinct slices: the layer you wear next to the skin – some form of underwear; the mid-layer – midwear garments such as fleece or fibre pile; and the outer layer – windproof or waterproof garments. Of course, there can be variations on the theme. A light polycotton jacket might form your protective layer over nothing more than underwear, or perhaps underwear and fleece, but if harsher weather comes along, it takes a subordinate role to your shell garments.

Cotton T-shirts might be fine for general leisure wear, but they're pretty uncomfortable once they're soaked in perspiration, and they take for ever to dry. In mid-summer, a loose cotton or poly-cotton shirt might be the best thing – something to keep you cool. But in more average conditions, a closer-fitting garment will be a lot more useful over a wide range of temperatures.

'Thermal' is a word that is rapidly slipping into the past when it comes to underwear. Not that you can't get warm underwear, but a lot of the specialist stuff for outdoors activities is made for year-round use. And the priority isn't so much to keep you warm, although that may come as a matter of course, but to keep you dry. They work either by absorption, or wicking – transfer of moisture by capilliary action – depending on the type of fabric.

Midwear garments are the ones you wear to provide some warmth. Traditionally, you'd be talking about woolly jumpers, while the hi-tech approach is taken up with the synthetics like fibre-pile and fleece. As an outer layer, they may be just right in cool, still conditions, or where you're under some exertion, but in breezier weather, or once you stop piling on the energy, they may need some wind-proofing. Some fleece garments come with outer shells of Pertex or other close-weave fabrics. They make the jacket windproof, but, you could argue, at the expense of some loss of flexibility in a complete layer system.

The final layer is the one which should keep all the weather nasties at bay. Also known as shell garments, they're the first line of defence against wind and rain. The properties of different waterproof fabrics are dealt with in more detail further on in this chapter, but suffice it to say here that the types of fabric used, and the design and construction of the garment, play a significant part in the overall performance of a layer system.

A non-breathable outer layer will obviously work against good underwear and midwear, and conversely, there's not much point in wearing a highly breathable outer shell if all you've got on beneath it is a cotton T-shirt and a cheap acrylic pullover! Many of the big clothing manufacturers have developed all the elements of layer systems so you can be sure they work in harmony.

The integral approach to layered clothing relies not just on temperature control, but in being able to deal with perspiration. Close-fitting underwear should take it away from the skin and, in contact with the next layer, should pass it on. That, at least, is the theory, although my own view is that if you're sweating that much, perhaps you'd be better off removing a layer! In any event, if the British climate maintains its traditional unsettled state, there's no doubt you'll find layering the key to new strata of comfort.

Typical waterproof and midwear layers.

Base Layers

When the temperature reaches a stifling 86°F (30°C), it's hard to imagine a need for clothes at all, let alone that most glamorous of topics for the outdoors activist – underwear! And, lest there should be any confusion, it doesn't necessarily have to be 'thermal'. Indeed, the priority these days isn't so much the extra layer of warmth, although of course it helps, as a layer which keeps you dry. It may add up to the same end result, but it arrives by a different route.

The ideal clothing for summer is lightweight and loose, giving the best opportunity to lose excess body heat and perspiration as quickly as possible. In winter, when you're trussed up in warmer clothes, with a windproof or waterproof layer on top, you still need to be able to dissipate perspiration, and the key to this is efficient underwear.

The trouble with cotton is that while it's comfortable enough in normal use, where you might not be sweating that much, it takes a long time to dry once it does get damp. Damp cotton next to the skin isn't terribly comfortable and, at worst, is a potential danger. Wet cotton has no insulation value and, in direct contact with the skin, it hastens chilling.

But alternatives are available, in both natural and synthetic fabrics, which do the job much better. Polypropylene is a widely used synthetic fibre, non-absorbent and, knitted into a stretchy fabric for a close fit, it offers both insulation and the capillary action which removes sweat away from the skin.

Helly-Hansen are without doubt the best-known company using polypropylene, with their Lifa underwear.

They can do all sorts of whizzo things with polyester these days. It can be texturized, so it weaves up into a fabric with a natural look and feel to it, and although naturally hydrophobic, it can be programmed to be hydrophilic. Malden's Polartec 100 has this, but with just the surface treated, so the inner core of the fibres repel, the outer surface attracts, thus creating a set of opposing forces which they say aids the 'wicking' effect.

Sub Zero's underwear made from ICI Tactel (hydrophobic) comes in two weights. Factor 1 is lightweight and stretchy – the basic fabric without any finishing, while Factor 2 is heavier, with a brushed fleecy inner surface for added warmth.

There are pluses and minuses with both natural and synthetics. Polypropylene, for example, will last only a few days without washing before the odour it takes on will be enough to test even the closest friendship, and constant use eventually degrades the treatment which enables polyprop to wick efficiently, after which it doesn't have an awful lot going for it. Also polyprop doesn't like much in the way of heat when you wash it. I once accidentally washed a polyprop T-shirt at too high a temperature – it came out at about the right size for a garden gnome!

The latest polyester base-layer garments such as Polartec 100, used by a wide range of British companies, incorporate an anti-bacterial treatment which inhibits the growth of the bacteria which produces the characteristic odour. Natural fibres like wool and silk – silk especially – are much better at coping with nasty niffs, but although they're capable of absorbing up to a third of their own weight in moisture without feeling unduly damp, there will come a point under heavy exertion when they become noticeably sticky.

Nevertheless, natural fibres have as strong a following as ever. Underwear made from wool no longer has to be of the itchy variety, and it has the advantage of generating a certain amount of heat when wet. It's a great favourite with the armed forces because it ignites only with difficulty and, unlike synthetics, doesn't make a horrible mess which needs to be removed surgically as a result of gunshot or burn injuries.

Not just the fabric for those chasing unashamed luxury and boxes of dark chocolates, silk makes superb underwear – highly absorbent, a good insulator and incredibly light. A silk T-shirt and long johns packs down to a very small handful.

Whatever sort of fabric you go for, the designs tend to be pretty much the same. Short- and long-

The Phoenix Phreeranger, a superb lightweight two-man tent.

sleeved T-shirts, long-sleeved shirts with roll necks and perhaps a short zip, and long johns. Amazingly, most mens' long johns still come with the traditional front opening, despite the fact that they tend to require a certain amount of contortion to use, or the close-fitting, stretchy nature of the garment means that the opening actually becomes a bit too open! Given that most modern briefs for men have now dispensed with this facility, it may be that the performance underwear manufacturers should look upon an updated design as a new opening rather than a stitch-up job!

Midwear

Perhaps one of the most all-encompassing terms in outdoors clothing, midwear really takes in everything which isn't underwear or shell garments. In the days before purpose-made clothing came about, you'd probably start off with a T-shirt, and put a woollen check shirt and woolly pully on top. Midwear made specially for the job allows you to control your temperature effectively, as well as getting rid of perspiration more efficiently.

For example, you can start out with a bottom layer, silk or wool if you like the natural fabrics, or polypropylene or nylon if you prefer to use synthetics. In fact, those thermal underwear type garments can be quite effective over a wide temperature range, so it may be that all you need on top is a lightweight windproof layer which keeps enough warmth in without letting you overheat. The poly-

cotton garments first brought on to the scene by Rohan and now made by the likes of Mountain Equipment and Abris, are ideal for this sort of thing. Most do an over-the-top type of windshirt, as well as zipped jacket designs and, of course, you'll be able to buy a matching pair of trousers.

Look for something with a little more warmth to slip under that windproof layer, and the choices really are wide. You could stick to the traditional woolly sweater, but that can be quite bulky when it's doing service in your rucksack. Fibre pile is an old favourite in its own right and, despite the advent of fleece fabrics, it still does well as a good-value, hard-wearing all-purpose insulator. Its drawbacks are that it isn't windproof, and that it tends to pill, which means it ends up looking about as well-groomed as the Dulux dog after it's chased rabbits through a hedge. But pile garments take on an extra versatility when they're combined with other fabrics, and one of the best examples has to be Hamish Hamilton's Buffalo pile and Pertex garments, which combine warmth with wind and water resistance all in one garment.

The alternative to pile is fleece, no more windproof, but a good deal more attractive. And whereas it once seemed to be the done thing for manufacturers to try and conjure up the most outlandish combinations of colour in one garment, the latest technology, which allows the fabric manufacturer to print patterns on fleece, has provided even more scope for imagination. It's a brushed polyester knitted fabric, which means that even after wear, it retains its looks a lot better than pile. Most of the fleece in the UK comes from the same source, the American company Malden Mills, and manufacturers making garments from the heavyweight

Polartec 300, or the lighter, more stretchy Polartec 200, include Berghaus, The North Face, Karrimor and Sprayway.

But there are other fleeces, including Karisma, a much denser brushed woven fabric which not only has excellent wind resistance, but remarkable abrasion resistance too. Of the non-run-of-the-mill fleeces, I'm particularly impressed with the very soft and cuddly ICI Tactel fleece from Sub Zero. It's nice in that it doesn't just exhibit good wind resistance, the fibres also have a hydrophobic coating, which means you might get a pleasant surprise if you get caught out in the rain without anything more substantial to slip on top.

Fleece with added windproofing is available in a variety of forms. Some manufacturers add a microfibre fabric shell, and may even make the garment reversible. Or there's Gore's Windstopper – essentially two layers of fleece sandwiching their magic membrane. And Maldens themselves have brought out their own version of windproof fleece fabric.

Fleece jackets started out as quite conservative garments. Since then, there's been an explosion in the colours available and in the way different coloured fabrics are combined in one garment.

Some of them aren't particularly tasteful and sometimes you may find function subordinated to the overall look, with designers combining panels of colour which don't seem to pay much regard to the fact that they create seams in places which can feel pretty uncomfortable underneath a rucksack.

Patterned fleece is now very popular. Most companies tend to use patterns as highlight panels, say around collars, rather than create entire garments in pattern. However, Eppik have gained their reputation from making fleece tops in the Austrian Thermovelour fabric with the wildest batik prints!

The people who make lightweight polycotton clothes generally tend to do some form of insulated garments too, not necessarily of the bulky Michelin Man variety, but using modern slimline insulating waddings, such as those made by the Swiss company Neidhart. Basically, they combine the windproof quality of the densely woven shell with a thin layer of insulation, a sort of high-tech version of the traditional sweater. The idea works quite well with trousers, too, although I find it actually has to be pretty cold for them not to be too warm! I like the idea of combining lightweight fleece with polycotton, something which Abris do rather well with their Jura Plus trousers, where you get extra warmth without the bulk.

There's no doubt that all the latest advances in fabrics point towards layering as the logical means

Useful all-purpose midwear, the Allinone made by Eppik.

Rohan's Classic Fleece pullover, a simple, stylish item of midwear.

Fleece tops don't get any more distinctive than these!

of keeping your personal micro-climate under control, whether you look at midwear garments as protection against a chill when you're out walking the dog or as part of a complete system on a mountaineering expedition. One thing's for sure – you don't need to weigh yourself down with heavy, bulky clothes to keep warm any more!

EXTREMITIES

Keeping head, hands and feet warm is pretty important if you want to ensure your comfort in cooler conditions. Your scalp is covered with a mass of sweat glands and blood vessels designed to regulate the temperature of your brain. Up to 70 per cent of total heat loss goes through your head, so when it's chilly, there's no doubt it pays to wear a hat. The heat loss is so great, that it may be that you'll find you can cure cold hands by putting some insulation on your head!

A simple woollen hat could be the answer, though some might find woolly hats a bit itchy. These days, the same companies which make fleece jackets and jumpers also tend to do a variety of headgear in fleece – everything from very basic tea-cosy hats to caps with waterproof outer shells and wired peaks. A balaclava is another good option, though the extra insulation around the neck may confine its use to colder conditions.

Keeping drafts away from your neck can be done with a scarf – and yes, you can get those in fleece as well – or the kind of all-purpose tube made from stocking knitted polyester or polypropylene – the kind of fabric normally used for thermal underwear. This kind of thing, of which the Bridgedale Headover is a good example, is wonderfully versatile – something which can be worn as a neck tube, scarf, pulled up into a hood or even rolled into a simple hat.

What kind of gloves you wear depends on whether you need to retain any kind of dexterity. A thick pair of mitts is super, but if you want to operate a camera or binoculars, you'll find them a bit restricting. For most conditions down to freezing, you'll find the lightweight gloves made from polypropylene or polyester fabrics to be as good as you need. I always tend to walk with my hands in my pockets to keep them out of the wind, though never when crossing difficult terrain.

It pays to invest in good socks for walking. They're the point of interface between you and your boots, and things like bulky or poorly located seams can make for excruciating agonies on the trail. Loopstitch socks provide good cushioning around the feet, and there are now several makes which even provide varying amounts of cushioning, with loopstitch panels around heel and toe, and a lighter construction over the rest of the foot.

If you're backpacking a heavy load, it's worth noting that, just as your boots will probably feel a bit different, so will your socks. You may want to consider the more traditional two sock set-up, maybe wearing loopstitch next to the skin and Norwegian rag wool socks on top. This also has the advantage of coping with perspiration quite well, as the synthetic loopstitch wicks it outwards to soak into the woollen outer sock.

WATERPROOFS

I don't know about you, but I have this strong aversion to getting wet. In cold, windy conditions, getting wet can be downright dangerous and, even in hotter climates, a drenching downpour can still be pretty bad for morale, as a friend of mine discovered when he led a party through days on end of unremitting torrential monsoon in Nepal.

In places where short, sudden, heavy showers are common, I reckon you can't beat a good umbrella. The time it takes to fumble through the contents of a rucksack after feeling the first spot plummetting out of the heavens can be long enough to get you thoroughly soaked and the rucksack half full of water! Much better to grasp your brolly and whip it up all in one deft movement, although it has to be said that the potential for hang-gliding is pretty interesting when the wind gets up. Umbrellas are also useful when furled for fending off over-friendly animals, and making one's way through crowds.

Elsewhere, I prefer a good set of waterproofs and, since British weather conditions can be as demanding as you'll find anywhere, you have to look no further than the stuff that's available in British outdoors equipment shops.

Traditional waxed cotton jackets, as exemplified by Barbour, might be fine if you're going to slip on your Hunter wellies and wander up to the butts with the 12-bore to have a go at conserving the local grouse population, but they're far too heavy and cumbersome for walking.

The most basic fabric for waterproofs is polyurethane coated nylon, followed by the more durable Neoprene coated nylon. Quality manufacturers tape-seal the seams so the garments are 100 per cent waterproof. The silicon proofed nylon garments which you can pick up in many department stores might be fine for light showers, but they're no good for anything more. All you need to do to determine a fabric's waterproofness is to pick it up and try to blow through it. If you can't force air through it that way, rain and wind aren't likely to have any better luck.

A waterproof jacket with a decent hood – essential protection in the hills.

The drawback with these impermeable waterproof coatings is that you can get almost as wet from condensation inside the garment as you can from not wearing it! But somehow, people have only found this to be a real problem since breathable alternatives have been offered. Under such circumstances, one or two layers of clothing between you and the waterproof might make things a bit more tolerable.

But, without doubt, the buzzword these days is 'breathability' – the means by which a fabric impervious to the passage of liquid water can transmit water vapour, thus eliminating that damp but not very pleasurable experience known as condensation. Climb up the price scale, and you arrive at a mind-boggling choice of breathable fabrics, designed to allow a certain amount of moisture vapour to pass through, while remaining waterproof. The performance factors are many and varied, not least the fabric's own ability to pass moisture vapour, with other influences such as the ambient humidity, temperature, and your own metabolism also coming into play.

It's so far advanced now that there are even different ways of making breathable fabrics work.

Gore-Tex, undoubtedly the best-known breathable waterproof fabric, is based on a thin membrane of expanded PTFE which can be laminated to a variety of facing fabrics for strength and visual appeal. Microscopic pores in the membrane allow water vapour to pass through, while keeping liquid water at bay. Manufacturers turning out good quality Gore-Tex garments include Berghaus, Phoenix, Sprayway, Mountain Range, The North Face and Karrimor.

The other route to breathability, favoured by many simply because there aren't any little pores to get clogged up by the inevitable accumulations of sludge which the average trail walker seems to attract, is the hydrophilic type of coating or membrane, specially engineered to pass water vapour through its structure along 'water-loving' molecular chains. There are laminates and coatings here too. Of the former, Sympatex is the best, since the membrane itself possesses formidable strength even without any reinforcing fabric. It's available in the UK in garments by Abris, Jack Wolfskin and Vau De. There are quite a few hydrophilic coatings about, including Milair, and a variety in the Peter Storm stable and, indeed, breathable PU coatings are tending to replace non-breathables even at the very bottom end of the market.

Long side zips are essential for waterproof leggings. These Extrem salopettes have full-length side zips.

Masters of lightweight outdoors clothing – Rohan make excellent waterproofs, too.

But if all that suggests the very latest high technology, you might be surprised to know that there was a breathable waterproof half a century ago. Cotton Ventile was developed originally for immersion suits for Second World War fighter pilots on North Atlantic convoy patrols to give them 20 minutes of survival time if they had to ditch in the water. It's been used by service pilots ever since.

Ventile has also been used since as a breathable waterproof with a good deal more comfort and handle than most synthetic varieties. The close-woven Egyptian cotton breathes naturally when dry, but as it becomes wet, the fibres swell to lock together into a waterproof barrier. The only drawback is the extra weight of the water when the garment's wet, but that's outweighed by its advantages. It works best when double layered, examples of which are available from Snowsled Vau De.

When you're walking in hotter climes, arid mountains or desert, where the chances of a good drenching are more of an exciting gamble, you might think full-blown waterproofs a bit excess to requirements. On the whole, showerproof, quick-drying garments are all that you'll need. The latest advanced polyester micro-fibre fabrics have a built-in water repellency which can't be washed out, unlike polycotton. I'd go for the same approach in hot rainforest conditions too, simply because if you do get wet, you're going to dry off in next to no time.

One thing you will notice with modern water-proof clothing is the amazing variety of gob-smack-ing colours and designs. Whether you go for colours which make you stand out or blend in with the environment is up to you. The most important thing is to check out the design. Rain will find any weak points, especially if there is a good blast of wind to help it along. The main zip of a waterproof jacket should have some form of protective flap – a double flap to cope with the worst conditions – fas-tened either by Velcro or press studs. Most water-proof trousers have a zip on each leg to allow you to slip them on over walking boots. Ideally, there

should be a gusset behind the zip to stop the rain getting through.

Make sure the hood of the jacket gives your head adequate mobility and that it doesn't restrict your vision too much when it's adjusted tight. Many of the higher priced waterproof jackets have specially shaped hoods with side cutaways to give improved peripheral vision – especially important when you're picking your way over uncertain terrain in the wet. You'll find the shorter jackets more useful than the traditional longer styles, especially when sitting on buses, mules and bicycles, and raglan cut sleeves/shoulders give the best mobility for arms.

The explosion in fabrics technology over the last few years has enabled manufacturers to produce modern shell garments with the performance required for walking and mountaineering, but with the looks, and feel, which make them perfect for casual use and travel. Apart from that, I still can't help thinking that the alternative for the essential eccentric wanderer has to be a brolly good idea!

The Trango Extrem, a top performance mountaineering jacket made from 3-layer Gore-Tex.

CLOTHING CARE

In most instances, you should have few problems washing clothes made specially for the outdoors, providing you follow the instructions on the label. Waterproof and insulated jackets sometimes pose a bit more of a problem. Not everything can be dry-cleaned, though I can't imagine many actually wanting to do that anyway.

What you may find with breathable waterproof clothing after a few washes is that you start noticing more condensation in wet conditions. What's hap-pened is that the facing fabric has lost its water-repellent treatment, with the consequence that it now takes up rain water into the fabric as far as the coating or membrane. If the facing fabric becomes water-logged, there's no way the coating or mem-brane can breathe.

The way round the problem is to apply a light sil-icone proofing to restore the water-repellency of the facing fabric. Performance is at its best when water hitting the fabric beads up and rolls off. The fluorocarbon finish applied to Gore-Tex facing fab-rics can actually be livened up for the first few washes simply by ironing the outside after washing. But while a cool iron will do the trick a few times, you will eventually need to use a spray to restore the 'as new' performance. It's even possible to restore waterproofness to membrane or coating based garments where the waterproof layer has

Ready to move on. Torridon, Scotland.

worn through or lifted off. One of the latest products from the Nikwax stable, TX.Direct, reproofs all leaky waterproofs by 'healing' cracks in membranes or coatings with a breathable polymer.

Other clothes can be proofed with Nikwax's TX.10 immersion proofing – there are types specially formulated for cotton and polycotton clothes, garments with synthetic insulation and down-filled products.

BOOTS

Most people like to think they've got the right kit for the job – whatever they're doing. But when they're walking, one or two people sometimes make do with footwear which cannot be regarded as being uppermost in their list of priorities. Like the time that true example of an English eccentric abroad, Christopher Portway, made a successful ascent of the 20 561ft (6 267m) Ecuadorian peak Chimbarazo, in a pair of plimsolls! And I suppose you could include Martha Scott, daughter of mountaineering legend Doug, who accompanied her dad to a similar altitude on Makalu at the age of nine, shod in a smart pair of red wellies.

In fact, for years, what was considered standard footwear for walking would actually have been more appropriate for mountaineering, or perhaps such boots might have served better as protective gear for walking through minefields! But while a whacking great pair of hefty boots might have looked pretty impressive, even while kicking steps up Mam Tor, it came at a price, and not just the horrendous erosion at the top of Mam Tor! With tough, unbending hide leather uppers and midsoles, they certainly provided the all-important support for ankles, but their weight and potential for propagating juicy great blisters before being properly broken in could hardly be an endearing prospect for anyone contemplating a stroll.

At the other end of the scale, there are still plenty of people to be found wearing the aforementioned plimsolls in all manner of rugged and slippery terrain, despite the fact that their soles will do about as much good as a cattle baron addressing a convention of vegetarians.

For good, all-purpose footwear for walks in undemanding terrain and travelling, you can't beat a quality pair of running shoes. They are, after all, built to protect feet against the infinitely more rigorous practice of pounding out marathons and the like, so it makes sense that they'll feel pretty comfortable if you cut your speed down to a more leisurely 2 or 3 miles an hour. They're built with shock absorption as a prime consideration, and specially shaped, closed cell foam insoles provide comfortable support for your feet. The latest Reebok pump running shoes are multi-functional enough to serve for walking, travelling and casual use. And when the going gets a bit more demanding, you can simply pump up the inflatable collar to provide a bit more support around the ankle. Other good makes include Adidas, Hi-Tec and Puma.

It's only when the going starts to get a little rough that you need to look at something on sturdier lines. Running shoes aren't waterproof, which can be a drawback in persistent rain, and the soles don't have the amount of grip or stiffness to be comfortable on wet or stony terrain. Having said that, mountain marathon runners cope quite happily with these disadvantages, but then they train their feet to get used to extra stresses.

The lightweight boot revolution came about when manufacturers realized that it would be possible to take the technology used to make running shoes and adapt it to walking boots. Early attempts by Karrimor, in conjunction with the Italian boot manufacturer Asolo, produced fabric boots which were incredibly light and comfortable, but in the end didn't match up to the walking public's expectations as far as waterproofness was concerned. That, at least, was how it was in the mid 1980s. By the end of the decade, with long, hot Mediterranean-style summers becoming more the norm in the UK, the sale of fabric boots rocketed. These days, the fabrics outnumber all-leather boots, though top-of-the range fabric boots are even more technical – with breathable waterproof liners made from Gore-Tex or Sympatex, and sophisticated shock absorption features.

But if the lightweight boot revolution did anything, it forced walking boot manufacturers to utilize modern manufacturing techniques, employing

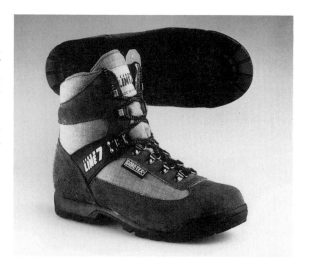

Fabric boots for trekking and summer walking are very popular now. Line 7's GT35 boots have Gore-Tex liners to keep wet weather at bay.

more gluing and less stitching than the traditional designs of boot. The uppers of a typical boot used for three-season walking tend to be calf leather – which is softer and therefore not so hard to break in. They feel a lot more comfortable the moment you slip them on, with linings either of leather or Cambrelle, an absorbent synthetic fabric.

Many of the better makes have graded midsoles of injection-moulded nylon, which means that you get a bit more flex in smaller sizes compared with the larger – generally providing the correct amount of stiffness for the weight of the wearer. And varying the overall thickness of the midsoles means the boot can be made relatively flexible for casual rambling, right through to totally rigid for winter mountaineering. But one of the biggest contributions to comfort underfoot has to be the shaped, closed cell foam insoles from running shoes, now almost universally found in lightweight walking boots.

If you bought your boots in the days before insoles, you can buy them separately, although you may have to reduce the thickness of the socks you wear to compensate for the extra space taken up by the insoles. You can also get purpose-made, shock-absorbing insoles such as those made by Spenco and Sorbothane. One manufacturer in particular, the American company Merrell, has made its name on a guaranteed good fit by making a range of different thickness insoles to ensure that anyone can get a 'perfect fit straight from the box'.

Many of the latest leather boots have a waterproofing treatment applied to the leather during

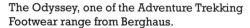

The Odyssey, one of the Adventure Trekking Footwear range from Berghaus.

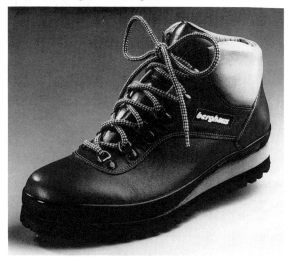

the tanning process, which means it's much longer lasting. When the leather does eventually get soaked by water, it also has the advantage of much quicker drying times. They tend to go by a variety of names – HS12, Aquastop – depending on the individual boot manufacturer.

Not even the very best all-leather boots can stave off water leaking into the boots for ever, although care of your footwear, and common sense when you're walking, can help to delay it. Some boots are made with breathable waterproof inserts of Gore-Tex or Sympatex, which are pretty effective. You can even get separate waterproof socks made from stretch Gore-Tex, sold by Berghaus, which keep your feet dry even when your boots or shoes are saturated. Alternatively, you can try halting the wet at the first line of defence with a pair of gaiters.

Without doubt the very best is the Berghaus Yeti gaiter, which completely encloses the boot. The very latest version has a redesigned rubber rand which not only seals around the sole of the boot, but provides protection over the toe cap as well. Yetis handle prolonged exposure to wet superbly and I've even waded streams in mine without experiencing any leaks.

If you aren't scrambling over terrain rough enough to warrant the ankle cuff of a full-blown walking boot, you should take a look at the various models of walking shoe available from the main boot manufacturers. Some, like those made by the French company Mephisto, or the American Timberland, are styled on traditional lines. Others, such as High Country and Merrell, have either gone for cut-down versions of lightweight walking boots or a sort of beefed-up trainer design.

Order of the boot. The Brasher Mountain Master, one of the highly successful range of Brasher Boots.

SCARPA, Zamberlan, Asolo, Daisy Roots and db Mountainsport are all good names for walking boots, manufactured in the heartland of quality boots in the Dolomite region of northern Italy. But unlike the narrow continental designs which tend to have a toe-scrunching, crippling effect on the majority of British feet, those on sale in the UK have been made on slightly wider lasts to accommodate our national peculiarity.

That's not to say there aren't some good home manufacturers, though. Most notable are Giffard Newton, the first walking boot manufacturer to win a British Design Centre Award a few years back with their High Country Lakeland, G.T. Hawkins or K. Shoes, former manufacturers of the best-selling Brasher Boot, now with their own range of walking footwear.

Fitting a new pair of boots

It makes sense to wear the socks you intend to use for walking when you pop along to your outdoors shop to buy your boots or shoes. Make sure there's plenty of room for your toes. Feet do actually expand when they get hot! An easy gauge is to slide your foot forward in the boot as far as it can go. You should then be able to fit your index finger comfortably between your heel and the back of the boot. You may find it difficult to walk like that, so with the heel comfortably at the back of the boot, and the laces tied, the boot shouldn't allow your heel to move about or your foot to slide forward.

Boots are made to fit ladies, too. High Country's Little Green Boot and Little Green Boot in Blue are made specifically for the female foot.

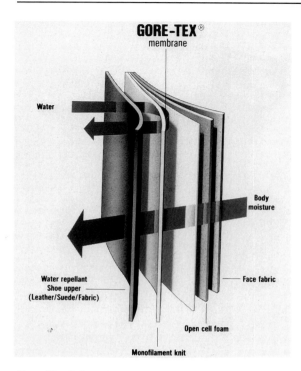

Gore-Tex is best known for its use in waterproof clothing. This diagram shows how it works when laminated to leather for use in footwear.

Any movement here will speed the onset of blisters and, predictably, descending steep slopes can be quite painful on the toes.

Looking after your boots

What's the first thing you do when you get your muddy boots home after a trip? No, you don't chuck them into a corner of the garage until the next time you need them. You should wash all the mud off and dry the boots off naturally. Resist the temptation to force the process by cooking them in front of a heater. Water expands as it heats up and, unable to work its way through the fibres of the leather quickly enough, tears it apart from the inside. It is even better to stuff your wet boots with newspaper, and put them in a corner to dry overnight – or, if the weather's fine, hang them out on the washing line!

Then go over clean, dry boots with a proprietary treatment like Nikwax, Mars Oil or Grangers G-Wax. A little extra warmth such as a gentle waft from a hair-dryer can help the treatment to penetrate further. Modern leathers with tanned-in water repellency such as Scarpa's HS12 or Zamberlan's Hydrobloc can simply be given a coat of shoe polish and then buffed up. Nikwax's latest product, Aqueous Nikwax, is a water-based product which can be painted on to the boots with ease, and can even be applied to wet leather, which can be particularly useful on multi-day treks where it might actually be a bit difficult to dry off the boots before reproofing.

Inevitably, there comes a point in the life of every pair of boots when they start to wear thin. Research has shown that people do tend to leave it too long before getting their boots resoled – a situation which could actually put your life in danger in the right, or should I say wrong, conditions. Get your boots resoled in good time and have any frayed stitching attended to at the same time. The Chorley-based firm Shoecare offer original replacements for all major brands of walking boot and running shoe, done either by mail order or through your local outdoors shop.

DAYSACKS

Given that you want to keep your hands free while you're walking, the best place to carry your spare clothing, sandwiches and so on is on your back. Unless you feel inclined to carry a month's supplies,

The Yetis make it a bit easier. Fording a stream in Finnish Lapland.

what most would regard as necessary for a day should fit comfortably into a bag with a capacity of no more than 35 or 40l. Without camping gear, I've found a 35l bag on its own quite sufficient to take everything I need for three or four days.

The smaller daysacks tend to have fairly straight-forward designs. A single compartment with a flap lid is the very simplest, and from there, pockets may be added to the top, front or sides of the pack, in a variety of combinations. The more modern teardrop design with a zipped front panel is quite popular, but unless there's some form of facility to strap things on the outside, you are limited by its capacity – inasmuch as a top flap can always be used to anchor something like a waterproof jacket not taking up space in the body of the rucksack itself. They're good for travelling, though. Apart from looking smarter, the fact that they have zipped openings with two pullers means you can lock the pullers together for security.

Carrying is generally by shoulder straps alone on sacks of around 20l or less, since it isn't likely that

you'd have much weight, with most sacks above this size equipped with at the very least a thin waist strap just to give the pack extra stability when negotiating tricky terrain. It's worth having any-way. If you don't use it all the time, you can simply strap it around the front of the sack to keep it out of the way. But you'll certainly appreciate it if you get involved in any sort of scrambling or anything else where concentration on your balance needs to be more finely tuned. And if you're mad enough to want to run while wearing your daysack, the waist strap stops it from bouncing about uncontrollably.

If the climbing style of rucksack appeals to you, then there's no reason why you shouldn't use one. Climbers' rucksacks tend to have a very clean pro-file, usually just one main compartment with per-haps a top pocket. It makes them less likely to snag on anything when they're being hauled up a rock face by rope. And they're more likely to have com-pression straps, which are very useful if you under-fill the sack, because you can pull the load in to stop it swinging about unnecessarily. And, of course,

Berghaus Dart 40, a useful daysack with enough capacity for winter walks.

The Cyclops II Cobra, a slimline 50 litre sack with a fixed length back.

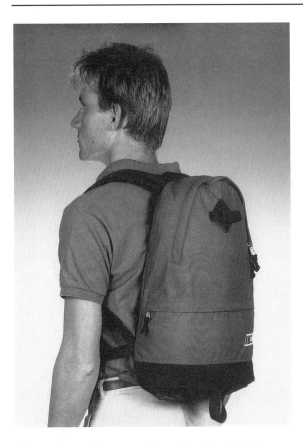

The Berghaus Blaze, a small rucksack suitable for short day walks.

you're guaranteed attachment points for ice axe and crampons if you do any winter hill walking. At the very least, rucksacks made for climbing tend to be that bit more durable.

Most pockets have zipped openings, and by far the easiest to get into, especially on small side pockets, is the zipped panel opening design. Those which open horizontally around the top of the pocket tend to be a bit more fiddly to use unless the pocket itself is fairly large.

Karrimor and Berghaus are the two biggest and best-known British rucksack manufacturers. Karrimor have been going for some 30 years, and associations with top climbers like Dougal Haston, Don Whillans, Joe Brown and Peter Boardman have produced classic rucksacks. They've pioneered several of their own coated fabrics such as KS100e, Silvaguard and their latest abrasion-resistant fabric, KS100t Granite. Their range of daysacks is extensive, from the basic Diddy sacks, with capacities from 16 to 20l, the Horizons, also ranging from 16 to 30l, to the larger Trails. Those who prefer panel-loading bags are catered for with the Vista 2 and 3 bags, the smaller of which also incorporates a mesh pocket on the front panel. They make good everyday bags too. I have a Vista 2 which quite often serves as a hands-free executive briefcase (albeit somewhat unsubtle with its bright pink, blue and yellow colour scheme!) – just the job for business trips and overnights.

Like Karrimor, Berghaus have brought about a good deal of innovation in their time. Their current collection of six Dart sacks ranges from 20 to 45l, three with side pockets, the other three with compression straps. Made from Ardura 1000, Berghaus's own texturized nylon pack cloth, they feature Advent fabric on the back and undersides of the shoulder straps. It's intended to combine the soft feel normally associated with cotton with the quick-drying characteristics and durability of a synthetic fabric.

Distributed by Europa Sport, Lowe Alpine Systems' soft daypacks are almost entirely zipped teardrop designs, with a couple of top-loading packs called Cloudwalker aimed more at climbers and ski tourers. Again, there is no reason why you shouldn't use something like this for walking and travelling, although you are paying extra for those holsters, straps and slings for attaching climbing hardware. There's also a more unusual design in the shape of the Arrow, a 25l teardrop sack with a central vertical zip opening on the front.

When it comes to buying, it pays to shop in the more reputable places if you want something which won't fall apart at the seams. Day rucksacks are the sort of thing which everyone and his dog seems to make. You can find no end of cheap rucksacks on market stalls, for example. But if you want something with a certain amount of robustness which will stand up to the rigours of hard walking, it's best by far to go for one of the more well-known names stocked in outdoors shops. After all, you want a pack on the back, not a pain in the neck!

CHAPTER 4

Where, When, How ... and With Whom

Planning where to walk

by Paddy Dillon

SOME PEOPLE will sit on grassy knolls and wait for inspiration . . . only to find it eludes them. Others may catch a chance remark at a noisy party . . . and find it provides the vital spark. Maybe a guidebook, magazine article or the recommendation of a friend inspires you to tackle a particular walk or expedition. One way or another you have an idea, a short-list or even a very long list of places to visit. Surely no one is bereft of a few ideas?

Before heading for the hills, it's a good idea to take a step back and look at your basic plan from a distance. Consider three things:

1 your personal fitness
2 the time of year
3 the nature of the route

Even if you're lacking in energy, a half-day walk in midsummer on the South Downs is unlikely to end in grief. If you feel very fit and confident, you may wish to test yourself to extremes with midwinter bivouacs in the Scottish Highlands. Almost anything goes at this stage – you can be as imaginative as you like without leaving your armchair. When you take a general overview you'll realize if you need to get fit, book your holidays for a particular season or choose a more appropriate route.

The next step is to look in greater detail at a particular walk. If you're going on your own, then you can either plan things yourself or seek advice from someone else. If you're going away with a group, then you'll have to bring them in at this stage, and make sure that everyone is fit and can spare the time for the trip. Usually, you'll be looking at the following things:

1 transport
2 breakdown of the route
3 accommodation

Transport simply covers getting from your home base to the place where you'll start walking. If it's a long-distance walk then you'll need to find transport home from the finishing point. Yes, you can drive a car to the start, but you might not want to leave it unattended for weeks – and you'll have to retrieve the thing at the end of the walk. Try and find a friend who will act as chauffeur. You could organize full vehicle support if a large group is going to be involved in a tough, challenging walk. Public transport will normally get you close to where you want to be, but you'll have to check timetables carefully. Look out for seasonal variations and lack of Sunday services. With public transport, you have to tailor your walk to suit their schedules.

The breakdown of the route depends on the nature of the walk and the time available in which to complete it. You could walk the Pennine Way in less than a fortnight, but there's very little leeway on such a tight schedule. A day of foul weather, or a blister or a shop which has closed for the day could delay you sufficiently to prevent the completion of the walk. Long, hard, challenging walks are fine, but don't be over-ambitious as repeated failure can be dispiriting.

Fifteen miles (24km) of rugged, mountainous country may well take as long to cover as 25 miles (40km) of gently rolling downland. You'll learn from experience how far you can walk in comfort on firm tracks, boggy moorlands, rocky mountains etc. You can stride out unimpeded on the Ridgeway Path over the Wessex Downs, but you'll have to hurdle hundreds of stiles on the lowland parts of the Offa's Dyke Path. On a Munro-bagging trip you'll always be tackling steep, rugged slopes, possibly in bad weather, with frequent stops for shelter or navigation checks. Remember – it all takes time.

When you start to break your route into manageable sections, you'll begin to see if appropriate accommodation can be found at the end of each daily stretch. There are generally three types:

1 hotels and B&Bs
2 hostels and bunkhouses
3 tents

In many popular walking areas you'll be spoilt for choice. With hotels and B&Bs, it's best if you can obtain lists in advance so that you can check prices, facilities and availability. You may need to book in advance – say for a summer trip around the South-west Way. The advantages are obvious. You'll have all the comforts of home and someone else is doing all the cooking and washing-up. On the minus side, it's the most expensive way to travel, you'll be tied to a fairly rigid schedule and you may find set meal-times awkward. The Ramblers' Accommodation Guide (see Useful Addresses at the back of this book) lists hundreds of 'walker-friendly' addresses throughout Britain.

Youth Hostels offer a fair range of facilities at budget prices, with a greater emphasis on doing things for yourself. Annual handbooks list hostels world-wide, noting prices and facilities. They're usually marked on Ordnance Survey (OS) maps, so you can see exactly where they are. Bunkhouses and independent hostels generally offer the same sort of accommodation. Many of those in Britain are listed in the Ramblers' Accommodation Guide, while in Ireland the Independent Hostel Owners (see Useful Addresses) produce an annual guide.

Backpackers carry their shelter with them and either travel very cheaply or pay nothing at all. Obviously there may be an initial outlay for all the gear, or you could borrow what you need. With a tent you can stop almost anywhere. You can use campsites, negotiate for a pitch on some other property or establish discreet, wild camps. There's a weight penalty – and you're going to be exposed to the elements. You need to pay particular attention to your safety. It's best to start cautiously and learn from experience.

When you're making your general plans there are other things you'll need to know about your route. You can bring all this together under the heading of 'Information'. If you're doing all your walking from a single base, then it's fairly easy to find out if it has a shop, pub, restaurant etc. When you're tackling a long-distance walk it's important to know where your next supply point will be. While it's fair to assume that a large town will be able to supply all your needs, a small village may have nothing to offer. On some walks there may be plenty of shops, while on others you may need to

carry two or three days' supply of food. So where is the next shop? Will it be open? Will it sell what you need? And where's the nearest bank? A sudden lack of food and money can bring even a tough walker to a complete halt. Usually, you'll be able to find the answers to some of your questions before you start your walk. Other information will need to be gathered along the way. There are three ways of gleaning information:

1 maps
2 guidebooks
3 information centres

Maps are splendid things and with patient study you'll be able to read them as easily as you read a book. Some of the symbols are very specific and will point to the availability of post offices, telephones, campsites etc. If you're very familiar with maps, then you'll be able to read between the squiggly lines and identify idyllic, sheltered, wild camps. The scale and style of maps you use is up to you, but generally a large scale, such as 1:25 000, will show good detail.

You may find a good guidebook which saves you an awful lot of planning. Ideally, a guidebook would tell you everything you want to know about your chosen route or area. A guide to a long-distance walk, for example, should have a route description and offer a specimen route breakdown. It should indicate what sort of accommodation is available. Shops, pubs and transport should be noted. There should be plenty of background information, so that walkers are informed about the history, wildlife and other features of interest. A guide to a particular area should offer several routes and give a clear picture of what you can expect on each of them. All guidebooks should include maps which can easily be used in conjunction with the appropriate OS maps. In short, a good guidebook will save you a lot of time and effort in the planning stages.

At the end of the day, there may still be odd things you need to know about places which are hundreds of miles away. The best thing you can do is to phone a nearby information centre. Usually, you'll be able to get a quick answer to a query about accommodation, transport, shops etc. In some particularly popular villages there may be an information centre which can tell you almost anything about the place. Annual booklets are produced by tourist offices which list all the information centres, so you can find one near to your 'problem' area.

One of the best ways of gaining information while you're on the move is by tuning in to the 'trail talk'. On a long-distance route you may find someone who has just come from the place you're heading towards. They'll warn you of the muddy campsite and the shop that closes at 3 p.m. The presence of a remote farmstead supplying teas and cakes will be the sort of thing which is revealed at this late stage. It's all worth knowing – it's up to date and it's useful.

A minor debate rumbles on about whether you should walk on your own or with a group. Quite honestly, it's not a subject anyone can preach about, and you must ultimately do as you please. There are advantages and disadvantages in both modes of travel, but the bottom line is safety. There's no accounting for folk – so consider this: some people may walk alone because they are social outcasts; some people may walk in a group because they hate their own company; some people may lead because they yearn to exercise power over others. Avoid these bores, leeches and tyrants!

The solitary walker may be happy to walk alone – and let's get this straight – being alone has nothing at all to do with being lonely. There are practical advantages in that you can set your own pace and route, start and stop when it suits you, alter your route on a whim without the need to consider others etc. A solitary walker is generally quiet and can

more easily observe the wildlife of an area. However, if you lose your way you've got to unravel the route for yourself. If you're benighted or injured, will anyone know where you are? And if you need to be rescued, people will point their fingers at you and use your unhappy experience to fuel the debate against solitary walking.

People who walk in groups are usually quite happy to do so. They prefer the company of others, and delight in lively conversation, and the sharing of knowledge and experience. However, a group must be competently led and proceed at a pace and along a route which is suitable for everyone. In case of an accident, help is readily available. If the route-finding is difficult, members may assist the leader. When things go badly wrong, everyone may suffer and the leader has to shoulder the blame.

You need to make your own choice about whether to walk alone, with a friend or with a group. Your choice needs to be based on your feelings, ability and experience. You must always consider your safety. If you're not happy with the first choice you make, then choose again. If you're happy with the choice you make, then stay with it and enjoy your walking experiences to the full.

UK AND IRELAND

Walking is a popular pastime in Britain. There are over 120 000 miles (193 080km) of public rights of way in England and Wales, plus a high degree of freedom to roam in many parts of Scotland. Walking is becoming more and more popular in Ireland too, where a network of waymarked trails is being established. Some walkers have favourite areas which they visit whenever they have the opportunity – the Lake District, Snowdonia, Scottish Highlands, County Kerry – or wherever. That's fair enough, and they'll certainly get to know their particular patches in great detail. Other walkers have itchy feet and prefer to wander from place to place – maybe spending a week in the Yorkshire Dales, a series of weekends bagging the Munros, a fortnight on the mountains of Connemara, a long walk along the Offa's Dyke Path and so on. There are endless possibilities for both easy day walks and more challenging, long-distance walks in Britain and Ireland. There follows a whistle-stop tour of some popular

walking routes and areas, which must necessarily be brief and selective. There are also a few pointers to quieter walking areas.

SCOTLAND

Scotland is bigger, wilder and more varied than many people imagine. There are a mere handful of waymarked long-distance trails, but you're free to link many long hill tracks and create your own cross-country routes. Hordes of walkers are becoming engrossed in summit-bagging and it must be admitted that Scotland is the place to head for the highest, wildest and most rugged hills. There are also several islands with varied walking opportunities.

Long Distance Trails

The Southern Upland Way

This is a coast-to-coast route across southern Scotland from Portpatrick to Cockburnspath. An easy start on good paths and tracks, but note that the hard surfaces can cause blisters. The surroundings gradually become bleak and rugged. Extensive forests on the Galloway Hills are negotiated via broad tracks. Forested hills are climbed beyond Dalry and Sanquhar. After visiting ruined lead mines around Wanlockhead, the route crosses the Lowther Hills and reaches the half-way mark around Beattock. Forest tracks lead over to the Ettrick Valley, after which the trail crosses to St Mary's Loch. A drove road runs over Minch Moor, then easier walking is found around Galashiels, Melrose and Lauder. The broad Lammermuir Hills are followed by easier walking from Longformacus to Cockburnspath.

Length: Over 210 miles (340km).
Time: Up to a fortnight.
Accommodation: B&Bs, hostels, campsites and a few bothies. There are some lengthy stretches with very little accommodation.

The West Highland Way

A popular choice for many first-time, long-distance walkers. The route starts on the outskirts of Glasgow and leads to Fort William. The beginning is easy at Milngavie, but becomes quite difficult along the wooded shore of Loch Lomond. Big hills start to build up near Crianlarich and Tyndrum, but a fine military road leads between them and continues across Black Mount and Rannoch Moor. Isolated hotels offer food, drink and lodgings. The military road zig-zags up the Devil's Ladder and takes the trail over to Kinlochleven. After passing through a lofty glen and going through a forest, the route descends to Glen Nevis and Fort William, at the foot of Ben Nevis.

Length: About 100 miles (160km).
Time: About a week.
Accommodation: B&Bs, hostels, bunkhouses campsites and a few bothies.

The Speyside Way

This is a simple route from Spey Bay to the fringe of the Cairngorms at Tomintoul. Easy riverside paths lead to Fochabers, then roads and tracks continue to Craigellachie. There's a spur to Dufftown you could include to boost the distance or you could head straight onwards by following an old railway trackbed to Ballindalloch. Paths head over heathery hills via Glenlivet to reach Tomintoul.

Length: 50 to 60 miles (80 to 100km).
Time: A long weekend.
Accommodation: B&Bs, hostels, campsites.

Other long-distance trails

Even the most remote wilderness areas in Scotland will feature some kind of path or track – often created for deer-stalking. Some of the most well-trodden hill tracks pass through the Cairngorm glens. A waymarked trail may one day be established through the Great Glen to link Fort William with Inverness. A partly waymarked trail goes around the coastline of Fife.

Over The Hills

There are various lists of summits which have been prepared and some walkers delight in visiting every listed point. It's a harmless pursuit, but it can become addictive and may earn you the scorn of fellow walkers. The premier list was drawn up by Sir Hugh Munro – hence all summits above 3000ft (915m) are known as 'Munros'. There are also 'Corbetts' between 2500ft (760m) and 3000ft (915m). There are 'Donalds' which are over 2000ft (610m) in southern Scotland. The latest list is of 'Grahams' which are between 2000ft (610m) and 2500ft (760m) in northern Scotland.

If you arm yourself with the appropriate lists and rise to the challenge of climbing to a thousand or so summits, then you'll certainly know Scotland's hills at the end of it all. If you simply want to look at a few of the best hillwalking areas, then try some of the following.

Ben Nevis

Ben Nevis is the highest mountain in Britain, so you'll probably want to climb it some time. You can extend the walk over Carn Mor Dearg to Aonach Mor and Aonach Beag – all summits above 4000ft (1220m). That's a hard day's walk. For a tough weekend walk, continue over the Grey Corries and return to Glen Nevis across the Mamores.

Glencoe

A well-known and much visited glen. Striking rock scenery rises on both sides. Scramble along the airy Aonach Eagach ridge on the northern side of the glen. Climb Bidean Nam Bian and neighbouring peaks on the southern side. The fierce-faced Buachaille Etive Mor can be found beyond the head of the glen.

Lomondside

Choose a base somewhere around Loch Lomond and you could travel to the Arrochar Alps and climb

A soggy day in Mullardoch, Central Highlands.

to the curious summit of The Cobbler – with the aid of a rope. An easier walk leads up Ben Lomond or you could wander across the huge, lumpy hills around Crianlarich. The nearby Trossachs is a compact area of great beauty and interest.

Ben Lawers
A lofty mountain. Notable on many counts, but also offering a fairly easy walk-in from a visitor centre. An ideal first Munro. More experienced walkers should consider the horseshoe route around several summits from Glen Lyon.

The Cairngorms
The Cairngorms represent wilderness at its best and most remote. Essentially there's a high-level, bouldery plateau fringed by steep slopes, cliffs and lonely corries. There are four summits above 4000ft (1220m) which walkers sometimes try and link in a hard day's walk – Ben Macdhui, Cairn Gorm, Braeriach and Cairn Toul. There's lots more besides,

but you'll need to carry in all your food and either camp or stay in bothies to explore the place properly. A well-walked through-route is the path through the Lairig Ghru.

Glenshiel
Splendid and easily accessible ridge-walks are found on either side of Glenshiel. This is a fine area for a weekend walk. You can extend your explorations into neighbouring Glen Affric or visit the forbiddingly rugged and remote Knoydart wilderness.

Torridon
Strange red terraced mountains rise up near Torridon. Climb Beinn Alligin and traverse its 'horns'. Scramble along the crest of Liathach and get to grips with the Am Fasarinen pinnacles. Explore Beinn Eighe and its neighbours. Slioch is also worth the effort – and don't forget lower hills such as Baosbheinn.

Ullapool
From this handy base you can travel extensively around northern Scotland. Trek into the Beinn Dearg or Fannaich groups of hills and enjoy their solitude. An Teallach's splendid terraced slopes and airy ridges aren't too far away. There's also the strange range of Sutherland summits which include Stac Pollaidh and Suilven.

The Islands
You can't beat Scotland for islands. Orkney and Shetland are usually shown as insets on maps, so that you don't appreciate how far north they really are. Try studying them on a globe! Shetland has plenty of rocky, boggy wilderness and an impressive cliff-line. Orkney is more pastoral, but be sure to visit Hoy, if only to see the famous sea-stack called the Old Man of Hoy. The whole island's fairly wild.

Have a look at a map of the Outer Hebrides and wonder what an end-to-end backpack would be like. How would you go through Lewis? Would you climb all the hills on Harris? Catch a ferry, then walk through North Uist, Benbecula and South Uist. Take another ferry to Barra – once short-listed as one of the world's most beautiful islands.

Moving to the Inner Hebrides – Skye is pre-eminent. The jagged Black Cuillin ridge furnishes some difficult scrambling, though some summits could be reached without too much effort. Basic rock climbing is necessary to reach the top of the Inaccessible Pinnacle. Away from the Black Cuillin ridge there's rugged Blaven and the more rounded Red Cuillin. Strange places can be visited on easier walks –

Macleod's Tables, the Old Man of Storr and the weird, rocky Quiraing.

Free walking is not necessarily automatic on Rum, where the Rum Cuillin offer splendid walking. Explorations of the 'Small Isles' need careful planning and studying of ferry timetables – the very essence of island-hopping. After visiting the solitary Munro on Mull, you'll realize that there are other hill walks and a fine coastline to explore. The sight of distant Jura and Islay will draw you on to Kintyre, which is such a long peninsula you feel it's an island. Arran is a great island for walkers and has some superb hills on its northern half. You'll find everything from easy coastal walking to scrambles along airy ridges. Goat Fell, Cir Mhor and A'Chir are rugged, rocky hills and a good start.

The Southern Uplands

The Galloway Hills draw walkers along their rugged ridges, and this remote, forested area is supplied with a few handy bothies. A tough circuit of Merrick and the Rhinns of Kells might be considered. Other parts of the Southern Uplands are becoming better known. You'd see most of the hill groups from the Southern Upland Way, but use Moffat as a base and climb White Combe, before heading northwards across Broad Law and its neighbours. Popular hill groups include the Pentlands, Eildons, Tinto and Criffel. By the time you're walking in the Cheviot Hills you're stepping into England.

ENGLAND

England has a tremendous variety of well-walked paths in both upland and lowland regions. There are several long-distance trails – some are state-funded National Trails while others may be waymarked by local authorities or voluntary groups. Some trails aren't specially waymarked, so you'd need a guidebook for details of the route. Other walks include 'challenge' walks which may have to be completed within a certain time. You'll find good walks almost everywhere, but many walkers like to tackle the long-distance trails or head for the wilder uplands which are usually situated in the national parks.

Long Distance Trails

The Pennine Way

This route is a popular choice for many first-time, long-distance walkers. The route wanders along the Pennines from Edale, in the Peak District, and eventually crosses the Cheviot Hills to reach Kirk Yetholm, in Scotland. The Peak District section is being repaired as the boggy moors of Kinder Scout, Bleaklow and Black Hill have been severely overtrodden. As the route passes through the South Pennines it crosses Blackstone Edge, Stoodley Pike, Withins and Ickornshaw Moor. A gentle walk leads across the Aire Gap to find wonderful scenery at Malham in the Yorkshire Dales. Pen-y-Ghent provides a stiff climb, then good tracks lead from Horton to Hawes. The broad, boggy Great Shunner Fell is crossed on the way to Keld.

Stainmore is a bleak area between the Yorkshire Dales and North Pennines. A gentle walk by waterfalls in Teesdale gives way to boggy moors on the way to High Cup and Dufton. The lofty Cross Fell range has to be traversed before the River South Tyne is followed through Alston. An interesting walk leads along Hadrian's Wall and takes the trail into Northumberland. Forests, farmland and low moors are found on the way to Bellingham and Byrness. The Cheviot section of the route is boggy and barren – a long, hard day's walk which takes you over to Scotland to end at Kirk Yetholm.

Length: About 270 miles (435km).
Time: Up to three weeks.
Accommodation: B&Bs, hostels, campsites and a few bunkhouses.

The Coast-to-Coast Walk

This is a well-walked, but unofficial route from St Bees Head to Robin Hood's Bay. The route runs from St Bees, across the Lake District, to reach Shap. After passing through Kirkby Stephen the trail leads through the northern half of the Yorkshire Dales to Richmond. A low plain is crossed between the Yorkshire Dales and the North York Moors. A trek across the rolling moors is followed by gentle walking before the route ends at Robin Hood's Bay.

Length: About 200 miles (320km).
Time: About a fortnight.
Accommodation: B&Bs, hostels, bunkhouses and campsites.

The Cleveland Way and Wolds Way

These two trails are quite different, but are joined together and offer a remarkably varied walk. The Cleveland Way leaves Helmsley and wanders around the edge of the North York Moors, following a heathery escarpment overlooking the Plain of York. Osmotherley and Kildale are passed, then the trail visits the little hill of Roseberry Topping before skirting Guisborough. The coast is reached at Saltburn, where the character of the walk changes suddenly. Cliff paths lead past charming places such as Staithes and Whitby to reach Robin Hood's Bay, Scarborough and Filey. On the wave-washed Filey Brigg we join the Wolds Way and follow it inland. Now we cross the broad, cultivated fields and narrow, steep-sided dales of the Wolds. Thixendale is one of the few villages actually on the route, located at a point where several dales meet. The Wolds Way ends on the Humber Estuary at Hessle, close to the graceful span of the Humber Bridge.

Length: Almost 200 miles (320km).
Time: Up to a fortnight.
Accommodation: B&Bs, hostels, bunkhouses and campsites. Sparse in some places.

The Peddars Way and Norfolk Coast Path

This is a trail which comes in two distinct parts. There's a long trek along the ancient Peddars Way Roman road, which starts near Thetford and finishes on the coast near Hunstanton. Castle Acre is an interesting village half-way along. The Norfolk Coast Path leaves Hunstanton and follows sea walls, shingle banks, dunes and marshes through Brancaster, Wells, Cley, Sheringham and Cromer. It's a good introduction to walking in East Anglia.

Length: Almost 100 miles (160km).
Time: Up to a week.
Accommodation: B&Bs, hostels, bunkhouses and campsites.

The Thames Path

Easy riverside walking from the Thames Barrier to Thames Head. The river provides an excellent running theme! After plodding through London an old towpath is usually followed, which passes many interesting towns and villages. Gradually, rural scenes open up and towards the end of the walk a series of field paths are used to reach the source of the river. The Thames path is a splendid way to explore an interesting and historic river.

Length: Almost 200 miles (320km).
Time: About a fortnight.
Accommodation: B&Bs, hostels and campsites. Some places off-route.

The Ridgeway Path

The Ridgeway is a splendid walk across the Wessex Downs and Chiltern Hills, which are rich in prehistoric remains. The first part of the trail follows the Great Ridgeway from near Avebury to reach Goring. This is a 5000-year-old route which crosses broad downs, and passes hill forts and burial chambers. From Goring, various paths and tracks take

the trail around the wooded Chiltern Hills, passing Watlington, Princes Risborough and Wendover to end on Ivinghoe Beacon.

Length: About 90 miles (145km).
Time: Up to a week.
Accommodation: B&Bs, hostels and campsites. Some places off-route.

The North Downs Way

This traces the North Downs from Farnham to Dover. The stretch through Surrey is largely wooded, while the stretch through Kent is largely cultivated. Some parts are aligned to the ancient Pilgrim's Way. Passes close to Guildford, Dorking, Reigate and Sevenoaks, but generally the route avoids towns and villages. The trail crosses the Medway Bridge near Rochester and passes close to Maidstone. After a long walk along the Pilgrim's Way walkers can choose whether to head straight to Dover via Folkestone or take a longer route via Canterbury.

Length: Up to 150 miles (240km).
Time: Up to a fortnight.
Accommodation: B&Bs and a few hostels.

The South Downs Way

A pleasant and popular walk, usually along the crest of the South Downs. Starts at Eastbourne with a walk over Beachy Head and the Seven Sisters, and ends in the historic city of Winchester. The South Downs are mostly open around Alfriston, Ditchling Beacon, Truleigh Hill and Amberley. Beyond the hill fort of Chanctonbury Ring the crest of the downs is largely wooded. The route used to end at Buriton, but an extension now takes it over Butser Hill and Old Winchester Hill to end at the King's Capital of Winchester.

Length: About 100 miles (160km).
Time: About a week.
Accommodation: B&Bs, hostels, campsites and a few bunkhouses.

The Cotswold Way

This is a well-walked 'unofficial' route which may be elevated to the status of a National Trail. The route runs from Chipping Campden to Bath and generally stays high on the Cotswold Hills. The route passes Cleeve Common above Cheltenham, and visits the curious Devil's Chimney near Birdlip. Stroud and Wotton-under-Edge are passed on the way to Bath – a city of fine Georgian architecture.

Length: About 100 miles (160km).
Time: About a week.
Accommodation: B&Bs, hostels and campsites.

A "view stop" is as good an excuse as any for a short rest!

The South-west Way

The South-west Way makes for an enormous coastal tour around the south-west of England, from Minehead in Somerset to Poole in Dorset. A route description is hardly necessary as the trail visits every coastal town and village. Cliff paths, dunes, beach walks and promenades are all included, and the route can be fiddly in places. Towns and villages are frequent, and often prove interesting to explore. It's essential to check ferry services across several inlets, or you might be faced with a long walk round. Walkers don't usually tackle the whole route in one go, but settle for particular stretches. The route is generally broken into five parts: the Somerset and North Devon Coast Path; the North Cornwall Coast Path; the South Cornwall Coast Path; the South Devon Coast Path; and the Dorset Coast Path. It's an immensely varied and interesting route.

Length: About 570 miles (920km).
Time: About five weeks.
Accommodation: B&Bs, hostels and campsites.

Other Long-Distance Trails

England is full of them! There are literally hundreds of walks which have been waymarked, written about or otherwise suggested. You can also study the rights of way network and create your own cross-country routes. You could link trails together – the Icknield Way links the Ridgeway Path with the Peddars Way, while the Downs Link joins the North and South Downs Ways. Cumbria could be explored via the Cumbria Way; Lincolnshire via the Viking Way. Long-standing 'challenge' walks include the badly eroded Three Peaks of Yorkshire and the Lyke Wake Walk. The list is endless and could go on to include the Isle of Wight Coastal Path, the Saxon Shore Way, the Dales Way, Hadrian's Wall and many, many more listed and logged for long-distance walkers.

Over The Hills

Most of England's loftiest, wildest and most challenging hills are found in the north. Summit-baggers have tended to concentrate their efforts on points above 2000ft (610m), but the 'Wainwright-baggers' have a highly individual list of summits in the Lake District to tick off. Many walkers heading for the hills will be found in the Lake District, Yorkshire Dales, North York Moors and Peak District

National Parks. Fewer walk in the boggy Cheviot Hills or the broad, bleak North Pennines.

The Lake District

Often overcrowded, the Lakeland Fells are suffering in places. There is virtual freedom to roam over most fells. Many walkers are to be found on the 3000ft (915m) summits of Scafell Pike, Scafell, Helvellyn and Skiddaw. You could link them all in a long, hard, day's walk. The Langdale Pikes, Bowfell and Great Gable are also popular choices. Celebrated horseshoe walks include the Fairfield, Mosedale and Coledale rounds, though there are much longer circuits of Buttermere, Ennerdale, Wasdale and Langdale. Tough scrambles are available in many places, though the classic, easy ones are Striding Edge, Sharp Edge, Jack's Rake and Lord's Rake. The Cumbria Way and Coast-to-Coast Walk pass through the fells. 'Wainwright-baggers' have over 200 summits to tick off. Some people walk all over the world, then return to the Lake District and declare that it has no equal!

The Yorkshire Dales

There are several lofty hills – none of them more badly eroded than the celebrated Three Peaks of Yorkshire: Whernside, Ingleborough and Pen-y-Ghent. For a change, try Great Whernside, Buckden Pike, Great Knoutberry, Wild Boar Fell and the wonderfully open Howgill Fells. The Pennine Way steers a fairly high course through the area.

The Peak District

This is a land of extended bogtrots! There are all sorts of long-distance walks and challenge walks in the area, with considerable overlapping. Those in the Dark Peak tend to follow broad, boggy moorland crests, though some follow firmer ground on hard gritstone edges. The White Peak is lower and contains a number of easier, long-distance routes, such as the White Peak Way.

The North York Moors

Although the hills aren't particularly high in the North York Moors, they are broad, bleak and barren. Several challenging through-routes and circuits have been devised, and these usually keep to the broad, moorland crests. There's a lot of overlapping of routes and classic crossings, such as the Lyke Wake Walk, are badly eroded.

The Cheviot Hills

These forbiddingly boggy hills have to be crossed by Pennine Wayfarers, but otherwise attract only a few walkers. Summit-baggers might like to cross all the 2000ft (610m) summits in a hard day's walk. There are plenty of lower hills.

The North Pennines

Not a National Park – or at least not yet – but this is the broadest, bleakest and wildest tract of upland in England. It's not known to many walkers, though the Pennine Way has some difficult moments there. There are plenty of summits above 2000ft (610m), which some walkers have started to visit, but for the most part you'd have the heights to yourself.

Lesser Hilly Areas

The Bowland Fells, Pendle Hill and the South Pennines are all places with fairly wild, upland country. Further southwards in England, the surroundings become rather tamer. There are reasonable hills and fine edges you could follow in Shropshire, and there's always the rugged ridge of the Malvern Hills. Dartmoor offers some challenging boggy walking over featureless moorland. The emphasis isn't so much on summit-bagging, but rather on visiting huge, granite tors or locating cunningly concealed 'letterboxes'. Concealed metal boxes contain stamp and ink pad to enable walkers to prove where they say they have been, eliminating bar tales. The idea of letterboxes has spread to Cornwall's Bodmin Moor, which is worth a visit, and also to neighbouring Exmoor. Upland walking is fairly limited in Exmoor, but go there anyway. On a clear day you'll be able to look across the Bristol Channel to Wales.

WALES

Despite the small size of Wales, this is largely an upland country and it has a fairly varied range of scenery. There are rights of way which allow you to plan all sorts of cross-country routes. There's only a handful of waymarked, long-distance trails, but there are wild stretches of coastline, mountainous national parks and plenty of opportunities for challenging walks.

Long-distance Trails

Offa's Dyke Path

Offa's Dyke is a lengthy earthwork which was raised in the Dark Ages between the Kingdom of Mercia and Wales. Some fairly lengthy stretches are followed closely by the Offa's Dyke Path. At other times, the path wanders elsewhere, and includes varied terrain between Chepstow and Prestatyn. This coast-to-coast route through the Welsh borders has upland stretches in the Black Mountains, Shropshire Hills and Clwydian Hills. Interesting towns such as Monmouth, Hay-on-Wye, Kington, Knighton, Montgomery, Welshpool and Llangollen lie on or near the route. There is an Offa's Dyke Visitor Centre at Knighton which you might like to visit before attempting the actual walk.

Length: About 180 miles (290km).
Time: About a fortnight.
Accommodation: B&Bs, hostels and campsites.

The Pembrokeshire Coast Path

This is a splendid coastal trail from St Dogmaels near Cardigan to Amroth near Tenby. The route is almost entirely confined to the Pembrokeshire Coast National Park. It's a very convoluted route which is fairly true to the coastline. There's a major diversion around the industrial inlet of Milford Haven and the Castlemartin Firing Ranges could upset your plans. Mostly, however, it's a scenic and interesting route with plenty of cliff paths. A waymarked route around the tidal Daugleddau can be used to boost the distance.

Length: About 180 miles (290km).
Time: About a fortnight.
Accommodation: B&Bs, hostels and campsites.

Glyndwr's Way

This is a waymarked trail through mid-Wales, which ties in with the Offa's Dyke Path and may eventually become a National Trail. Walkers leave Knighton and wander through low, hilly country to Llanidloes. After climbing a distant shoulder of the sprawling Plynlimon, the route descends to Machynlleth. The walk wanders over the hills to the Vyrnwy Dam and continues through gentler country to end at Welshpool.

Length: About 120 miles (195km).
Time: About a week.
Accommodation: B&Bs and a few hostels, bunkhouses and campsites.

Other Long-distance Trails

A waymarked, high-level route through Wales was once suggested, but ultimately dismissed. However, the idea appeals to many walkers, and there are suggested routes and guidebooks which are being followed. You can make such a trek as difficult as you like, as there are no shortages of hills to include.

Over The Hills

Lists of Welsh hills above 2000ft (610m) have been prepared if you feel inclined to join those who are ticking them all off. You'll be drawn to both popular and unfrequented areas. There are high, exposed moorlands in the Brecon Beacons National Park, quiet and unfrequented country in mid-Wales, and mountainous country in Snowdonia.

The Brecon Beacons

The National Park comes in three parts – the Black Mountain, Brecon Beacons and the Black Mountains. One of the greatest challenge walks in the area is a walk across the full width of the National Park, starting high above Llandeilo and finishing high above Hay-on-Wye. There are also dozens of long, broad moorland ridges which offer good, high-level through-routes or can be linked to form long circuits around upland valleys. If you go northwards from the Brecon Beacons you'll reach the lonely Mynydd Eppynt. Southwards lie forested hills and the post-industrial sprawl of 'The Valleys'.

Mid-Wales

Mid-Wales is an area often neglected by walkers. There's Glyndwr's Way, which gives a fair tour through the region. Summit-baggers tend to be drawn to the sprawling Plynlimon, lonely Drygarn Fawr and Radnor Forest. Travelling between these areas, you'd realize that there are possibilities for long, quiet, upland walks.

Snowdonia

Several 3000ft (915m) summits are sometimes linked by walkers. This takes in the Snowdon massif, Glyders and Carneddau. There's some scrambling on the way, and you could either make a long, hard day of the tour or spread it across a weekend. There are plenty of other walks, such as the classic Snowdon Horseshoe, the circuit of Cwm Idwal or a climb to the shapely summit of Cnicht. If you wander from hill to hill you'll find yourself being drawn along the Lleyn Peninsula or towards the rugged Cader Idris. Find time to explore the rocky Rhinogs, lonely Arenigs or the broad and bleak Aran and Berwyn ranges.

Lesser Hilly Areas

Look out for small areas of low hills where you could enjoy at least a day's walking in fairly wild surroundings. Visit the Gower Peninsula and enjoy its fascinating coastline. Walk along the Mynydd Preseli range in Pembrokeshire. Climb Yr Eifl and its neighbours on the Lleyn Peninsula. Study the rugged coast of Holy Island, climb up Holyhead Mountain and look across the sea to Ireland.

IRELAND

It's taken Irish walkers a while to find their feet, but more and more walkers are taking to the hills. For British visitors it's 'the same thing but different'. General landforms are on the same scale as in England and Wales, but there are areas which have wilderness more akin to parts of Scotland. There is a series of waymarked trails being developed, while in upland regions there is a high degree of freedom to roam.

Long-distance Trails

The Wicklow Way

This was the first trail to be established in Ireland and it proves to be a popular choice for first-time, long-distance walkers. It starts on the outskirts of Dublin and keeps to a fairly high level through the Wicklow Mountains. After crossing Three Rock Mountain and the slopes of Djouce, the trail passes Lough Dan and heads towards Glendalough. Splendid monastic remains abound here. After climbing Mullacor and wandering through forests near Aghavannagh, the route goes through gentler country near Tinahely and Shillelagh to end at Clonegal.

Length: About 80 miles (130km).
Time: Up to a week.
Accommodation: B&Bs and hostels.

The South Leinster Way

This trail starts at Kildavin, near Clonegal, so it can be linked easily with the Wicklow Way. The route crosses the slopes of Mount Leinster, then follows a stretch of the River Barrow to Graiguenamanagh. The forested slopes of Brandon Hill are crossed on the way to Inistioge. Forests eventually give way to more open country and there is a final road-walk to Carrick-on-Suir.

Length: About 60 miles (100km).
Time: A long weekend.
Accommodation: B&Bs only.

The Barrow Towpath

The Barrow Towpath comes in two parts. The northern section is a spur from the Grand Canal, running from Lowtown, through Rathangan and Monasteravan to Athy. The River Barrow itself is followed from Athy, through Bagenalstown and Graiguenamanagh to its tidal limit at St Mullins.

The towpath is generally easy, and the countryside is gentle and interesting. The canal and river provide a good running theme.

Length: About 70 miles (115km).
Time: Up to a week.
Accommodation: B&Bs only.

The Beara Way

This trail makes a complete circuit round the Beara Peninsula shared between County Cork and County Kerry. There is some coastal walking, but the route generally keeps a step inland, and uses old bog roads and hill tracks. There is some splendid mountain scenery. Towns and villages visited include Kenmare, Allihies, Castletown Bere and Glengarriff. Spurs from the main route can also be included to reach odd headlands and Bere Island.

Length: 90 to 130 miles (145 to 210km).
Time: About a week.
Accommodation: B&Bs and hostels.

The Kerry Way

This is a popular route which makes a complete circuit of the Iveragh Peninsula. It starts in the Killarney National Park and passes by mountain ranges such as Macgillicuddy's Reeks. Visit coastal towns such as Glenbeigh, Cahirciveen, Waterville and Caherdaniel. Makes use of old bog roads and hill tracks across rugged slopes. It is a scenic and interesting route which is a sort of walkers' version of the scenic 'Ring of Kerry' tour. The trail ends with a walk over a high gap between Kenmare and Killarney.

Length: 110 to 135 miles (175 to 220km).
Time: Over a week.
Accommodation: B&Bs, hostels and campsites.

The Dingle Way

This trail offers a complete circuit of the Dingle Peninsula in County Kerry. Fairly easy tracks lead past small villages and several ancient monuments. The only towns are Tralee and Dingle, but there are a number of small villages. The route is often close to the sea, but there is also a high-level stretch near Brandon Mountain which is frequently shrouded in mist. There is good mountain scenery and towards the end some lengthy coastal walking.

Length: About 100 miles (160km).
Time: About a week.
Accommodation: B&Bs and hostels.

The Western Way

The Western Way is a long and scenic route which wanders between the mountains of Connemara, passing the Holy Mountain of Croagh Patrick, then going round the Nephin Beg Range to reach the northern coast of County Mayo. The trail starts at Oughterard and visits Leenaun, Westport, Newport, Ballycastle and Ballina before ending on a boggy gap in the Ox Mountains. There are some long, boggy sections on this walk and some parts are remote from habitation. A spur from the route, known as the Bangor Trail, uses an old drove road from Newport to Bangor.

Length: About 150 miles (240km).
Time: Up to a fortnight.
Accommodation: B&Bs and hostels. Some parts have very sparse accommodation.

The Ulster Way

It is probably the most rugged of all the waymarked trails, yet the Ulster Way is fairly short. It starts in Pettigo and runs through County Donegal to reach the northern coast at Falcarragh. There are forests near the start around Lough Derg, then a boggy walk leads towards Lough Eske. Rugged, boggy ground is crossed around the Blue Stack Mountains on the way to Fintown. The slopes of Moylenanav and the Poisoned Glen are difficult to negotiate on the way to Dunlewy. After wandering around the splendid peak of Errigal and along Altan Lough, the trail reaches its end at Falcarragh.

Length: About 70 miles (115km).
Time: Up to a week.
Accommodation: B&Bs and a hostel. Sparse in places.

Other Long-distance Trails

These are being developed apace. When the Munster Way is fully open it will provide a link between the South Leinster Way and the Kerry Way, so that walkers will be able to follow a waymarked series of trails from Dublin to the south-west coast of Ireland. Other long-distance trails are being established along the towpaths of the Grand and Royal Canals. The Ballyhoura Way is being steered through the midlands and a number of shorter one- or two-day routes are available around the country. It should be noted that many of the trails in Ireland have some lengthy stretches along tarmac roads or forest tracks. To avoid blisters, it's often a good idea to have a pair of comfortable trainers in reserve.

Over The Hills

Some walkers are drawn towards bagging all the 3000ft (915m) mountains, which are spread across country from Wicklow to Kerry. A few tackle the 2000ft (610m) mountains. This is a fairly good way to get to know the mountainous areas, but many walkers simply head for County Kerry, where most of the mountains are to be found. Some of the classic, high-level walks include the traverse of Macgillicuddy's Reeks, the Coumloughra Horseshoe or the ridges of Brandon Mountain. There are plenty of good routes which seem seldom trodden.

Throughout the rest of Ireland, it seems that every mountain range has its day, when some organization encourages walkers to undertake the traverse of an entire range. Classic routes include the Lug Walk through the Wicklow Mountains; the Galty Ridgewalk through the Galty Mountains; the Maumturks Walk along the Maumturk Mountains; the 'Marathon' which runs from Muckish to Errigal in County Donegal. There are plenty of other traverses you could cover – in the Comeraghs, Knockmealdowns, Nephins, Blue Stacks and so on.

Lesser hill groups include well-known heights such as Slieve League, Carlingford Mountain, Slieve Blooms, the limestone Burren and so on. Most heights in Ireland have some legendary or historical significance and usually some sort of access route.

NORTHERN IRELAND

Walking is fairly popular in Northern Ireland, but it tends to be concentrated in a few areas. The place gets a bad press, so doesn't attract the numbers of visitors it really deserves. Rights of way are being recorded, but aren't yet shown on maps and only a few are signposted. However, there is the waymarked Ulster Way and a number of upland areas are good for walking.

Long-distance Trails

The Ulster Way

This enormous trail encircles Northern Ireland and even slips over the border in a couple of places. It visits most of the main walking areas and can be summarized in an anti-clockwise direction from Belfast: first are the broad, boggy Antrim Mountains – overlooking Belfast and the coast. These are moorlands with steep sides falling to the Nine Glens of Antrim. Next is the North Antrim Coast, which takes in the cliffs of Fair Head, the stunning White Park Bay and the ever-popular Giant's Causeway. From Downhill the route heads inland and crosses the broad, bleak, forested Sperrin Mountains.

Dungiven, Glenelly and Gortin Glen Forest Park are visited on the way to the Ulster American Folk Park. The route climbs Bessy Bell and wanders through Lough Bradan Forest to reach Pettigo. The Fermanagh Lakelands feature some stunning views of lakes, plus the Marble Arch Caves and Florence Court Forest Park. Forests and minor roads are a feature of South Tyrone, then in North Armagh there's a peep at one corner of the immense Lough Neagh. The Newry Canal leads from Portadown to Newry and has a good towpath. The Mountains of Mourne are climbed, then the route includes a series of coastal walks, leading around Strangford Lough and Belfast Lough to return to Belfast.

Obviously, the route is hardly ever walked in one go, so walkers tend to select scenic sections and cover them over a week or even a weekend. It deserves the attention of more long-distance walkers, as it's an interesting and varied route.

Length: About 570 miles (920km).
Time: About five weeks.
Accommodation: B&Bs, and a few hostels and campsites. Some areas have very sparse accommodation.

Over The Hills

The Mountains of Mourne are shapely and compact, and rise from the sea in County Down. A popular circuit follows the stout, solid Mourne Wall around the main summits. A bagful of 2000ft (610m) summits are found here. The Sperrin Mountains are about as high, but walkers are discouraged from wandering over the main summits. The vast, sprawling moorland of Cuilcagh straddles the border, and offers tough walking and wide-ranging views. Lesser hills include the broad and boggy Antrim Mountains, which you could explore via the waymarked Moyle Way. Solitary hills include Slieve Gallion and Slieve Gullion – both of which bear forest tracks.

THE ISLE OF MAN

This island is a sort of 'pig-in-the-middle' kind of place which often gets left out of things. However, it's a walkers paradise. There's a 100-mile (160-km) coastal circuit, and cross-island routes such as the Millennium Way and Herring Way. A whole range of hills is available and there's a solitary 2000ft (610m) summit called Snaefell. Views from this point embrace Seven Kingdoms – Scotland, England, Wales, Ireland, the Waters Above, the Waters Below . . . and of course the Kingdom of Man!

TREKKING THE WORLD

BY STEVE COOLING

These days world travel is cheap, and there's been a boom in people heading overseas for treks and trips into the wilderness. Going to some far-flung destination can seem daunting at first, but with sensible planning, the world's your oyster.

NORTH AMERICA

From the 19 680ft (6000m) peaks of Alaska to the canyons of Arizona and a whole lot in between, there is a host of trekking possibilities in North America. Most wild landscapes tend to be in the west, including the Rockies, but there are less spectacular wild areas in the east such as the Appalatian range. There are excellent trekking possibilities in many areas including the Sierra Nevada, especially in the Sequoia/Kings Canyon and Mount Whitney region. If you're really switched on by the 'Wild West' there's always the 2585 mile (4160km) Pacific Crest Trail to aim for.

In summer, trekking conditions tend to be ideal and many trails become heavily used. Put it another way – you're unlikely to find the solitude you might be seeking. In most National Parks you'll need to get a 'Backcountry Trekking' permit, which limits you to certain camping areas and routes. These are easily obtainable and free, from National Park information centres and ranger stations, but for ultra-popular destinations, such as Grand

Mount Liberty Bell, North Cascades, Washington State, USA.

Canyon National Park, you'll have to book many months in advance to get hold of a permit. If you trek without one then expect a stiff fine. The Canadian Rockies are less crowded, perfect for the authentic wilderness experience. Jasper/Banff and Yoho National Parks have miles of excellent trails, while for day walks the Lake Louise area is unrivalled. In North America, trail guides and maps are of a very high standard, and getting hold of freeze-dried food and fuel is easy.

Trekking the Virgin Narrows

Zion National Park, Utah, USA

The two-day trip following the narrow and deep canyon of the Virgin river in Utah's Zion National Park is a spectacular introduction to the region's trekking possibilities. It is a trek with a difference; one that leads deep into the earth with views of rearing canyon walls of red and yellow water-sculpted sandstone, with just a slit of blue sky above.

The route starts outside Zion National Park at the lonely Chamberlain's Ranch, 19 miles (30km) down some rough tracks. For those without their own transport, the National Park runs a special bus up to the trail head, leaving most days during the summer season.

From here it's downhill all the way; at first through pleasant meadows, then gradually deeper and deeper into the canyon. Route-finding is no problem, as there's only one way, and that's in the stream. Boulder-hopping soon gives way to wading. The rock scenery on either side is stupendous, with the Navajo sandstone carved into the most incredible shapes, and numerous narrow side 'slot' canyons which demand exploration.

Although the trip through the canyon is only around 12 miles (20km), most people choose to do it over two days, and camp for the night in the canyon. Due to the possibility of flash floods, it pays to camp as far above the water level as possible – luckily there are many convenient sandy terraces which provide ideal sites.

The next day's walk, more of a wade in reality, is through the most impressive section of 'narrows' where the canyon's walls are only a few metres apart, rising vertically for hundreds of metres. Each bend reveals new vistas of towering red sandstone.

Eventually the narrow, slot-like canyon widens and a concrete path leads to a car park, and, likely as not, milling hoards of tourists.

Distance and times: Around 12 miles (20km) from the trail head at Chamberlain's Ranch to the car park in

Zion Canyon. A quick trip without any side canyons could be done in a long day, but most people choose to spend at least two days in the canyon.

Difficulty and dangers: Given low water conditions, typical in the summer months, the deepest water that is likely to be encountered is waist deep, but conditions in the canyon change frequently and it pays to check locally. The canyon is prone to sudden flash flooding, so get an up-to-date weather forecast before setting out.

Season and weather: The best time is from June to September when the water is warmest. Outside the canyon temperatures are hot, frequently topping 90°F (35°C), while the canyon's depths remain pleasantly cool.

Equipment: Basic backpacking outfit, including walking stick for support while wading. Fabric boots dry out better than leather ones after a soaking.

Permits: Best obtained locally at the headquarters of the Zion National Park, in Zion Canyon.

You don't have to go in search of high mountains and snow. Canyons and deserts make for interesting and challenging walking, too.

SOUTH AMERICA

South America is another continent offering immense potential to the keen trekker. With the world's largest tropical rainforest, biggest river and the impressive Andes Mountains culminating in the great rock towers of Patagonia, there's plenty of scenery to soak up.

Unless you stick to the popular routes such as the Inca Trail, Ecuador's volcanoes and the more accessible parts of the Peruvian Andes, you'll have to be a hardy traveller and able to cope with route-finding (the maps are generally poor) in addition to language barriers. Little English is spoken, so a smattering of Spanish won't go amiss in most South American countries. There's also the worry of the Shining Path, a guerrilla outfit which has seriously disrupted tourism in Peru. If you're a tough traveller, and looking for an adventure, South America might be the place for you.

Trekking in Peru's Cordillera Huayhuash

After the Himalaya Mountains, the Andes is the next greatest range on earth, stretching the length of the South American continent, from Columbia in the north, to the wild island of Tierra del Fuego in the south. Geological instability is a feature of the whole area, and earthquakes and volcanic eruptions are common. There is a great contrast between the lush, eastern slopes of the range, nourished by moist air currents from the Amazon basin, and the harsh desert of the Pacific coast.

The Huayhuash forms a supremely rugged range, heavily glaciated with six summits over 21 000ft (6100m), and many high alpine lakes. The whole area is remote and unspoiled, and trips into the range have an expeditionary flavour lacking in more popular regions. More effort is required, but then the rewards are much greater.

From Huaraz, the main town in the area, getting to the trail head at the village of Llamac is something of an achievement. Peruvian buses tend to be crowded and hardly comfortable, and you may end up travelling in a truck. The route heads off into the mountains and, in crossing the continental divide twice, offers experiences of the lusher eastern slopes and the parched high altitude desert in the west – and of course, superlative views of the icy peaks high above.

The walking is tough and the trail crosses many high-altitude passes in excess of 16 500ft (5030m).

Time for a break. On trek in Bolivia.

Remote villages are passed *en-route* but don't rely on these to stock up with supplies. It's best to be totally self-sufficient and carry everything you expect to need. This means carrying heavy packs. Sometimes it's possible to hire *burros* (mules) which, along with their *arrieros* (owners), can add an extra dimension to a trip and ease logistical problems considerably.

Distance and times: Around 100 miles (160km), taking up to two weeks.
Difficulty and dangers: This is a remote region, so experience of remote and rugged mountains is desirable. Many high passes are crossed and in order to avoid altitude-related problems correct acclimatization is essential.
Season and weather: The Peruvian Andes are tropical mountains and there are no seasons as such. Heavy rains are experienced in northern and eastern areas from October to April, and the best weather usually occurs from June to mid September.

Equipment: Basic backpacking outfit, including tent and cooking equipment. Due to the high altitudes encountered, temperatures can be very low so warm clothing is required.
Permits: Not required.

ASIA: THE HIMALAYAS

To most people, trekking in Asia means one thing: the Himalaya. This is where commercial trekking began and there's immense scope for the independent trekker too. Combine incredible scenery with friendly people, especially in Nepal, and you have a trekker's Mecca. In most of the Himalaya there are two main seasons for trekking: the pre-monsoon, during March and April; and post-monsoon, in October and November. At these times of year the air is clearest and the weather most reliable. As there are few roads most trade and 'traffic' goes on foot, and trails are generally good.

There's more to Asia than the Himalayan mountains, however. There are trekking possibilities in

Trekking in Bolivia.

the lodges and probably little English spoken. For a first visit, it's probably best to head for one of the more popular areas, maybe at the tail-end of the season when fewer trekkers are about. Kathmandu must have more 'outdoor' bookshops than any-where else, and you'll certainly be able to get hold of maps and guide books there. There are many equipment shops too, but don't be fooled by 'gen-uine' kit offered at low prices. Much of it is locally made and certainly not real Gore-Tex or Lowe, for example! Take care with food and drink. Nepal is full of Westerners who have succumbed to gut rot – or worse. Filter or use iodine to sterilize all water.

Pakistan and India

Pakistan and India are not so geared up to trekkers, but if you're self-sufficient and willing to carry a heavy pack, including tent and food, there's plenty of scope for some interesting treks into some spec-tacular areas. Ladakh in Northern India and Pak-istan's Karakoram range are not subject to the monsoon, and are therefore a safer bet in the sum-mer months. In many places maps are non-exis-tent, so you'll have to rely on locals or guidebooks for directions. Getting hold of packaged food is diffi-cult, if not impossible, so make sure you buy such things back in the UK. You'll be able to replenish food stocks in the mountains, as in most areas there are many villages, but don't count on getting any-thing fancy.

Getting hold of fuel in the mountains can be problematic, so a multi-fuel stove will make life easier. In some areas, paraffin is available in moun-tain villages, but don't count on it. Check out the red-tape situation before heading into the wilds, as you may need permits for some areas – Sikkim and Kashmir, for example – and the regulations are always changing.

Apple Pies around Annapurna

The Annapurna circuit is a two- to three-week trek which circumnavigates the impressive Annapurna Himalaya in central Nepal. With the mountains of Dhaulagiri, Manaslu and the Annapurnas forming the ice-shrouded backdrop, frequent trekkers' lodges *en-route* and the friendly Nepali people, it's no wonder that this is one of the most popular treks in the Himalaya.

Most people choose to tackle the route in an anti-clockwise direction, by trekking up the lush Marsyandi valley to the town of Manang. Tackling the high Thorong La pass is easier from this side, as there is considerably less altitude to gain. It takes ten dusty hours by bus from Kathmandu to reach

Malaysia's jungle-clad mountains, in the Golden Triangle area of Thailand and many other areas, including the highlands of New Guinea.

Nepal

In Nepal it couldn't be easier to organize a trek. Kathmandu is home to many trekking agencies, who will arrange everything from porters to food for you. It's also easy to do everything yourself and head off into the mountains, stay in the many lodges and have a fantastic time without spending very much. Don't leave town without first getting hold of a trekking permit. The Everest and Anna-purna regions tend to be very popular, and find-ing accommodation in the high season can be troublesome.

Luckily there's much more to Nepal than these popular areas. Once off the beaten track you'll find the real Nepal. Unspoiled yes, but with many has-sles for the inexperienced – no Western menus in the road head at Besi Sahar. From there the route gradually gains height as the trail leads through medieval-looking villages and past steep, terraced fields. Accommodation is in lodges, found in every village, which are surprisingly good and very cheap. The staple food is 'Daal Bhat', curried lentils served up with vegetables and rice. It's delicious, too. Some lodges have cottoned on to Western tastes, and even offer pizza and chips, and apple pies!

Manang, a small village of flat-roofed houses at 11 500ft (3500m) is spectacularly situated below the peak of Gangapurna, which rears above a tangled ice fall. It's a good place to spend a few days acclimatizing before the crossing of the Thorong La pass 17 600ft (5400m), which is the high point of the route. It's a steep 3300ft (1000m) pull up to the pass, and in the thin air heart and lungs certainly feel the strain. The top is marked by a large cairn decorated with many tattered prayer flags and the view extends north into Tibet.

Far below, the green fields of Muktinath beckon, standing out in stark contrast to the desolate stony desert all around. The remainder of the route is down the valley of the Kali Gandaki, supposedly one of the deepest on earth. Half-way down you have the option of taking a side trip up into the Annapurna Sanctuary, a high valley ringed with icy summits and an inspiring place to spend a few days.

Arriving back at a road and catching a truck or bus belching out diesel fumes to Pokhara is all a bit of a shock after a routine of daily walking amidst stunning scenery and the friendly Nepali people.

Distance and times: Around 155 miles (250km) from the trail head at Besi Sahar to Phedi, near Pokhara. Allowing up to three weeks will give you time to soak up the atmosphere of the villages and head up into the Annapurna Sanctuary, a high valley surrounded by peaks.

Difficulty and dangers: Most of the walking is fairly easy and on good trails. Assuming that you're reasonably fit, you shouldn't have any problems. It pays to take time to acclimatize properly before tackling the Thorong La pass, which can be a killer. Take care with food, especially water, which must be filtered or sterilized using iodine before drinking.

Season and weather: Pre-monsoon, April and May, and post-monsoon, October and November, offer the clearest views and best conditions.

Equipment: Basic walking outfit including sleeping bag. Ice axe not needed.

Permits: Trekking permit obligatory, obtained in Kathmandu or Pokhara.

AFRICA

Africa is a vast continent with tremendous trekking possibilities. The mountains of East Africa are the most popular destination, offering treks through jungle-clad lower slopes up to moorlands of weird plants topped by glaciers and eternal snows. Mount Kenya and Mount Kilimanjaro are very popular with independent trekkers, and both have huts and good trails, though these days, a trip up 'Killy' is expensive. For more of an adventure, Uganda's Ruwenzori Mountains offer a challenge. There is now a network of huts, and within a couple of weeks it's possible to circumnavigate the range and climb a few peaks too. Rain and mud are typical conditions, so be warned! The town of Kasese is the start point and all arrangements, including the hire of porters, can be made there.

Many other parts of Africa offer exciting trekking opportunities, including South Africa's Drakensberg Mountains, the Ethiopian Highlands and the High Atlas in Morocco. Political instability, a harsh climate and a lack of accurate information can be problematic in Africa, but that's the price of getting off the beaten track . . .

Exploring Uganda's Mountains of the Moon

Imagine a range of spectacularly rugged peaks hung with glaciers rising from the hot savanna grasslands of equatorial Africa. The first white people to see the distant peaks nearly dismissed them as mere clouds, but long before, the Greek astronomer Ptolemy had predicted that such a range of mountains would exist in the middle of the Dark Continent. How he knew, nobody knows . . .

Even in these days of jet travel, the Ruwenzori Mountains – as they are better known – offer a challenge to trekkers and mountaineers. Luckily the trekkers' lot has become much easier of late, as the old huts which were in a poor state of repair have been superseded by a series of excellent new huts allowing a complete circumnavigation of the range in comfort. They are spaced a day's walk apart, and have bunk beds, but little else. You'll need to carry food and cooking equipment. It's customary to hire porters for the trek, and the men from the Bakonjo tribe are cheerful and hardy, many coping with the thick mud and roots with bare feet!

From the trail head at the small village of Ibanda the trail climbs unrelentingly; first through 13-ft (4-m) high elephant grass, then through thick, tropical rainforest, where moss hangs from every branch. Gradually the forest gives way to a sort of moorland, where the plant life seems to have gone crazy. Here the heather towers 40ft (12m) high, and the weird cabbage groundsel and giant lobelias look more like the creations of a science fiction writer than the process of natural selection.

The thick vegetation and boggy conditions make the going tough, and views of the surrounding peaks rare. But when the clouds do part, often just before sunset, the peaks of Stanley, Speke and Baker look inspiring, the steep rock walls and hanging glaciers offering formidable defences. But appearances can be deceptive and one of the features of this trek is that its possible for a suitably equipped party to climb the major peaks. Many of the climbs are not technical and would be well within the scope of experienced trekkers.

Distance and times: About 43 miles (70km) round trip from Ibanda, near Kasese. The route described could be completed in a week, but allowing up to two weeks will give you time to climb some of the peaks and do some exploring.

Difficulty and dangers: Most of the walking is quite tough, conditions underfoot are frequently boggy and rooty, and it rains for much of the time! The mountains are a complete wilderness and all food has to be carried. It pays to take time to acclimatize properly before crossing any passes or climbing any high peaks.

Season and weather: As the mountains are almost bang on the equator, there are no seasons as such. The so-called 'dry seasons', December to March and May to September, offer the clearest views and best conditions.

Equipment: Basic walking outfit including good waterproofs and boots, sleeping bag and cooking equipment. Pack ice axe, crampons and ropes if you intend to climb any of the peaks.

Permits: Not required, but check locally as rules frequently change.

AUSTRALASIA

New Zealand

A land of tremendous contrasts, New Zealand has many spectacular wilderness areas, including Fiordland, one of the world's wettest places (over 315in (8000mm) of precipitation annually), and the Southern Alps, with 12 346ft (3764m) Mount Cook the highest peak. There are many excellent wilderness treks in Fiordland, including the popular Milford and Routeburn Tracks. 'Tramping', Kiwispeak for trekking, is very popular, and you even have to make reservations on the popular Milford Track. Escape the hoards on other equally impressive routes nearby, including The Dusky, Hollyford and Kepler tracks.

Most tracks are well served by huts which are paid for on an honesty basis. They're a welcome haven from the hoards of marauding sandflies and frequent precipitation. Don't forget to pack 'Dimp', the local brand of Diethyltoluamide, better known as insect repellent. The small town of Te Anau is the tramping capital of the South Island and the place to get local trail information. As for the rest of New Zealand, it has loads of wilderness, very few people and vast potential for the trekker.

Australia

Most people don't realize the tremendous trekking potential in Australia. It has the lot, from hot deserts and rainforests, to Tasmania's vast wilderness. In the summer months, temperatures can get a little too hot for comfort and water can be hard to find. As a result, most people choose to trek in winter (the same time as the British summer), when conditions are often ideal. There are many National Parks, and most are well served with trails. The Blue Mountains, near Sydney, are cool in the summer, and Mount Kosciusko near Canberra is the highest peak and a good area for trekking. The island state of Tasmania is home to one of the world's largest temperate wildernesses, protected in several world heritage areas, and with outstanding trekking opportunities. The South West Coast Trail, the Overland Track and the Western Arthur Range are all in unspoiled wilderness areas. Some of the trail heads are only accessible by air! The weather can be temperamental, and watch out for the tiger snakes and bogs too! After trekking in Australia you'll understand why the Aussies are fond of the term 'bushwalking'.

Tasmania's South Coast Trail

This magnificent walk traverses a wilderness area of stunning beauty; vast sandy beaches, rugged mountains, boggy 'button grass' plains and rainforest are all encountered. The 59 mile (95km) trail keeps close to the coast for most of its length, and splendid camps above the beach are an endearing feature of this trek.

Apart from walking in and back, there's only one way to the trail head, and that's by air. Several companies fly into remote Melaleuca, an abandoned mining settlement deep in South West National Park. From there it takes a minimum of five days to walk out to the roadhead at Cockle Creek, but most people choose to spend several 'rest' days exploring the coast. Allowing eight or nine days to complete the route would be a good idea.

In most places, the trail is fairly easy to follow as it wends its way through thick bush. Think of it more as tackling an obstacle course which includes deep, gloopy mud, boulders, branches and roots, and you begin to get the picture. A length of 59 miles (95km) may not sound much, but Tasmanian trails demand more respect than most . . .

The wild and remote beaches offer a welcome respite from the arduous sections of bushwhacking, and after a hard day's walking it's great to explore a deserted beach and wash muddy feet in the Southern Ocean.

Although the trail is relatively level for most of its length, crossing the high Ironbound range involves a hard slog up 3000ft (900m) of boggy hillside. The stunning views are adequate compensation for all the effort. Far below, the New River Lagoon, later crossed by rowing boat, and immaculate Prion Beach beckon.

Arriving at Cockle Creek and dumping heavy packs on the ground is a good moment, but such is the beauty and charm of this magnificent coast that most people vow to return . . .

Distance and time: About 59 mile (95km) round trip from Melaleuca to Cockle Creek. The route described could be completed in five days, but allowing up to nine or ten days will give you time to do some exploring or wait out bad weather.

Difficulty and dangers: Although the trail is well defined, most of the walking is hard and conditions underfoot are frequently boggy. Tasmania is famous for its bad weather and storms can cause creeks to rise fast. The whole area is a complete wilderness and all food has to be carried. Encountering snakes is quite likely and since all Tasmanian species are venomous, it pays to tread carefully!

Season and weather: The summer months of December to March are best, although foul weather can strike at any time.

Equipment: Basic walking outfit, including full camping equipment, good waterproofs and boots.

Permits: Not required, although may soon be introduced. Check locally.

EUROPE

What could be easier than trekking in Europe? Although there are few true wilderness areas, there are many spectacular mountain ranges from the Alps and Pyrenees to the rugged Pindus range in Greece. For trekking without hassle, Europe has to be high on the list of destinations. In many mountain areas, especially the Alps, trails are of an excellent standard, and well served with huts where cheap(ish) food and lodging can be found. The trouble is that in many parts the trails are as busy as the M25 and people jams are a serious possibility.

France has a splendid network of GRs, otherwise known as long-distance footpaths. GR10 follows the Pyrenees from the Atlantic to the Mediterranean and is a challenging walk. If you like your mountains wild and prefer cooler regions, then head for Scandinavia where the sun never sets in summer. In general, maps are excellent (except in Greece and Spain), as are the many guidebooks. With the opening up of Eastern Europe there are bound to be some interesting 'new' areas, such as the Polish Tatras, for trekkers to escape the madding crowds of the Alps.

The High Pyrenees

The Pyrenean mountains stretch from the Basque country in the west to the Mediterranean in the east, and by linking up various trails, it's possible to walk the length of the range, from coast to coast. The best part of the range is in the central area, and this route dips in and out of both France and Spain as it wends its way from the village of Lescun in the west to the tiny country of Andorra in the east.

The route is generally on good trails, but there are plenty of ups and downs, many opportunities to camp out in impressive mountain surroundings, and frequent refuges (huts) providing cheap food and accommodation.

Lescun is a delightful village with impressive views up to the spiky limestone summit of Pic d'Ansaberre which dominates the valley. The trail heads out of town through forests of beech and fir, and gradually climbs up to a rocky cirque where peasants bring their animals to graze for the summer months. If you're lucky they may even have some spare milk or cheese! From here there are many high passes to cross, and it pays to carry an ice axe, as even late in the season snow can make some of the descents tricky.

There are great contrasts between the French and Spanish sides; to the north the villages are thriving and prosperous, while on the Spanish most have long since been deserted by their inhabitants and now lie ruined, gradually succumbing to advancing creepers and plants slowly reclaiming lost ground.

There are plenty of opportunities to scramble up to some summits *en route*. Aneto 11 165ft (3404m), the highest summit in the Pyrenees, still holds some small glaciers, but is easily climbed, the final rocky arête offering some exciting scrambling and far-ranging views.

Further east, the Sierra de los Encantados are every bit as enchanting as their name suggests. A myriad of granite peaks rise from a plateau of rocky tarns, where camping is a delight and seeing another person is rare.

Distance and times: Around 155 miles (250km) from Lescun to Andorra. The route described could be comfortably completed in around three to four weeks, but allow more time if you intend climbing many peaks *en-route*.

Difficulty and dangers: Most of the trails are well marked and route-finding is not difficult, although marking is generally not as good on the Spanish side.

Season and weather: Summer, from July to September, is the best time to tackle this route. Foul weather can strike at any time and violent summer thunderstorms are common, especially in the afternoons.

Equipment: Basic walking outfit including camping equipment/bivvy bag for nights in remote areas where there are no refuges. Ice axe recommended for some steep, snowy descents.

Permits: Not required.

EXOTICA: GREENLAND, ANTARCTICA, SPITSBERGEN

Strictly for the hardiest and most experienced individuals, but such areas offer the true wilderness experience. If you have the expertise, equipment and skills, there are some outstanding opportunities in these cold regions. Getting there could prove expensive and you might feel more like an explorer than a trekker. Comprehensive insurance to fully cover eventualities such as being stranded by blizzards – it has happened – should also be seriously considered.

THE NECESSITY OF WILDERNESS PROTECTED AREAS

BY ROLAND SMITH

Thousands of tired, nerve-shaken, over-civilised people are beginning to find out that going to the mountains is going home; that wilderness is a necessity; and that mountain parks and reservations are useful not only as fountains of timber and irrigating rivers, but as fountains of life.

The opening words of wilderness guru John Muir's book *Our National Parks*, written over a century ago and published in 1901, are just as relevant in today's world.

In Muir's day, much of the American West which he was describing and for which he was such a passionate protagonist could still truly be described as untouched wilderness. Today, as the real wilderness areas of the world continue to shrink at an alarming rate, there has never been a time when it has been more important to keep the wild places wild, for exactly the reasons so eloquently expressed by Muir a century ago.

More and more citizens of the late twentieth century are realizing Muir's 'necessity of wilderness;' the need to escape to places where humankind's influence is either absent or unseen, to recharge their mental and physical batteries in wild country.

And few places are more suitable to do that than the National Parks and other officially protected areas. The story of the international National Parks movement could be said to have begun in the English Lake District. It was here, in his 'Guide 'through the District of the Lakes' published in 1810, that the poet William Wordsworth first suggested that 'persons of pure taste' should join him in deeming that the district should be 'a sort of national property, in which every man has a right and interest who has an eye to perceive and a heart to enjoy.'

Yet it was to be another 60 years before the first National Park in the world was set up by far-sighted pioneers like John Muir at Yellowstone on the borders of Montana and Wyoming, in 1872. Muir's encounter with President Theodore Roosevelt in 1903 at Glacier Point, overlooking the spectacular Yosemite National Park of California, which had been established in 1890, has been described as one of the turning points in the history of the conservation movement. Other state-run National Parks soon followed in various New World countries and the first in Europe were set up in Sweden in 1909.

Although Muir was born in the small Scottish fishing town of Dunbar in 1838 and never forgot his ancestry it seems ironic that, even now, there are no National Parks in Scotland. The uninhabited, state-owned wildernesses that larger countries like America could afford to set aside bear little resemblance to the privately-owned landscapes of the small and heavily-populated island of Britain. And Scotland's case for or against National Parks has always been quite different from that of the rest of Britain.

The first statutory attempt to set up National Parks in Britain was James Bryce's Access to Mountains Bill of 1884. This and later attempts were all ultimately frustrated, and it was not until the Addison Committee of 1931 reported on the desirability for National Parks in Britain that the possibility gained real political support.

The post-war Labour government was firmly committed to the outdoor movement and in 1945 it appointed John Dower, an architect and town planner, to write the report which was to form the blueprint for the British National Parks system. In his report, Dower gave the generally-accepted definition of a British-style National Park. It was, he wrote:

an extensive area of beautiful and relatively wild country in which, for the nation's benefit and by appropriate national decision and action:
(a) the characteristic landscape beauty is strictly preserved
(b) access and facilities for public open-air enjoyment are amply provided
(c) wild life and buildings and places of architectural and historic interest are suitably protected, while
(d) established farming use is effectively maintained.

When Sir Arthur Hobhouse reported two years later, Dower's definition was accepted and 12 parks (including the Broads and the South Downs) were proposed with an administration system which was incorporated in the long-awaited National Parks and Access to the Countryside Act of 1949.

The same Act also set up the mechanism for a second tier of landscape protection for areas in Britain not within a National Park but which 'appear(s) . . . to be of such outstanding natural beauty that it is desirable that the provisions of the Act relating to such areas should apply thereto.' They were to be known as Areas of Outstanding Natural Beauty (AONBs).

There was much heated debate on the splitting up of landscape and nature conservation, and eventually the two functions were separated by the creation of the National Parks (later Countryside) Commission and the Nature Conservancy Council (now known as English Nature). The latter organization was made responsible for the designation and management of National Nature Reserves (NNRs), many of which, of course, were within National Parks and AONBs.

During the early 1950s, ten National Parks were designated, although only the first two, the Peak and the Lakes (which eventually received National Park status 140 years after Wordsworth had first suggested it), were administered by the independent planning boards recommended by both Dower and Hobhouse. The others – Snowdonia, Dartmoor, the Pembrokeshire Coast, North York Moors, Yorkshire Vales, Exmoor, Northumberland and the Brecon Beacons – were all run by special committees of their respective county councils. The Norfolk and Suffolk Broads eventually joined the family as a National Park in all but name in 1989, and the government has recently announced that the New Forest in Hampshire will soon be similarly designated.

The Edwards Review of National Parks, published in 1991, was the first major review of the working of the parks for 15 years. It proposed that all parks should be administered by independent boards as originally recommended and that the purposes of the parks should be restated to expressly refer to 'quiet enjoyment and understanding, and to the conservation of the wildlife and cultural heritage'.

Over 30 AONBs have been designated since 1956, the latest and largest being the North Pennines, covering the wild moorlands between the Yorkshire Dales and the Tyne Gap, in 1988. Other AONBs cover such beautiful countryside as the Cotswolds, the Shropshire Hills and the Gower in South Wales.

But the protection of these equally precious areas remains imperfect, with a duty on the local planning authorities only to consult the Countryside Commission for advice on development plans, and to take appropriate action to preserve and enhance their natural beauty.

Today the 11 National Parks of Britain are widely regarded as the jewels in our countryside crown. They cover 10 per cent of the land area of England and Wales, and range from the gentle coastal scenery of the Pembrokeshire coast and Norfolk Broads, to the more rugged landscapes of Snowdonia and the Lake District.

In 1992, the parks received over 100 million day visits and, with increased leisure time, these figures are bound to grow as we approach the turn of the century. But 40 years on, and despite being among the nation's best-loved landscapes, Britain's National Parks still suffer from an identity problem.

Despite their name, they are neither 'national' in the international sense, nor that of being owned by the nation. Neither are they 'parks' in the normally accepted, urban sense. They are frequently confused with the National Trust and still have not established themselves as part of the nation's culture as they have in America, where the British pioneer John Muir is far better known than in his native land.

In Britain, National Park designation does not change land ownership, nor does it normally allow any special rights of access to the public. Except in areas where access agreements have been negotiated with landowners (most notably in the Peak), walkers have to stick to the rights of way system just like anywhere else in Britain, and wild country campers should usually seek the landowners' permission. The same laws apply in National Parks as anywhere in Britain, so respect the property and rights of the 250,000 local residents.

The National Park authority's main task is to act as the local planning authority; controlling development and trying to ensure that harmful change does not take place. The first priority is always to protect the landscape, so that future generations can continue to enjoy it. National Park authorities are also charged with providing suitable quiet, open-air recreational opportunities for visitors, and with protecting the wildlife and historic heritage of the parks. They must also always have due regard to the interests of those who live and work in them.

One of the most difficult problems faced by National Park authorities is reconciling their dual, and sometimes conflicting, aims of conservation and recreation. For example, allowing free access to ramblers on open moorland can upset the ecologists, because that moorland is often the breeding ground for rare birds of prey and serious disturbance could be caused.

Three-quarters of the expenditure of British National Park authorities comes directly from the government by means of a special grant, which in 1990/1 was about £18.75 million for all 11 Parks – less than the grant given to the Royal Opera House, Covent Garden and equivalent to the cost of a newspaper annually per head of the population.

The other 25 per cent of National Parks expenditure comes from a precept on the local authorities within which the National Park falls, in return for which the park authority carries out the local planning function. National Park authorities also now earn a significant proportion of their income from their own activities.

The membership of National Park authorities is made up of two-thirds from local county and district councils, and one-third direct appointments by the Secretary of State for the Environment, specifically to look after the national interest. For the dedicated backpacker and wild country enthusiast, the British National Parks, AONBs and other protected areas represent rich areas for exploration and 'getting away from it all'. Even for those who enjoy a veneer of civilization, there are usually well-marked and maintained footpaths and good campsites.

Many of our best-known long-distance paths or national trails also run through the National Parks. The Pennine Way, for example, crosses three, the Peak, Yorkshire Dales and Northumberland, as does Alfred Wainwright's Coast-to-Coast route, which runs through the Lake District, Yorkshire Dales and North York Moors.

With such a wealth of trail walking opportunities, it is hardly surprising that some of our National Parks are now suffering as a result of their own popularity. Footpath erosion on the best-known and publicized routes, such as the Pennine Way, the Yorkshire Dales' Three Peaks and the popular routes to Snowdon's summit, is now a severe problem to the hard-pressed National Park authorities and represents a severe drain on their limited resources in expensive footpath maintenance schemes.

But true wilderness seekers can still find the solitude they need by avoiding the crowds and finding their own routes into what is left of Britain's wild country in these protected landscapes.

The benefits were best expressed by John Muir, perhaps the greatest wilderness sage:

Climb the mountains and get their good tidings. Nature's peace will flow into you as sunshine flows into trees. The winds will blow their own freshness into you, and the storms their energy, while cares will drop off like autumn leaves.

CHAPTER 5

The Walkers' Bible

Mountain navigation

by Terry Storry

THE SKILLS of mountain navigation are still much neglected. Many find out too late that they cannot navigate. Few would contemplate going to sea in a boat without having a good groundwork in navigation. Yet many go into the hills thinking they will find their way using a 'sense of direction'. There is no such thing. If you are caught out in bad weather and rely on a sense of direction you will go round in circles, or worse still wander over a cliff face!

A very high proportion of mountain accidents are due to bad navigation. Accidents are often reported as being due to exposure, or slipping on snow or wet grass, but in many cases the accidents would not have happened without an initial error in navigation. The first part of this chapter outlines the skills of good mountain navigation. These skills can be summarized as map reading, compass bearings and distance estimation.

Everyone gets lost, including me. You cannot spend all your time peering at a map, nor would you want to; there are better things to do in the hills. So you need to know how to relocate yourself as well as how to stay on course. The second part of this chapter suggests what to do if you get 'temporarily misplaced'!

THE SKILLS OF MOUNTAIN NAVIGATION

Map Reading

The two map scales most useful to the mountain walker are the 1:50 000 and 1:25 000. The latter covers half the area but gives twice the detail. It is therefore very useful for bad visibility navigation. It is not so useful where permanent snow cover hides the features shown – walls, streams, and lakes for instance – or where the land is already featureless – moorland or high plateau areas. In that case the more closely packed contours on the 1:50 000 map can make it easier to 'read' the land forms.

The most important symbol for map reading is the contour. This is a line joining points of equal height. The shape of these lines shows the shape of the hillside and the spacing of them shows the steepness. With practice you can look at the contours and picture the shape of the hill in your mind.

A good compass is essential. This one is a sighting model, the Silva 15T Ranger.

You will then be able to identify your position and plan your route. Other important symbols to help you read the map in the mountains are crags, walls, streams and lakes.

Planning a route off a map is harder than it might at first appear. This is because of the unknowns. From a map you cannot tell how deep the river that you have to cross will be, or the degree of tree fall and undergrowth in a forest on your route, or the amount or condition of the snow on the tops you want to traverse. Local knowledge is invaluable, sometimes essential.

Having said that, there are a number of useful route-planning 'rules of thumb'. First of all look for routes that gain height early and then stay high. This keeps you out of boggy ground, gives you good views (hopefully) and above all prevents the extra work involved in reascending.

Second, when planning the ascent or descent avoid very close contours. The best way through mountainous country is by ridges or valleys. The slopes on either side of these features are often unpleasantly steep for walking, although sometimes excellent for climbing.

Third, avoid boulder fields and marshes. These two features are particularly unpleasant and time-consuming to walk through. Boulder fields are in fact only marked on 1:25 000 maps, as is the more useful navigational feature of walls/fences; this map is therefore useful for planning in combination with the 1:50 000 map on which contour features are better highlighted.

Finally, pick a route that has a number of alternatives. The alternatives may be more attractive once you are out there, so try not to commit yourself at the planning stage. Some alternatives should also be escape routes if the weather deteriorates or you have overestimated your fitness.

COMPASS BEARINGS

As an instrument for navigating in the hills, the compass is best used working from map to ground. You take bearings from a known position to an intended position and then walk on that bearing, probably for a certain length of time or number of paces. Below I describe how the compass will enable you to take a grid bearing (measure the direction of travel angle on a map) and walk on that bearing (use the magnetic needle).

Grid Bearings

To take a bearing from the map the compass is used like a protractor. It measures the angle of intended direction from grid (map or geographical) north. The measurement is done in three stages.

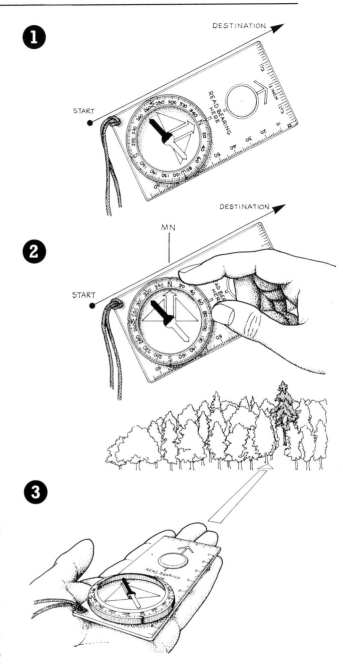

1 Place the side of the compass on where you are and where you intend going, with the direction of travel arrow pointing towards the latter.
2 Turn the compass housing round until the orienting lines are parallel with the eastings (grid lines going from north to south on the map) with the orienting needle pointing north.
3 Read off the bearing where the direction of travel arrow intersects the compass housing.

It will be best to get someone with experience to show you how to make this measurement. Even after much practice, however, you should always estimate the angle/bearing before measuring it. This obviates the frequent errors caused by mis-aligning the direction of the travel arrow on the base plate or the orienting arrow in the compass housing.

Magnetic Variation

Unfortunately, for those who have to navigate with a magnetic compass, magnetic north does not coincide with grid north. The magnetic pole is somewhere north of the Hudson Bay in Canada at the moment. In Britain, magnetic north is to the west of grid north. In other parts of the world it is to the east of grid north. A further complication is that the magnetic pole moves, so the variation between magnetic and grid north is changing. In Britain the variation is 5° at the time of writing decreasing by about ½° every three years.

The crucial thing of course is to know whether to add or subtract this variation when working between map and compass, and vice versa. Bearings on a compass are measured in a clockwise direction from north (0/360°) to east (90) to south (180) and then to west (270). Since in Britain the magnetic pole is west of the geographical pole, a compass bearing will always point further left (anti-clockwise) than a bearing taken off a map – by 5° at the moment. To compensate for this you must, after taking a bearing from the map, and before following that bearing on the ground, move the compass bearing to the right (clockwise) – in short, add 5°.

The opposite also holds true. If you take a bearing on the ground – to identify your position from some recognizable feature as described below, for instance – you must, before transferring it to the map, move the compass bearing anti-clockwise (left). In short, subtract 5°. Otherwise the bearing, taken from the magnetic pole, would be too large or, to put it another way, point too far right on the

Understanding the reason why we add or subtract the magnetic variation is the best way to remember what to do, but there are a number of tricks and rhymes that will stand in its stead. Here are three.

1 The ground is bigger than the map so you must add if moving from small to big (map to ground) and subtract if going from big to small (ground to map).
2 Grid to mag(netic) add, mag to grid subtract.
3 G (grid) comes before M (magnetic) in the alphabet so you add if moving in that direction and vice versa.

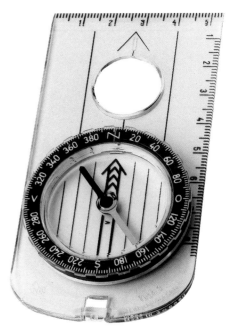

A good compass for beginners, the Silva 3NL.

Because the magnetic variation is relatively small in Britain at present, for the next decade it may be ignored for purposes of getting a rough direction of travel or for 'setting' the map (aligning the map to the ground for the purposes of identifying features).

Walking on a Bearing

To walk on the *magnetic* bearing you align the magnetic needle with the orienting needle in the compass housing and follow in the direction indicated by the direction of travel arrow (on the compass base plate). Walking on a bearing is usually combined with pacing or timing to determine distance travelled.

Unless you use a sound and practised technique you can easily walk off your bearing. A 12° error in your bearing will result in a 20 per cent error at the end of your 'leg' (intended distance), i.e. on a leg of 1km you will be 200m from your intended destination. Some error is inevitable given that a mountain compass is not an accurate instrument and a small sweep search may be necessary at the end of your leg to find your desired destination. But good technique will do much to reduce the area of search.

There are four main methods of walking on a bearing:

1 Leapfrogging

Send someone out ahead on the bearing while you remain stationary. Stop them at the limit of hearing and visibility (whichever comes first); they turn to face you (particularly at night when torches are used) and then align themselves on the bearing following your instructions. Remember that your left and right will be different from their left and right as they face you; decide whose left and right you will use before starting the exercise. Satisfied they are on the bearing, you then join them. This is the slowest but most accurate method, useful only when pinpoint accuracy is essential. Leaders (without assistants) should not use this method because it necessitates novices leading into unknown ground, possibly in bad conditions.

2 I Spy

Take a bearing on an object and walk to it. This is accurate and fast, but cannot be used at night or in white-out conditions. Do not make the mistake of taking a bearing on an object which cannot be reached either because it moves (like a sheep) or because it is too far away (like a distant silhouette, light or summit); in both cases you can walk off the bearing without realizing it. And make sure the object of your desire is distinctive. One bunch of heather, pointed rock or jumble of boulders looks much the same as another once you have taken your eye off it.

3 Swingometer

Walk along trying to keep the magnetic needle over the orienting needle. When first using this method you may end up face first in bogs and boulder fields! Aligning the arrow and looking at your feet at the same time is not easy. Always remember the bearing, because having landed in the aforementioned bog or boulder field, your compass may have been jolted off course.

Do not reject the swingometer because of hurt pride or painful bruises or, indeed, because, as its nickname suggests, it is the least accurate method. Its accuracy improves considerably with practice and it is the only possible method if walking for any length of time in very bad visibility (leapfrogging is dangerously slow). If accuracy is important, to locate a small, isolated feature for instance, timing or pacing will enable a sweep search or box search to be conducted at the end of the 'leg'. A 6° error over 1km would lead you to be 100m out, and if legs are kept to less than 500m, you will not have to look far when you arrive at the end of your pacing.

Alternatively, you could use the swingometer for a long approach to a large feature, and then finish off by leapfrogging to the pinpoint. If walking all

Good map reading helps keep you on track.

night, it is best to go for large features every time; that way the swing on the swingometer becomes irrelevant. Junctions are a good way of defining your position (e.g. wall/stream, ridge/forest, path/fence) and the swingometer method is best used here in conjunction with aiming off.

4 Aiming Off

Rather than walk directly on a compass bearing at an object, it may be better to aim off to one side. This takes account of the fact that taking and walking on bearings is necessarily inaccurate. Aiming off is only appropriate if there is a linear feature close to your objective, a track, stream, wall, valley or ridge, a feature big enough to allow for inaccuracies in 'aim', and which will lead you on to your objective.

If, for example, you are heading for a bridge over a stream in bad visibility, you can deliberately aim (take a bearing) upstream or downstream of the bridge. Once you 'hit' the stream you will know whether to turn left or right for the bridge. If you had aimed directly for the bridge and missed you would not know whether to go upstream or downstream, and Murphy's Law suggests you would first search in the wrong direction.

Clive Tully atop Ryan Mountain, Joshua Tree
National Monument, California.

Estimating Distance

There is little point in walking on a bearing unless
you know when to stop. To estimate distance you
will either have to count paces or watch the time.
Pacing and timing necessitates measuring distance
on the map. This is done with the millimetre scale,
or more easily with a romer, a graduated scale
etched into the base plate of more expensive compasses.

Timing

A reasonably fit hill walker with a rucksack should
be able to maintain a speed of 3mph (5kph) over
flat and even ground. The variables are weight of
rucksack and weather conditions; moreover this
speed does not allow for rest or lunch stops. If you
are going uphill add on half an hour for every 300m
climbed (this is 1 minute per 10m contour). Walking downhill you should be able to maintain your
flat speed unless it is very steep. An ascent of Snowdon (3 560ft/1085m) from Pen y Pass (1168ft/
356m) by way of the Pyg track (4 miles/6km)
would therefore take about 2½ hours. Add on
1 hour for stops and you have 3½ hours as a realistic estimate of ascent time.

Timing is most useful as a general estimate of
what distance can be covered in the time available
or what distance has been covered in the time
elapsed. It can be used with practice as an estimate
of distance over short legs – after walking for 6 minutes on the flat you will have covered about 500m –
but where navigation or visibility or terrain necessitates a 'stop–go' walking style, it is less accurate
than pacing.

Pacing

When walking on a bearing in bad visibility or at
night an accurate estimation of distance is essential.
Pacing is the best way to do this. An average person
will do between 120 and 130 paces to 100m on flat
ground. Going uphill and/or over difficult terrain,
you may have to increase your paces by up to 60 or
70 for every 100m. To find out your number of
paces to 100m you will have to measure that distance off the map and pace it over various types of
terrain going uphill and downhill.

When you are using pacing on the hill, count
every other pace – in other words each time you
place your right or left leg, and start again after
every 100m. That way you should never have to
count above 100 even when going steeply uphill –
keeping to small numbers means there is less
chance of losing count. However, you will have to
have some means of remembering each 100m.
Thumbing a numbered 'clicker' fixed to the side of
the compass is the best method. Coins or pebbles
transferred from one pocket to another is a less reliable alternative.

Altimeters

Altimeters are expensive, but are of value to the
trail walker needing to navigate for long distances
in bad weather or over featureless terrain. Setting
off from a known height, you can use an altimeter
to discover how much height you have lost or
gained. Over distances of more than ½ mile (1km)
this is simpler and more accurate than pacing or
timing.

An altimeter can also help if you are traversing a
slope. The tendency here is to 'fall off' the contours
or, for those aware of this tendency, to over-react
and start climbing. An altimeter will help keep you
on the level.

An altimeter works on the principle that atmospheric pressure always decreases with height. Since
pressure does not remain constant during the day,
the altimeter should be reset when passing any spot
height marked on the map.

Fast-moving trekker in Turkey's Aladaglar Taurus mountains.

TEMPORARILY MISPLACED? OR LOST?

You're a long way from home. The clag's come down. It's getting dark. You don't know where you are. You're on your own. Has this ever happened to you? I suspect it has, but you don't like to admit it. Can you get yourself out of trouble?

Even good navigators can get lost. If this happens, the first thing to do is to admit you don't know where you are. The better you are at navigation, the harder this is. But without a problem there is no solution. Do not press on regardless. That way lies disaster. Admit you have made a mistake and

consider your options. If you can select the appropriate option, you will, with some justification, be able to claim you have never been lost, only temporarily misplaced. The next section outlines the options open to you.

Option 1 Retrace Your Steps

You can do this in your mind first before you do it in body. Ask yourself the following questions. Can you remember anything you passed that will help you relocate – a stream, wall, lake, crag, valley or ridge? Can you identify anything around you on the map? Perhaps there is a prominent summit, or a deep valley or a sheep fold close to you? Were your navigational calculations from your last known point – bearing, pacing and timing – correct?

If none of these questions has helped you to relocate, then you may have to walk back to your last known point and start again. In the unlikely event that you can see where you have come from, take a (back-)bearing on the position and locate yourself in that way (assuming you know, or can estimate, the distance). If you cannot see or find your way back to your last known point because you have been wandering aimlessly, then proceed to options 3 or 4.

Option 2 Search

If retracing your steps – in mind or body or both – has proved to your satisfaction that you are in approximately the right place, then you should search the area. Below I outline two ways of doing this depending on whether you are alone or in a group. Crucially, with both methods you can always regain your original position, or pinpoint your new position in relation to it, in the event you do not find your objective. If you choose any other method, it must at least incorporate this characteristic, otherwise you really will get lost.

Spiral search

The expanding right-angle spiral search is useful if you are by yourself or perhaps walking with one other person. Choose a point on the ground at the limit of visibility from your position and pace count to it on a bearing. To simplify matters this original bearing should be a cardinal point on the compass – north, south, east or west. Turn 90° to the right and search for a distance equal to twice the visibility (i.e. twice your last pace count). Turn 90° to the right and search for a distance equal to three times the limit of visibility. And so on until you find your objective, or give up and return to your original position.

Your ice axe makes a useful "third leg" for winter hill walking.

Sweep search

The circular sweep search is useful if you are in a group of three or more, but the bigger the better. The group spreads out along a line of known bearing and distance, keeping within sight of each other. Person A stays at the original point and the group rotates around him or her. If the objective is not sighted once the line has returned to the original bearing, the whole group can then pivot around person E who was originally at the far end of the line. The process can be repeated in one direction (bearing) or in different directions. To regain the original position prior to going in a different direction, simply return along the bearing by the correct multiple (the number of sweeps) of the line distance.

Option 3 Back-bearings and Re-section

As a walker you will frequently follow line features – ridges, valleys, slopes, rivers, streams, footpaths, tracks – using them as 'handrails' without knowing exactly where you are along them. After all, walking would be pretty boring if you spent your whole time looking at the map. Suddenly you notice the weather is changing, or it is getting late, and you want to know exactly where you are so you can concentrate on the route or change your plans.

Knowing you are somewhere along a line feature means you can take a bearing back from a point feature off to one side – 90° is the ideal angle to identify your position. After subtracting the magnetic variation from the bearing, transfer it to your map by putting the side of the compass base plate on the point feature and rotating the whole compass until the orienting lines in the compass housing are parallel with the eastings. Now draw a line (imaginary or real) along the side of the compass base plate; where it intersects your 'handrail' is your location.

Another method of using a single (back-)bearing for relocation is to take the aspect of the slope. If you are contouring a slope – in other words using an (invisible!) contour as a handrail – and want to know where you are along it, take a bearing at right angles to the slope (i.e. directly down it) and transfer that to the map (remember to subtract the magnetic variation). Keep the orienting lines parallel with the eastings, and slide the base plate across the slope until the side of the compass intersects the contour lines at right angles – that is how far along the contour you have travelled. This technique works best if the aspect of the slope you are on, in other words the direction the slope faces, is changing rapidly as you traverse it.

Less common is the situation where you are completely lost, (I mean temporarily misplaced), but can see, and recognize on the map, prominent landmarks around you. This is an unlikely combination since if the visibility is good enough for you to identify features, you will usually have a rough idea of where you are. But let us suppose you don't because you are in featureless terrain (like the Cairngorm plateau in winter), yet surrounded by obvious distant peaks. If you take (back-)bearings on the peaks and transfer them to the map, their point of intersection indicates your position.

A breathtaking winter day in the hills. Sunshine and snow on Sharp Edge, Blencathra.

In point of fact such is the inaccuracy of 'sighted' bearings with hand-held compasses that you never produce a 'point' of intersection, but rather a 'triangle of error'. Your position will be somewhere within the triangle. Prismatic or 'optical sighting' compasses are best for back-bearings and re-section, although not as good as protractor or 'orienting' type compasses for the more crucial map-to-ground compass navigation. The really well-equipped party will therefore have both types of compass.

Option 4 Escape Routes

Let us imagine that you are temporarily misplaced in bad visibility, you cannot retrace your steps and have searched but failed to find your objective. You will now be looking for some escape from this situation.

I have to assume that you at least know what part of the map you are on to within a mile or two. What you need to find is a line feature that will 'catch' and relocate you when you walk towards it (on a bearing) from wherever you are. Anything will do, a road, river, wall, fence, forest edge, valley or ridge, as long as you are bound to cross it (ideally your bearing/direction of travel should be at right angles to it), it is immediately recognizable, and – an important point – it is not dangerous. A cliff top, particularly if it was corniced with snow, would not be good at 'catching' you.

It is rare to run out of options or for there to be no escape. Occasionally, however, you will find yourself ringed by cliffs, or avalanche-prone slopes,

and your only option is to shelter for the night, or sit it out and wait for the mist to clear. In this case you will undoubtedly rue your original lack of concentration, for there is no doubt that time spent in navigation is time saved in the end.

Natural Methods of Orientation

There are a few ways of orientating yourself without a map or compass, but they rely on good visibility and/or the presence of unreliable natural signs.

Stellar navigation
North in the night sky is indicated by the Pole Star. It is not a very bright star and its position is indicated by the pointers of the Plough constellation.

Solar navigation
During the day, in clear skies, you can find south by using your (analogue) watch. Point the hour hand (ignore the minute hand) at the sun, and divide the angle between it and 12 o'clock. That direction is south. In British Summer Time subtract one hour from the time.

Botanical and zoological navigation
Mosses like shade and therefore tend to grow on north-facing slopes. The prevailing wind in Britain is from the south-west, so exposed bushes and trees tend to lean to the north-east. And finally, the long-eared owl (April Foolus) tends to fly on an east–west axis when hunting under a waxing moon!

CHAPTER 6

Under the Stars
Backpacking

by Clive Tully

BACKPACKING opens up a whole new world to the trail walker. No longer are you tied to getting to a car park or bus stop in time to get home, and neither are you restricted to day walks which inevitably have to be based on a circular route. Don't think that backpacking is solely for the young, the ultra fit or the macho – modern backpacking gear is lightweight and extremely comfortable, so provided you're reasonably fit, and you take it gently at first, you'll have no problems. Rucksacks are made to distribute the load efficiently, with a padded hip belt to take most of the weight off your spine, and transfer it to the part of your body best able to take it – your hips.

Mind you, the way camping gear has progressed over the last few years, you'll find that you don't actually need to carry a huge weight anyway. Having said that, I have done the odd backpacking trip with a rucksack weighing rather more than I would have liked. It was 60lb (27kg), but that included more camera equipment than most would normally take, a pocket computer and a lot of extra food. Most people should be able to work on the basis of about half that weight as a realistic maximum.

For many, the idea of departing from the comparative security of a single day walk is quite a big step, but if you take things in stages, it isn't as daunting as it may first seem.

First of all, it pays to get used to walking with a load on your back. My first backpacking trip was in the Peak District, and I just wandered from one campsite to another. If you've already been camping with motorized transport, you'll already know that campsites vary enormously in their styles and facilities. You may want to wean yourself gradually from the heated swimming pools, supermarkets and hot showers. It's certainly nice to take in a top-class site occasionally, especially if you want a good clean up, but as you progress, you'll realize that a lot of this is superfluous.

I much prefer to camp on small sites, well away from the crowds. But while they tend to have fairly basic toilet facilities, such sites are quieter, usually with more character and, of course, they're cheaper! You can plan your day walking to fit in with your own level of confidence – either sticking to lowland footpaths or more ambitious routes across wild terrain. The important thing, whatever kind of countryside you walk through, is not to be over-ambitious when you plan your route. You can't expect to cover ground as quickly with 30lb (14kg) on your back – at least not straight away – and it does make an important difference to the way you tackle terrain which is either loose or slippery. That extra weight will show up deficiencies in your boots, the rucksack itself – not to mention your legs!

Where you go backpacking depends very much on your walking tastes. It is, after all, just a means of extending what you already enjoy. The National Parks of England and Wales are popular with backpackers, as are the Scottish Highlands. Lofty hills, secluded valleys, wild moorland – they're all here. There's no shortage of national trails and other long-distance footpaths to choose from, or you might prefer to devise your own route. Alternatively, you might just like to look on your rucksack as a portable hotel which allows you to move about from one place of interest to another as the mood takes you. That way, you can set up camp somewhere, and use it as "base camp" for day walks in the area.

While the rucksack is perhaps the most outwardly visible sign that you're a backpacker, it isn't the first item of kit you should buy. First you get what has to go in it – tent, sleeping bag, stove and so on. The weight and bulk of these items varies considerably depending on the type and quality of what you buy, so it's only once you've sorted out what you're going to carry that you look for something suitable to carry it in!

RUCKSACKS

Take a look at how people all over the world tackle the problem of carrying loads, especially heavy ones. In many countries, the standard way is to balance the load on the head, perhaps using some sort of pad in between to make it a little more comfortable. Some use huge baskets, carried on the back, and held in place by a long strap which runs around the wearer's forehead. Having actually tried carrying one such as this in Nepal, I have to say I still think you can't beat a good rucksack!

Without doubt, the best place to carry a load is strapped to your back. Early rucksacks were nothing more than crude wooden frames with shoulder straps and the load lashed to the frame. These days, rucksacks have probably become as efficient as they're likely to get, with hip belts and chest straps to share the load with shoulder straps, and frames which can be bent to correspond to the shape of the wearer's back, allowing the load to fit that much closer – all giving the best possible comfort and stability.

Most people's idea of a 'real' rucksack was the army Bergen, with its metal frame, leather straps and canvas bag. Those who wore them, I gather, thought differently, but then there wasn't much better to be had 20 or so years ago. Climbing sacks, backpacking sacks and even small day sacks would be made of heavy cotton duck, with leather shoulder straps (no hip belts) and metal buckles. Cotton duck is pretty hard-wearing, but it does suffer from one major drawback – it weighs a lot when it gets wet. And in very cold conditions, the wet material may well freeze, and make the sack extremely difficult to handle. Leather straps tended to be rather thin and consequently were uncomfortable to the wearer.

The breakthrough really came with advances in synthetic materials. A coated nylon fabric could provide the same strength with a fraction of the weight and keep the weather out much more efficiently. And foam padding for straps took a leap forward with the introduction of closed-cell foam, which doesn't absorb water. More recently, the technology to come up with coated fabrics with the strength of nylon, but the pleasing texture and feel of cotton has added weight to the 'fashion' boom in rucksacks.

For average backpacking, the smaller capacities of 65 to 75l may well be sufficient. Longer trips might dictate a larger sack, anything from 85 to 100l. You'll need to be pretty strong if you contemplate anything like this, because such sacks are made for people carrying 50lb (23kg) or more! It's generally accepted that you should carry no more than one-third your own body weight. Even with the advanced harness designs in modern rucksacks, you can do yourself a serious injury if you carry too much. It's worth noting that the first British casualty after the San Carlos landings in the Falklands conflict was a soldier whose pack was so heavy he broke his back stepping into a small ditch! But even if you're carrying weights within the bounds of common sense, it pays to get used to carrying it, especially if you're planning a long hike.

The majority of rucksacks available in Britain are the more ergonomically shaped internal frame rucksacks. External frame sacks are still quite popular in other countries, particularly where very large loads are being carried.

Good backpacking rucksacks, such as those made by Karrimor, Berghaus, The North Face, Jack Wolfskin and Lowe Alpine have generously padded hip belts. This is where most of the weight is carried and an unpadded belt can be sheer torture when you're carrying 30lb (14kg) or more. The padding is usually a high-density foam, sometimes double density, with the softer foam next to the wearer and the harder material keeping the shape of the belt. If, like me, you're on the skinny side, you'll appreciate the padding, as it helps keep bruises around the hips at bay. The better packs have conical or specially shaped hip belts – extremely comfortable to wear, with no tendency to slip down. Cheaper rucksacks have hip belts which are straight and are therefore more likely to slip under a load, no matter how tightly you fasten them.

Shoulder straps shouldn't be too thin, either. If you're down to a T-shirt, a lot of weight pulling on thin straps can be most uncomfortable. Most of the quality rucksack manufacturers now provide chest straps as standard. They're especially useful at keeping the shoulder straps from slipping sideways and do away with the need to latch a thumb behind each shoulder strap to keep the rucksack comfortably up against your back without over-tight shoulder straps. The better ones are either completely elasticated, or have a short elasticated section, so there's a bit of give. There's usually a choice of positions for chest straps, and it pays to take the time experimenting with it set at different heights to ensure you get the setting which is most comfortable. You don't want it so tight it impedes your breathing!

Perhaps the most significant advance in rucksack design has been that of the adjustable harness, to cater for a variety of back lengths. It makes sound commercial sense as well, because retailers would have to stock a selection of one-size rucksacks,

Sunshine and snow. A rare combination in the Cairngorms, and one to be savoured.

Previous page: Don't forget to take time to enjoy the view!

Backpackers in Glencoe.

Spot the famous climber . . . a fine day on
Great Gable.

Heading for a scramble on Erlspitze, in Austria's
Karwendal Mountains north of Innsbruck.

On the summit of Eggenipa, a graceful 1340 metre mountain in Norway.

Karrimor's state of the art SA7000 rucksack shoulder harness.

Karrimor Condor, featuring the SA7000 harness.

High altitude mountaineering kit in the Karakorum Mountains, Pakistan.

Yeti gaiters are the best first line of defence for dry feet.

leaving them with more likelihood of unsold stock. A rucksack which can be made to fit nearly anyone is a much better proposition. The owner can achieve a much more personal fit, which is very important for carrying comfort. And, of course, the rucksack can be lent out to other members of the family or friends, and they too will benefit.

The vast majority of rucksacks work on the principle of being able to move the shoulder harness up and down, and anchoring it in whatever position is required. Different harness designs have come and gone, like the racks and pegs of the Berghaus AB system. One which has survived the years, and which has been filched by numerous less creative manufacturers, is Lowe Alpine's Paralux system. Basically, the shoulder harness is attached by a buckle to a strap running up the back of the rucksack, which is retained by a web of parallel straps. It's a simple but effective method of adjusting the position of the shoulder harness.

Most popular now is the stepless type of adjustment using straps and buckles, such as Karrimor's SA harness, featured on their Condor and Jaguar models. The Berghaus Laser system literally turned previous thinking upside down. It has a fixed shoulder harness for maximum stability, and the hip belt adjusts for back length by sliding up and down a pair of alloy rails anchored to the rucksack body. The very latest development from Berghaus, the FGA system, adjusts from the middle of the sack, so both shoulder straps and hip belt are fixed in the optimum position for stability. If you intend backpacking over rough and uncertain terrain, make sure you look at the various models very closely, as some of the cheaper Far East import rucksacks of this type tend to lack stability around the shoulders. The last thing you want is a heavy rucksack slopping about on your back, threatening to throw you off balance as you pick your way across a scree slope.

It's also encouraging to note that an increasing number of manufacturers have recognized that female backpackers are somewhat different in shape and build, and have produced models accordingly. One-size rucksacks for women generally have shorter back lengths, hip belts designed to take account of the fact that women have less distance between the top of the hips and the bottom of the rib-cage than men, and shoulder harnesses which allow for narrower shoulders, with straps designed to avoid cutting into the bust.

When it comes to buying a rucksack, it pays to try it on in the shop with some sort of load in it, so you can get the proper feel of it. Apart from anything else, it's important to get the right size if you're buying a fixed back length model. Don't risk

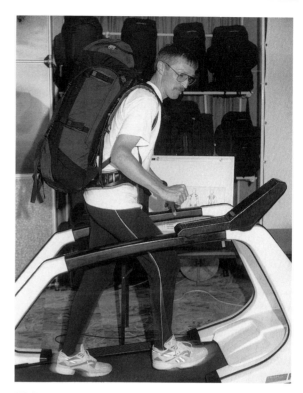

Walking quickly, getting nowhere. Clive Tully treadmill testing Karrimor's Aurora rucksack with SA7000 harness.

buying if all you can do is try it on without any weight in it. Most outdoors shops are pretty helpful on this point, and will be able to recommend the most suitable pack for your requirements.

But apart from the actual carrying system itself, what other features should you be looking for? The number of compartments is really down to your own taste and how you like to organize your load. Most packs have either a single main compartment and some have a separate bottom compartment, some have a movable divider so you can have either.

Fixed side pockets tend to be favoured by UK backpackers. While older design rucksacks tend to have pockets with flaps fastened by strap and buckle, most use zipped openings these days, and by far the easiest to get into, especially on small side pockets, is the zipped panel opening design. Those which open horizontally around the top of the pocket are tricky to get at on smaller sizes, but acceptable with larger diameter pockets. By contrast, continental backpackers prefer packs without fixed pockets, but attaching accessory pockets when required. You'll have no problem finding either type of rucksack in all the big names' ranges.

Straps and fastenings have moved with the times as well. Quick-release fasteners are commonplace now, with larger sizes for hip belts. They're particularly useful on profile straps, the straps which hold the rucksack lid down, as you can get into a rucksack more quickly and with less fiddling about. While the original Fastex buckles are perfectly adequate, they can tend to nip unwary fingers. Several manufacturers, including Berghaus and Karrimor, have come up with their own, more user-friendly designs.

Driving rain always manages to find its way into a rucksack. The better models have bound seams inside which, owing to the complexity of the construction, offer about as much protection against seams letting in water as you can expect. Some manufacturers like VauDe have actually managed to produce totally waterproof rucksacks, while others have produced ingenious liners which do the same thing. Even so, my own insurance is still the tried and tested dustbin liner, along with one or two supermarket carrier bags for the side pockets!

On top of all the functional design, you have the aesthetic element, or lack of it, to contend with – everything from the anonymous browns and greens to retina wreckers in all manner of vivid colour schemes. Actually, a lot of the really bright rucksacks aren't quite so dazzling once they've been chucked around for a bit. But whatever style and colour you go for, don't get carried away. That's the rucksack's job!

Loading up

Packing your rucksack isn't just about making sure your bar of chocolate is within easy reach. Just as ships and aircraft are loaded to ensure the best stability in transit, so care in packing your rucksack will make all the difference between a comfortable, stable carry and something which will make you feel as though the next few miles could crucify you!

By and large, the best way to pack your rucksack is to get the heaviest, densest items close to your back, thus as close as possible to your own centre of gravity. Modern, ergonomically styled, internal frame rucksacks allow you to do this fairly efficiently, but if you have a frame rucksack, which holds the load further away from the back, it's better to concentrate the heavy stuff higher up. Bear in mind, too, that you need to incorporate accessibility to certain items of gear into the equation. So it is that your sleeping bag will most likely find its way to the bottom of your rucksack, tent and food items close to the back, and spare clothes around the

front of the sack, with waterproofs and other essential items at the top, ready to come out at a moment's notice (and a moment is often as long as you get!).

The only other main point to bear in mind at this stage is that there's a right way and a wrong way to get a rucksack on your back. The wrong way entails bending over at the hips, picking up the sack and swinging it up on to your back. If it's under 20lb (9kg), it may not matter, but anything more and you risk doing yourself an injury. It's the sort of thing you do without thinking, and it happened to me one time when I arrived at Harwich with minutes to spare for a ferry to Sweden. I picked up my 40lb (18kg) sack in just such a fashion and regretted it bitterly for the next two weeks!

Weight-lifters always keep their backs straight and bend at the knees, and so should you. Don't try to swing the rucksack up from the ground to your shoulder in one move – instead, lift it up and rest it on your thigh. With your knee bent, the thigh is at enough of an angle to perch the sack on while you get one arm through a shoulder strap. Getting the other arm into its shoulder strap and the hip belt fastened is then fairly straightforward, with no danger of injury to your back. If you're daft enough to have an extremely heavy sack – and remember, you should never attempt to carry more than one third of your own body weight – it's better if you can perch the sack on some sort of ledge and reverse into it.

Convertible travel bags

While a rucksack is without doubt the most efficient way to carry your luggage (show me an Interrailer who doesn't use one), it does have its drawbacks as far as air travel is concerned. Dangling straps can get caught in luggage carousels or they can get tangled up if the rucksack is jammed into too tight a space. And although it's usually the cheap, flimsy models which succumb, I've seen rucksacks which have been torn apart and had frames mangled in the process of air travel.

Having a rucksack can be very useful when you arrive at those destinations where you're likely to be pestered mercilessly by people soliciting taxi fares or simply to carry your bag a few yards in return for a generous donation. If it's already on your back, they can't do as I have seen at some airports, where they literally force your suitcase out of your hands and then expect to be paid for it!

But elsewhere – customs halls and expensive hotels in particular – there's the minus side of carrying a rucksack. There are some places where they tend to think that rucksack carriers are hippies, drug pushers or just plain undesirables. You can almost sense the barriers going up as you stride across the plush carpet of a hotel lobby. And even if you're heading into the wilds, you may still need the odd night here or there in a hotel.

The answer comes in travel bags made with real travelling in mind. Many of them offer the perfect compromise – travel bags which convert into rucksacks. Typical examples made by major rucksack manufacturers such as Berghaus, Karrimor and Lowe are panel loading bags, usually with one main compartment, but sometimes with a smaller compartment attached to the front of the bag and a zipped back panel which conceals the rucksack harness. Made from the same tough, hard-wearing rucksack materials, convertible travel bags are without doubt the best means of carrying your belongings.

TENTS

It tasted good, whatever it was. I licked my lips again. In those brief moments between sleep and complete wakefulness, I couldn't quite fathom the reason why I should be drinking and lying semicomatose in my sleeping bag at the same time. It hit me, literally, as I turned my head, and the next huge droplet which had penetrated both flysheet and inner tent on that rain-lashed mountainside splatted me in the eye.

In the normal run of things, it has to be pretty exceptional weather before a good-quality tent starts to spring leaks, especially as more and more of the UK's manufacturers are adopting the technology developed for waterproof clothing, and tape-sealing all the major fly and groundsheet seams. As it was, the ultra lightweight dome tent in question had a flysheet made from ripstop nylon with a silicon elastomer coating so waterproof that the adhesives normally used to tape-seal seams on polyurethane-coated fabrics wouldn't stick to it!

There's no doubt that the humble tent deserves a lot of credit. Without the portable shelter afforded by a tent, visits to more inaccessible and inhospitable regions might not be so comfortable or, indeed, possible. Up until around 30 years ago, tents had remained pretty much the same sort of canvas ridge design with upright poles and no groundsheet.

One of the first to break the mould was Vango's Force Ten, a sturdy cotton tent with 'A' poles for greater stability and ease of access, and a welded

PVC groundsheet. In the greatest traditions of British design, the Force Ten was born from an outline sketched by designer Hamish Hamilton on the back of an empty packet of Senior Service cigarettes. In over 25 years, more than quarter of a million Force Tens have been sold, and its robustness continues to make it a firm favourite for expeditions, trekking companies and educational establishments.

Apart from durability, one of the great assets of a Force Ten is that its straightforward design makes it easily repairable in the field. It certainly proved extremely versatile the time I borrowed one from a friend in Iceland and arrived at the camp site at Thingvellir to discover one of the 'A' frames, which support each end of the tent, was missing. I still had a good night, though – the only time I've ever slept in a tent held up at one end by a camera tripod!

Strangely enough, the other occasion on which I was grateful to be sleeping in a less than lightweight tent also happened to be in Iceland, when a US Navy Sea Stallion helicopter flew at 50ft over the remote campsite at Landmannalaugar. He'd flown in from the NATO base at Keflavik, 100 miles through appalling weather to evacuate the unfortunate young lad in my party who had suddenly gone down with appendicitis. And without fear or favour, the Sea Stallion bombed straight across the camp, the enormous downdraught buckling tents of more dubious quality, with smaller items like peg bags borne aloft like chaff in the angry turbulence and vanishing into the next valley!

The whole thing was made worse by the fact that the site is compacted volcanic ash and rocks. Tent pegs wilt at the mere sight of the stuff, and the only things which penetrate well enough to anchor flysheets are 6-in nails banged in with a hefty hammer, and a good helping of aggression! With a handful of nails, and plenty of rocks, we'd just about got through a gale the previous day, with rips appearing in a couple of flysheets. So there you go – a sturdy Vango Force Ten is just the job for keeping helicopters at bay!

The need for lighter-weight tents for backpacking has produced an interesting variety of shapes. The early solution was simply to reduce the height of the tail end of the tent, producing a sloping ridge. The headroom was wasted there anyway, and pitched tail into the prevailing wind, it improved stability.

Whilst there's still very much a place for traditional ridge designs, the emphasis is now on getting the maximum usable space in a tent, with the least weight penalty. The significant advances in fabrics have contributed, of course, but designers have also exploited just about every shape imaginable using

A lightweight tent such as this one made by The North Face makes the perfect travelling home.

one or more flexible poles. Made from glass fibre or alloy, these long, thin poles slide into sleeves constructed in the tent, and tensioned to anchor into a semi-circular shape. A single hoop makes a sort of up-to-date ridge tent, such as you can find with the Saunders Spacepacker or Phoenix Phreerunner.

Two parallel hoops give a spacious tunnel design like the Vango Hurricane, and three hoops all crossing in the middle give the classic dome tent shape – a sort of giant brolly – typified by the now sadly defunct Ultimate Phazor dome. There's an added advantage at this level, where tents are self-supporting, in that you can pick them up and move them to another spot if you find a nasty lump under the groundsheet, or you want to change the view out! From there, extra hoops produce even more complex shapes – the so-called geodesic domes, where some of the hoops are offset to provide greater strength.

But while providing more usable space, some of the more basic hoop designs do need to be well guyed, or pitched when possible using natural

cover in extreme weather, simply because flexible poles can mean a flexible tent. I've slept in one or two domes and tunnels where high winds have had me pinned to the ground! At the very least, a tent wobbling around like a demented jelly can prove a touch disconcerting.

Of course, it really isn't reasonable to expect your average 5 or 6lb (2kg) backpacking tent to withstand the sort of high winds which might be whipping off roof tiles and unseating chimney pots at home. Tents built for the harsher environments encountered in high-altitude expeditions still weigh a good deal more!

There are arguments for and against designs which pitch inner first or flysheet first. On the one hand, the inner first types of design favoured in North America, and produced in the UK by firms like The North Face and Wild Country, are very easy to erect, with generously cut pole sleeves made from the softer material of the inner tent allowing you to thread the poles into position quickly. And you get nice, taut inner walls, which can be a plus if you're spending any amount of time in the tent.

The minus side is that while fine for drier continental conditions, inner first pitching isn't so popular in the UK simply because there's more than an even chance that it'll be chucking it down with rain when you pitch camp. Logically, you want to get the flysheet up then everything else, including whipping the inner into place, can be done under cover. Top tent manufacturers Phoenix also argue that a flysheet first design makes it a lot easier to attach guys directly to the poles for greater stability.

If poor weather is likely to be your camping norm, you need a fully enclosed flysheet. A flysheet with any sort of cutaway is unsuitable for mountain use, simply because rain can get underneath and, in more extreme conditions, you could even find snow drifts reaching the parts that snow others do! A fully enclosed flysheet also means you can have a covered porch, useful for storing kit you want under cover, but not inside – muddy boots, soggy rucksacks – and you have somewhere sheltered to cook.

Phoenix's Phreerunner is a single-skin tent, made in Gore-Tex, and supported by a single longitudinal hoop, with a short cross-piece to increase headroom at the top. You might think this would be a recipe for disaster as far as stability is concerned, but you couldn't be more wrong. All points on either side of the hoop are pegged to the ground, unlike a tunnel or dome, where a panel can be between two hoops, giving much more potential for flexing.

With an efficient if slightly fiddly guying system, the Phreerunner hugs the ground like a vacuum cleaner on a plastic bag and hardly quivers, even in the liveliest storms. There's a two-skin version called the Phreeranger and a new stretched version, the Phreebooter, with its extra hoop and extended roof support pole.

The Saunders Spacepacker is another single-hoop tent, and there is a 'Plus' version, which is better suited to taller backpackers. The layout is rather like the old transverse ridge tents, in other words, with the ridge going across the sleeping area rather than along, only this time it's a hoop. Bob Saunders has made it his life's work to perfect a tent which weighs almost nothing and every year he seems to get closer to that goal! The two major contributing factors are his use of high tenacity nylon – very light but incredibly strong – and designs which don't waste space.

The Spacepacker pitches easily, flysheet first, with the inner pegged out and suspended by two hooks. There's plenty of room in the porches on each side for gear storage and cooking, and while it's wide enough for two, it serves better as a spacious tent for one. The Spacepacker Plus is much better for two and still not too heavy. It, too, is available in a stretched version, the Galaxy.

When it comes to high mountain use, or you just want to get three or four people together in one tent, you have to start talking about a bit more weight. But whereas a traditional four-berth ridge might weigh a (literally) staggering 20lb (9kg) or more, the equivalent accommodation in a lightweight dome tent might weigh 10 to 12lb (4.5kg). Again, it's the use of lightweight materials that makes all the difference. The larger geodesic domes such as those made by Wild Country, The North Face and Phoenix are compromised least when it comes to stability, because the poles are arranged in such a way that the loading from a gust of wind in any direction is spread over the whole tent.

Unless they're very well guyed indeed, the simpler dome and tunnel shapes can be a bit animated in high winds. I've slept in some where the roof of the tent has bounced down on my nose. The answer, wherever possible, is to pitch the tent in some sort of shelter, even if it's only behind a large boulder.

My first requirement for a tent used in British hill conditions, and anything which approximates that, is to have a tent which pitches flysheet first, so the inner remains dry, and which has a covered porch for gear storage and cooking in bad weather. In drier continental conditions, inner first pitching tents are more acceptable and, indeed can be quite handy if all you want is to pitch the inner on its own to keep insects at bay. Excellent tents for this sort of use are those made by The North Face and Wild Country.

It's important to feel confident that the person who designed your tent has actually spent a few nights in his creation. I never miss an opportunity to harangue manufacturers for a couple of recurring design disasters. As it is, you'll still find tents, sometimes from respected companies, but more often than not from budget manufacturers, with features which just haven't been thought out, such as the zip-down inner doors made from the same impervious coated material as the groundsheet. The theory is that the door makes an extension groundsheet into the bell end of the tent when it's zipped down. It sounds really useful, but the reality comes home when the tent is zipped up. It becomes a condensation trap, which leaves water dribbling into pools around your sleeping bag. I've had some wild and windy nights when the only thing I needed to complete the picture was a bar of soap to go with the shower I got every time the wind shook the tent!

Condensation is inevitable with any synthetic tent, because the waterproof coating of the flysheet, usually polyurethane, doesn't breathe. Single-skin Gore-Tex tents work pretty well in most conditions, although they are quite expensive. A couple of tent manufacturers have toyed with the new hydrophilic, breathable coatings, but concluded that while they work well in waterproof clothing, they offer no significant advantage used on the fly-sheets of two-skin tents. So the important thing is to make sure condensation can run down the underside of the fly without cascading on to the inner tent. This is where good clearance between flysheet and inner tent is important.

That, however, is less than half the story. It's also essential to have ventilation in the inner, as an all-nylon tent can feel pretty airless on a warm night. Some have a small mesh panel, but, ideally, a full mesh door or doors should be included. The first point to watch is that cheap tents tend to have insect netting which assumes the minimum size of any likely marauding insect is on a par with that of a rabbit.

And where they do fit full mesh doors, they thoughtfully attach them to the inside of the inner tent door rather than the outside, hoping that any mosquito will curb its blood lust, and politely remain outside while you unzip the inner tent in order to roll back the doors and then zip the mesh screen into place. Tent manufacturers whose faith in entomological nature is less well founded play safe by locating their fine mesh screens on the out-side of the inner tent doors, thus obviating the need to open up the tent in order to get extra ventilation.

The sight of a flysheet sailing through the air can be quite amusing when you know it isn't yours, but it's a good reason nevertheless for making sure your own tent is well pegged out, not just when it's up, but when you're erecting it and taking it down.

While they're a lot lighter than steel, the stan-dard aluminium tent pegs do have the annoying habit of bending when you push them into stony ground, and unless you double peg and heave mas-sive rocks on top, they can pull out too. I've encountered some places where the only things to penetrate the ground were 6-in nails banged in with a hefty hammer! The North Face have come up with a high-tech alternative, a lightweight peg made from a super-strong alloy.

Looked after properly, a good tent should give years of service. Don't store it away without drying it thoroughly first and attend to any loose stitching before it opens into a gaping hole. A little bit of sili-con spray on your poles is a good idea if you're stor-ing the tent for any length of time – this makes sure the alloy doesn't corrode. You can usually get repairs done by sending your tent back to the man-ufacturers. The main thing is to get out and use it. Longfellow showed he was obviously no camper when he wrote:

The cares that infest the day
Shall fold their tents, like the Arabs,
And as silently steal away.

Take my advice. Stay put at night and pack up next morning!

SLEEPING BAGS

Never skimp when it comes to buying a sleeping bag. If you don't sleep comfortably, you certainly won't get any enjoyment out of camping, and it could well put you off for a long time! You can spend anything from £20 to £200 on a sleeping bag, but the principle on which they all work remains the same. Insulation is the name of the game. The body is constantly producing and giving off heat, and the moment you start losing heat at a greater rate than it's produced, you feel cold. A good sleep-ing bag slows down this heat loss to a balance by providing a layer of insulation.

Just like double glazing, the best means of insula-tion is a layer of still air. The way a sleeping bag does this is with its filling, the fine filaments of down or synthetic fibres trapping pockets of air. Poor quality of filling, or just less filling, traps less still air, and consequently doesn't insulate so well. Broadly speaking, there are two main types of fill-ing, natural and synthetic, and a range of qualities is available in each.

Choosing a sleeping bag isn't easy. Bags are designed to cope with different conditions and some may perform better in a range of circum-stances than others. If you were camping with a trailer tent, for example, you wouldn't necessarily need the same sort of insulation that you might for backpacking. Here, it's quite likely you'll encounter temperatures from hot, close summer evenings, to the occasional drop down to freezing in spring or autumn (or summer if you happen to be camping up high). So how do you decide what's best?

Ideally, you would have more than one sleeping bag. That way, you'd only need to take a bag of the required performance for any particular trip. If weight and bulk are the prime consideration, you'll obviously feel better for saving a couple of pounds by taking a one-season bag for summer use. But most of us have to make do with a compromise – one bag, which will hopefully not stifle us in the summer and still be able to provide enough warmth for the cooler months. If you have a yearning for winter backpacking, and high-level stuff, then you

The ultimate sleeping mats. Self-inflating
Thermarest mattresses.

must accept that you'll need a warmer bag as well.

Your basic choice concerns the kind of filling you want.

Down

Down is the plumage with fluffy tendrils obtained from the breasts of water-fowl. Don't think you'll be saving the species by buying synthetic. Down is a by-product, as the birds are farmed mainly in China for the dinner plate. If you're after minimum bulk and light weight, a down-filled bag is the answer. It's also much more forgiving of long periods of storage in a stuff sack – something you'd never do with a synthetic-filled bag. In fact, the RAF vacuum-pack down sleeping bags into incredibly small packages to fit into jet fighter pilots' seat-pack survival kits.

A certain number of feathers are always present as well, and the quality of the down depends on just what proportion of feathers have been removed. Down is allowed up to 15 per cent feathers before it has to be called feather and down, rather than pure down. It used to be the case that goose down was ranked better than duck, but the technology for removing the 'stalky bits' has improved over recent years, so it is possible to get similar grades, and thus similar performance, from either duck or goose.

For efficiency, it beats all other forms of insulation – for any given weight of insulation, down provides more warmth than a synthetic filling. A synthetic bag will last in average use three to five years, with its performance gradually deteriorating as the

fibres lose the 'spring' which enable them to provide the insulating loft.

So a down bag can be made much lighter for any given value of insulation. It does have disadvantages as well, although sensible use can minimize them. Down loses its effectiveness when it becomes damp. The furry tendrils clump together and no longer trap warm air, and once in this state, they take a long while to dry out. The answer here is not to let your sleeping bag get wet in the first place. The stuff sacks supplied with the majority of sleeping bags aren't waterproof, so slip the whole thing into a plastic bag as well. It's best to use a plastic bag such as a dustbin liner inside rucksacks, which should keep the weather at bay. The other main disadvantage is that a down bag requires a lot of care when cleaning – again, if used properly, it shouldn't need to be done too often. A liner or underwear worn in the bag will help stave off this event!

Synthetic

It's here that the synthetic sleeping bag wins. Synthetic insulating materials are basically polyester, manufactured in a variety of forms, some being more efficient insulators than others. It absorbs very little water, typically only 1 per cent of its weight, and while the filling may become water-logged, its performance suffers very little. The drawback is that to achieve a level of insulation comparable with down, you need more of the stuff, so consequently, synthetic bags tend to be somewhat heavier and bulkier than their natural counterparts, although depending on the quality of the filling, those differences aren't always that marked. The Isodry filling in Snugpak's 'Softie' bag, for example, comes very close to down performance in both insulation and compressibility.

Perhaps the most versatile synthetic bags are those made by Buffalo, not with fillings as such, but using fibre pile. Sold in a variety of inner and outer bags, with windproof, water-resistant Pertex shells, it's possible to tailor a set-up for any given conditions. They're extremely robust and they pack down well too.

Most manufacturers quote the suitability of their bags to different situations in terms of seasons ratings or minimum temperatures. It's not really so cut-and-dried, though. The humidity level can play an important part. Damp cold may feel worse than 10 or 15° lower of dry cold. And just as one anorak or jacket may feel warm and comfortable to one person, that doesn't necessarily mean to say it will feel right on someone else. We don't all have the same metabolism, so some people can get by with less insulation than others, while some need more. You should know whether you're a cold or warm person, so you could adjust up or down one season rating to your planned usage, to give a certain amount of compensation.

Season ratings

Season ratings are used to describe the level of performance of sleeping bags, and occasionally tents, based on valley use. Therefore, if you decide to do a lot of high-level camping (where it will obviously be colder than down in the valley), allow at least an extra season rating or be prepared to wear extra clothing in bed.

Approximate minimum temperatures for each rating are as follows:

	°C	°F
1 Summer only	10	50°
2 Summer, plus late spring and early autumn	0	32°
3 Spring, summer and autumn	–5	23°
4 All year	–15	5°
5 Expedition	below –15	below 5°

Unless you plan on summer camping only, discount any bag without a hood straight away. The whole point of a sleeping bag is to maintain an equilibrium between the amount of heat produced by the body and the amount which is lost. The head has no fat to supply natural insulation, indeed, it has a rich supply of blood vessels just under the skin and giving off heat. So make sure you keep your head warm! A full-length zip makes life a lot more comfortable in warmer weather, preferably a two-way one with a puller at each end. That way, you can vary where, and how much, you ventilate.

If you camp mainly in the summer months, with perhaps just a little bit of cold-weather camping, you could get away with a lighter-weight sleeping bag and uprate it for the odd occasion which demands a little more warmth. The simplest option is just to wear more clothes! If you feel you prefer things a little more civilized, you could buy a liner, which should allow you something like an extra ten degrees protection to whatever minimum rating you started off with.

Construction

The way the bag is constructed is all-important. Stitched-through quilting is adequate for summer bags, but no use where the weather is cooler. Good down bags have a system of baffles to maintain an even, deep loft and synthetic bags use a double layer of filling with the stitch lines offset to give better performance.

Sleeping bag designs vary quite a bit, from fairly ordinary straight bags, generally the type sold for family camping, or straight tapered ones, to 'mummy' and 'tulip' shapes. This is where it helps to go to your local outdoors shop and look at what they have. Some bags have a pronounced difference between the widest point, either at the shoulders, or slightly further down, and the narrowest, at the feet. You need to decide whether you like a fair bit of room at your knees and feet or whether you prefer more space to move shoulders and arms.

Your feet need enough free space around them to prevent the bag pulling tight over them and compressing the insulation. A fishtail shaped or boxed foot gives the tail end of the bag enough height to accommodate feet. Don't go for a bag without this unless you're short enough in relation to the bag you're after for it not to be a problem.

Unless you plan to bivvy out in your bag, the material used for the outside covering isn't critical. Down bags use a very close-weave nylon, either plain or ripstop, as the down has a tendency to work its way through most other fabrics. In fact, the

lighter the outside covering, the more effective a bag should be (in theory), since there is the least possible weight to compress the filling and thus lose the loft.

What goes inside makes a big difference though. If you sleep *au naturel*, you'll find a nylon lining cold at first and then, as it warms up, it sticks to you! Pertex shelled bags are much better at coping with this because they can dissipate any moisture more efficiently. Cotton is the most comfortable, although such bags will be up to ½lb (0.2kg) heavier than nylon. Some very acceptable linings made from polycotton are available in many bags now, and these are a good compromise, although I have found some to have a clammy feel about them. If you sleep with underwear on, then the only trouble you might find with a nylon lining is that it slithers all over the place. I always remember waking up to the plaintive bleating of my alarm wrist watch one morning and wondering why my eyes had flickered open to pitch darkness. Answer? My sleeping bag had done a 180° and the hood had ended up over my face!

Size

Some bags are made with a second option on size, usually large. It's worth taking stock here, for if you have a bag which isn't quite long enough, you may

Wild camp in Joshua Tree National Monument, California.

be able to fasten the hood all right, but the other end may be a little tight around your feet. If this happens, you're guaranteed to get cold feet! If the shop won't let you actually try a bag for size (without shoes, of course), you can at least stretch out on the floor with the thing beside you. Similarly, persons of more compact dimensions should check they're not buying a bag which is too large. A big bag takes longer to warm up and certainly won't be as efficient as one which fits comfortably in all directions.

Care

When not in use, sleeping bags should always be stored loose – many have hanging tabs so you can suspend them from a clothes-hanger. Synthetic fibre waddings are particularly susceptible to damage if packed away in their stuff sacks. When it comes to washing, you'll probably find the average family washing machine too small unless it's a very lightweight bag. The options are to take it to a launderette or to wash the bag in the bath. Use a low lather soap and make sure you rinse it thoroughly.

Future trends

As far as future trends are concerned, it seems that even the advances of the last few years in the technology of synthetic fibres will do little to overcome the natural advantage of down. Certainly synthetics have improved considerably and are now less bulky, soft and springy, but they still lack the long-term wear and durability which down affords. Still, who knows what may be just around the corner . . .

At the end of the day, you want to ensure that you get something suited to your particular needs. If you buy an expedition-type bag for four-season backpacking, you'll probably be wasting your money on something which is too warm, and heavier than a decent four-season bag. A decent sleeping bag is your highest priority when it comes to camping gear. If you don't get a good night's sleep, you won't enjoy the next day's activities. So buy the best you can afford. It'll repay you with the sweetest of dreams!

Underneath

Once you've chosen your sleeping bag, don't forget something to lie on. Whether it's down or synthetic fibres, the filling compresses beneath you and provides very little insulation from cold striking up from the ground. A closed-cell foam mat such as the Karrimat is best, if somewhat bulky. For a little extra weight, but less space, you can get a self-inflating foam mattress such as the Thermarest, which provides both insulation and a fair degree of comfort. Traditional air mattresses are not suitable in cold weather, because the air inside cools down and conducts your body heat away. If you can't do without an airbed, then a good trick in very cold weather is to slip a Karrimat under your sleeping bag and on top of your airbed.

Bivvy bags

Once upon a time, the idea of sleeping out without a tent was abhorrent to the vast majority of regular campers, and only attempted by climbers passing the night while nailed to some precipitous cliff. Yet really, it was only because of the state of available equipment. If you wanted to do without a tent in order to save pack weight, you had to be content with constructing your own rough shelter, using an old groundsheet or polythene survival bag to cover yourself or, in better weather, to chance it and lay out your sleeping bag on the ground in the fervent hope that any water in the sky would stay above 3000ft.

Gore-Tex fabric has very much led the way in making bivvying almost as comfortable as camping with a tent. Not all 'breathable' waterproof fabrics are suitable for bivvy bags which can be totally zipped up, because they don't have a high enough oxygen transmission rate – the reason why only first-generation Gore-Tex is used (the second-generation Gore-Tex used for clothing has a thin, hydrophilic coating to prevent the porous PTFE membrane from being contaminated by dirt).

Bivvy bags made by Phoenix and Wild Country fit generously over a sleeping bag, and a large hood takes care of equipment storage. Most have a zipped entrance across the bag, at shoulder level, with a Velcro-fastened flap to keep the weather from penetrating the zip.

Apart from its prime use, a bivvy bag is a very good means of uprating a sleeping bag for use in a tent in colder weather. Used like this, it should extend the range of your bag by around 10°C.

You might think you ought to have an uprated sleeping bag for bivvying. You aren't in any less shelter than you would be in a tent, and in fact you're likely to be warmer. The only way you could be worse off would be if the weather was pounding you so hard that you might lose a certain amount of loft in your sleeping bag. Your low profile and choice of sheltered spot should avoid this.

If the main thing you want from bivvying is a light pack with little bulk, then it follows that you should use a lightweight sleeping bag. Down provides the best performance for weight and bulk, although with bivvying even more so than general camping, you do have to be careful about keeping it dry. Synthetics will keep you comfortable and take a fair amount of misuse as well.

Buffalo's fibre pile sleeping bags have the added advantage that you don't need a separate waterproof bivvy bag. The Pertex shell dissipates rain, and even if it does penetrate both outer and inner bags, you won't feel cold as a result. They're pretty rugged, too – the sort of thing you could easily jump into with your boots still on and not have to worry about causing any damage.

Unlike tents, there's no space to sit up or move about in a bivvy bag and some might find it all rather claustrophobic. The next step up is a bivvy tent. Most are nothing more than a bivvy bag with a small hoop at the top end to keep the roof off your face, but some, like the ingenious Bivvybug Niche, combine a bivvy bag with a very small tent at one end.

Taking on water. Trekking in Bolivia.

FOOD

Food is pretty heavy stuff when you load up more than two or three days' supply. For short trips, you can easily stick to a variety of fresh or tinned foods, since the extra weight won't be too crippling. But if you're going off on longer trips, you can save a fair amount of weight by taking food with the heaviest element removed – the water – which you simply add from your sparkling mountain stream.

The range of dehydrated foods available is quite reasonable in the UK, even if the number of different manufacturers can be totted up on the fingers of one hand. There's a whole variety of main meals, available in packs serving either one or two, some intended as 'eat from the bag' meals, others requiring a little preparation in your cook pot. I must say that, without question, even the so-called instant meals taste a lot better if they have been tipped into

a pot and soaked for a while before heating. The trouble is that no matter how well you stir the contents of the bag, the bits lurking in the corners never seem to soak up any water! Unless it's tipping down with rain, it's a good time-saver to get your meal soaking first before you start putting up the tent.

Apart from main meals, there's a fair choice of desserts and breakfast cereals as well, though some of these items can be pretty expensive when you compare them to what you can do using your own ingenuity. Breakfast cereals are easy. I usually bag up my favourite kind of muesli. For short-term trips, it's even possible to take fresh eggs. Don't try to protect them in their shells, though. Crack them into a wide-necked poly-bottle, and you can pour them out as you need them. They'll probably scramble themselves as you walk along (which saves you the trouble) and, stored like this, the eggs will stay fresh for two or three days.

Other packaged meals worth a look at if you can get hold of them are the kind of things made for the hotel trade. They usually come in fairly nondescript, silver-grey pouches, but contain *haute cuisine* meals to which you simply need to add some instant mash potato and dried peas. Delicious!

STOVES

'Oh look, the cook house is on fire.' Our trek leader's casual comment very nearly interrupted my cup of tea. And, indeed, that shepherd's hut in the Garhwal, purloined as a base for our cook and his helpers had flames and smoke shooting through its thatched roof. Fortunately, the fire was extinguished without further disruption to our evening meal.

Then there was the celebrated time on a winter backpacking trip when my stove refused to light in sub-zero temperatures and gale-force winds – even inside the tent! I used up a bottle of priming meths, normally enough for a couple of weeks, wore a groove in my thumb from extended use of the lighter and, when we finally reached what might have been the critical moment and the promise of enough heat to brew a cup of tea, the thing flared up, nearly engulfing the tent in a fireball!

Under more controlled circumstances, fires are the essential element in providing hot food and drink. As long as you have an adequate supply of dead wood, an open camp fire can be quite pleasant and, in places, pretty useful at warning off inquisitive animals. They're fine, too, when people clear up the mess the next morning. An awful lot move on, leaving their little circles of stones and charred ground ready to spoil the wilderness experience for the next person.

For most purposes, a stove is a much more efficient way of cooking your food in the wild, and it's a lot tidier. Most stoves are made to burn a particular type of fuel, and here you have to decide just what sort of use you intend. Travellers visiting all corners of the globe will discover that airlines tend to frown on your carrying butane cartridges. If you're likely to be visiting somewhere where the supply of cartridges is doubtful, then it's probably best to go for a petrol stove. Fuel for that is available virtually anywhere.

Gas

Liquid butane gas burns cleanly, is cheap and comes in a variety of pressurized cartridges. Most stoves are designed to be used with one particular size, although some made for resealing cartridges can take different sizes. Butane doesn't need priming, so the stove lights instantly. But as the fuel uses up, the pressure in the cartridge reduces, so your cooking times get longer as the gas dwindles. Butane burners are easily affected by the wind and the liquid gas becomes less willing to vaporize when it's very cold. Ironically, it works better in sub-zero temperatures at altitude, where the low air pressure counteracts the effects of the cold.

Resealable cartridges offer a bit more flexibility for backpackers. With its valve and threaded connection, the cartridge can be removed from the stove for ease of transport or can be swapped for a fresh cartridge once the flame starts to get a bit lazy.

Pure propane burns without any loss of performance below freezing. Primus and Coleman both do propane cartridges, but there are disadvantages. The problem with propane is that the pressure at which it can be stored in liquid form is much higher than butane, so consequently the container needs to be heavier. However, propane and butane are available in a 40 to 60 per cent mixture which works very well in low temperatures, and is available in most standard sizes of cartridge – making virtually any gas stove suitable for winter use.

Meths

Meths is convenient to use. It smells great, but tastes horrible! It's good for stoves, though, because it doesn't need priming, nor does it have to be pressurized. It'll bring a kettle to the boil noiselessly, if a little slowly, and leaves no nasty lingering smell if spilt. Stoves designed for burning meths (Trangia, Optimus Trapper) are weatherproof and very stable. On the minus side, meths is rather a sooty burner and you tend to get through your supplies of fuel fairly quickly in comparison to, say, petrol.

It can also be quite difficult to obtain. While you can get it from most hardware stores in the UK, there are places where you may either be asked to sign the poison register or you may not be able to obtain it at all. It's generally available in plastic bottles from ½l upwards and, for safety's sake it's best to transfer the contents into a metal container such as a Sigg or Markill fuel bottle.

The Trangia is probably the best known of all meths burners and very efficient it is too. The aluminium body surrounds the pot or kettle, shielding the flame from the wind, while the ventilators in the bottom half of the body can be turned into the wind, feeding the flame from underneath and producing the famous Trangia roar.

In a similar vein is the Optimus 81 Trapper, except it does have an interesting plus – if you knock it over, it doesn't flare up. The meths is stored in absorbent padding inside the stove, so if some clumsy twit kicks the thing over, it remains safe and it doesn't even go out!

Petrol

A number of stoves on the market burn automotive petrol, that is, the leaded petrol still used in many cars in Britain, although built primarily for use with 'white gas' – petrol specially made for camping stoves. Now, of course, it's much more widely available.

Environmental considerations aside, burning leaded petrol clogs up the burner, which needs frequent cleaning. Some stoves have built-in jet pricking needles, which makes an otherwise fiddly and messy job straightforward.

Petrol stoves do need a little practice before you can drive them proficiently. It also goes without saying (although I am saying it here!) that you should never use a petrol stove inside a tent. Apart from the fire hazard, there's also the danger of carbon monoxide poisoning.

On the plus side, it's fast when you want to boil water. A pressurized petrol stove on full throttle will blast away at such a rate that its burner glows red hot! Many petrol stoves are built into a compact metal box, with the burner and a small fuel tank sitting side by side – these do tend to be rather heavy though. The Optimus Hunter and Shinabro 170 GR are good basic petrol stoves, and the Optimus Climber (Svea 123) is a compact, cylindrical, lightweight stove. Coleman's Peak 1 stove has an 'X'-shaped windshield built into the burner, which improves efficiency.

Multi-fuel stoves, such as the Optimus Ranger, generally give you the choice of petrol, paraffin or meths. Although horrendously expensive, the American multi-fuel MSR X-GK stove together with its even lighter brother, the MSR Whisperlite is much lighter than most petrol stoves. Instead of having a built-in fuel tank, the burner connects to a fuel feed and pump unit which screws into a standard MSR or Sigg fuel bottle. Since you have to carry a fuel bottle anyway, why not use the same bottle for the stove's reservoir, and save weight? The burner itself is very squat and, with the fuel tank acting as an outrigger, the stove is extremely stable.

Paraffin

Paraffin has to vaporize before it burns efficiently, so the type of stove which burns it is pressurized, like a petrol stove. The fuel itself is reasonably cheap and easy to obtain. It is rather smelly, though

MSR multi-fuel stoves – the X-GK (left), Whisperlite (right).

and, once spilt, won't evaporate readily. The stove needs a volatile fuel such as petrol or meths to prime it, or alcohol paste, which is available in tubes. Once burning, paraffin provides a good, hot flame.

You can get stoves which burn just paraffin, but I don't see much point in buying them. It's better to get a multi-fuel stove, so you can burn more efficient fuels, but have the capability to use paraffin when that happens to be the only stuff to hand.

Then, of course, there's dung. Markill's Wilderness Stove burns anything from bark and pine cones to dung. Basically, it's a ventilated pot which contains whatever combustibles you can find, with a battery-driven fan beneath it to speed up the airflow to get the stuff burning. Hmmm . . . I think I'll stick to something more conventional!

The main thing is that you have to balance convenience against boiling speed. Butane is generally quick and easy to light, but slow to cook. The other fuels require more care, but the reward is a quicker brew. Consider too that with any stove burning petrol, diesel, paraffin, turps, avgas or whatever – until the burner heats up, and the fuel starts to vaporize and burn properly, it can flare up, so make sure this part of the operation is performed outside the tent. Once it's burning properly, which usually only takes about 20 to 30 seconds even on a cold day, you can bring the stove under cover of your open bell end, but *never* inside the tent!

LOGISTICS

Apart from deciding where you want to do a back-packing trip, and hopefully Chapter 4 will have set your mind ticking over nicely on that score, there's the other element of planning which I always enjoy – the logistical side. Mind you, if you get it wrong, you can turn your trip into something less than the pleasure you might have hoped.

Essentially, you need to decide how much you need in the way of food, fuel and other consumables, plan how much you need to carry at one time and likely points of resupply.

Food

If you're carrying dehydrated food, you can probably carry a week's supply reasonably comfortably. You may have to carry more than that in a remote wilderness area, but if you analyse your consumption and take as much as you need with maybe a day or two's supplies extra (just in case of emergency), you can probably stretch it. But bear in mind that as your pack weight increases beyond the point of being a pleasure to carry, those extra supplies become a liability rather than an asset.

As you plan your route, you should be able to assess where there may be villages or towns where you can either buy food or pick up a parcel of your own supplies which you've posted on previously. All you do is address a parcel to yourself 'poste restante' at whatever post office you want to pick up from. If you include some packing materials in the parcel, you can also get rid of anything you've finished with – maps, exposed films etc. – by posting them back home.

Fuel

You can't send fuel through the post, and you can't travel with it by air, so in many cases you'll find yourself limited by the fuel available in the area you plan to walk. It's always best to try and get your full fuel supply in a large population centre before you head for the wilds. Even in Europe, you may well find that small mountain villages are unable to come up with your particular gas cartridge. On the other hand, if you use a petrol stove, you'll be extremely unlucky if you can't persuade someone to let you have some, even in some tiny hamlet.

In places with a good network of trails and huts – Scandinavia, for example – you can pick up food and fuel (generally for meths burners) at staffed mountain huts.

Other consumables

Maps can take up a fair amount of rucksack space on a very long walk, particularly if you're using large-scale ones. This is something else you can parcel up to pick up and drop off at intervals.

CHAPTER 7

The Green Backpacker

by Clive Tully

CHOOSING YOUR PITCH

THE LOGICAL EXTENSION to backpacking from one campsite to another is camping wild. But unlike in Sweden, where everyone has a right to roam unimpeded, and is allowed to camp anywhere provided it isn't within a certain minimum distance from houses, we in Britain must always bear in mind that sadly such a basic right does not exist, even in the wildest countryside. In theory, you should always ask landowners whenever you want to camp on their land. In practice, if you're 2000ft up a hill in remote country, no one is going to mind if you do. But such fragile tolerance can only continue provided backpackers behave responsibly. And that amounts to making sure that they leave no trace whatsoever that they've spent the night on someone else's land. And besides, it's your responsibility to ensure your campsite remains as attractive to the next backpacker as it was to you.

Part of the sport is finding a decent pitch that offers a certain amount of shelter, which is reasonably level, not too lumpy, not too far away from running water and, of course, with a nice view! You shouldn't have to hack the ground about to suit your needs – you adapt to what you find.

If you can't find any sort of natural windbreak, make sure you pitch your tent with its entrance on the lee side of any prevailing wind. This isn't always as easy as it sounds, as wind tends to swirl in eddies on a lumpy hillside. If you do end up with wind coming straight into the entrance, it's only likely to be a problem if it's fairly strong, and it's for this reason that a lot of tents have more than one entrance, so you can be sure you'll have at least one that is out of the wind.

The nice thing about backpacking in wild country is that you aren't tied to any schedule, so within reason, you can stop walking when you feel like it.

In practice, it often doesn't work out like this, since, once you develop an eye for what makes a good pitch, you'll discover that they can often be thin on the ground, so to speak.

Ideally, you need to start looking out for a good pitch at least half an hour before the time you decide you want to be the limit for the day's walking – and even that might not be long enough. But if you're starting to feel a little weary, it's easy to allow yourself to become blinkered into searching for pitches along the route itself. It may be that you've walked past half a dozen because you weren't scanning the ground more thoroughly on either side.

So what do you look for in the ideal pitch? It should be level, if at all possible. It should be reasonably flat. Mind you, lumps and hollows can actually be quite comfortable – orthopaedic even, if you manage to get them situated just right! I always lie down on the ground where I plan to put up the tent, just to test out the comfort factor.

You don't want the ground to be very boggy, although that's something you may have to take pot luck on. Most tents have good enough groundsheets to withstand wet, muddy ground, but it increases the chance of splashing mud and gunge inside your tent and of course it adds to the delight of packing up the following morning. You don't really want to walk with half your pitch still attached to the bottom of the tent, do you?

If the ground is rocky, by all means move what might make life uncomfortable beneath the tent, but don't go in for wholesale earth moving. Similarly, use rocks if you need to for extra security on guy lines, but don't leave them concentrated in a pile when you move on. Strew them around the site the way you found them.

A good wild pitch is one with a view. It's better still if you get a good sunset or sunrise on show through the doorway without having to get out of your sleeping bag! On a more practical note, it's

Clean teeth make a bright smile, but don't forget not to pollute water sources when you perform your ablutions.

quite handy to be pitched on the side of the valley which the sun hits first thing in the morning. That way, it'll warm up the tent quickly, and start drying the dew off the outside and the condensation inside.

And if you'd rather not have a chilly night, don't pitch down at the bottom of a hollow. Cold air sinks and collects in such places. Better to remain a little above, even if you are somewhat more in the breeze.

Running water is pretty handy to have close by. In some countries I've backpacked, I've either had to carry several gallons with me, or at the very least, walk half a mile or so from my pitch to find a stream. It is possible to overdo it, though. Camping near a babbling mountain stream is one thing, camping right by a fast-flowing river is something else. Not exactly the soporific gurgling you were hoping for!

At the end of the day, and this, of course, is when you're actually going to be confronting all these problems, getting a decent pitch inevitably becomes a compromise. Put safety above comfort and don't camp anywhere near places where things can fall on you or get blown on you. A good tent can withstand a good blast of wind, but is less robust if rocks start bouncing off it!

MINIMUM IMPACT CAMPING

It was one hell of a blizzard. Not so bad that visibility was totally obscured, but a vicious wind swept the hailstones horizontally across the hillside and, despite the good fortune of walking with my back to the oncoming weather, it was hard and cold enough to make me wonder whether I really did have any warm clothing beneath my Gore-Tex waterproofs. As it was, my rucksack kept the worst off me, apart from the minor irritation of my pockets filling up with hailstones!

So it was that a slightly battered backpacker found his way off that high mountain ridge. I'd already decided to look for a pitch down in the valley, perhaps somewhere near the river which swept purposefully through the mountains.

To my relief, the weather let up. A shaft of golden sunlight lanced through heavy black clouds and dripping trees sparkled. I found what I was looking for – an idyllic pitch, or so I thought. There was a nice, flat patch of grass close to the river – a wonderful spot to spend a night in the tent, far from the madding crowd.

But what I saw made *me* mad. A huge circle of charred ground surrounded by blackened stones and, sprinkled here and there, one or two even decorating the surrounding gorse bushes, were empty soft drink cans and beer bottles. So much for camping wild in remote mountains.

I believe the phrase 'Leave nothing but footprints, take nothing but photographs' had its origins in the US. It's a good rule of thumb for anyone, whether travelling through a remote wilderness or just going on a local, woodland walk. In fact, with the heavy erosion of popular trails very much a problem these days, it would be a distinct advantage not to leave the footprints, either!

I wonder just how many really think about the consequences of their actions. Is it really rational to assume that all your rubbish will biodegrade harmlessly before an animal chokes on it? How do you

Some British paths have been over-used. Steps leading to Pen y Ghent, Yorkshire Dales National Park.

feel about the prospect of litter greeting you as you travel through what's supposed to be beautiful countryside? If you aren't bothered, maybe you shouldn't be there.

Whether solo backpacker or as a member of a large party, your responsibility remains the same. To quote another much used American backpacking phrase: 'If you pack it in, pack it out'. Burying your rubbish might put it out of sight for a while, but animals can still dig it up and, if it doesn't biodegrade, it's there for all time.

A camp fire can be quite jolly if you're with a group, but it's also an excuse for an open rubbish tip. Not everything thrown on a camp fire burns – the plasticized foil containers for some dehydrated foods, for example. And so it is that the remains of the fire, complete with all manner of half-burned refuse, are left as an ugly scar. Those who practise the arts of the backwoods will tell you that the white ash left when you burn wood makes very good soap. They're right, it does. But it's a pity the fastidiousness and ingenuity which finds a cleaning agent in the remains of a fire so often falls short of clearing up the remains of the fire itself.

Even the wildest areas popular with backpackers suffer from this problem. Inevitably there are places which make ideal campsites and the experienced eye always picks them out: a nice, flat pitch in a beautiful setting and preferably not far from running water. The illusion you have to create for yourself is that you really are the first person to have pitched here. This is difficult when you start finding soggy cigarette stubs and the ring pulls from drinks cans as you peg the tent out.

Popular wild campsites – beside some of the high mountain tarns in the Lake District, for example – suffer because some of the backpackers who camp there don't behave properly and leave all manner of litter – drinks cans, cigarette stubs, food wrappers and so on. Apart from anything else, some rubbish can be harmful if livestock come along and eat it, but if you do behave so disgustingly, it simply shows you don't belong.

Another anti-social practice which I try to discourage is that of digging trenches around the tent. It stems from the days when tents didn't have sewn-in groundsheets, and a trench was the only way of ensuring the occupants weren't flooded out in a rainstorm. These days, trenches around the tent are unnecessary and unsightly, and just another example of the outdated concept of 'taming the wilderness'.

There are other problems that are distinctly more unpleasant. How can you become at one with nature when you're standing in a spot where 20 people have answered its call? When one or two 'nip behind a bush', there's no great harm done, but when scores of people do it in the same place, day in, day out, as can be found in places along some of the popular Himalayan trekking routes, it isn't just horribly unpleasant, it's an unnecessary health hazard.

The answer, whether you're travelling on your own, or with a group of 50, is to dig a proper latrine at each campsite. If, or perhaps I should say when, you get taken short during the day, you can still scoop a shallow pit in the ground or perhaps uproot a small rock which can then be replaced once you've finished. Lots of water and a left hand makes the least impact as far as the environment is

concerned, but I suppose the presence of pink or white toilet paper peering up from the ground does at least signal where someone hasn't had the consideration to properly bury their faeces. Can you wonder why the route to Everest Base Camp was dubbed 'the Kleenex Trail'?

It's important when setting up camp close to a stream to ensure you don't become a polluter yourself. Your toilet area shouldn't be anywhere near it, and washing should be done by taking water in a pot, and any soaping off and rinsing should be done well away from the stream. Don't use the stream in the same way as you might a running tap at home, and always bear in mind that just as you could be upstream of others, someone could be upstream of you. Several outdoors companies now sell environmentally friendly wash kits, with soaps, toothpaste and deodorants made from natural and biodegradable products, all of which fosters a responsible attitude.

If you have to take water from a still source – lake, tarn or puddle – you must either boil it (and keep it boiling for a good five minutes), or use purifying tablets or filtration devices. This is much more important if you start backpacking abroad, since even in the squeaky-clean wilds of North America, the chances are you'll have unpleasant little bugs like giardia to contend with.

I always have a cheap, disposable lighter with me so I can burn my used toilet paper. It isn't as rapidly biodegradable as you might think. And perhaps environmentally conscious trekkers and backpackers should consider using unbleached paper so as not to leave their own little legacy of dioxin in the ground.

Everest Base Camp is perhaps one of the best (or should I say worst) examples of the contempt which some people show for beautiful wilderness areas. Leftover equipment and garbage from over 30 years' worth of climbing expeditions had turned the base camp area at 17 500ft (5334m) into the world's highest rubbish tip. Much of the rubbish was of the mundane variety – food packaging, tin cans and cardboard boxes. There was also a good deal of what you might call the more exotic castoffs – oxygen bottles, tents, chairs, typewriters, video recorders and computers!

The excuse seems to be that it would be too expensive to hire porters to carry the heavyweight stuff out again. I can't help thinking that if the expedition members had bought the stuff themselves instead of getting it free from sponsors, they might have felt less inclined to dump such equipment! And yet recent expeditions to clean up Everest Base Camp have managed to collect several tons of combustible rubbish and put a match to it. If they

HRH Prince Charles gets away from the crowds with a short walk after opening the Peddars Way National Trail in North Norfolk.

could do it, why was it left there in the first place?

The first expedition to clear up after nearly two generations of climbers and trekkers decided that what couldn't be burned would be thrown into crevasses in the glacier – the theory being that the huge weight of ice would gradually grind it down to dust. And incinerators were left behind to encourage future visitors to treat the place with the respect it deserves.

People who smoke are a menace. Unless there's an ashtray immediately to hand, it seems as though the automatic reflex action is to ditch the finished stub without thinking. I suppose it provides employment for street sweepers in the city, but out in the wilds, it isn't just another example of an unthinking or uncaring attitude – it's downright dangerous. In the UK, for example, 1991 saw 35 forest fires destroying a total of 282 acres (114ha). That's pretty small fry compared with the losses in other countries and, while not the only cause, it is certain that some of those fires were caused by discarded cigarettes.

Some will tell you that fires start by the sun focusing through a piece of broken bottle at the right angle. This is absolute rubbish. I've tried no end of bits of broken bottles in places where the sun is a good deal stronger than it is in the UK and haven't even managed to get the object I'm trying to ignite vaguely warm. Using light to start a fire requires a powerful magnifying glass held at exactly the right focal distance from the intended conflagration. The fact that broken glass doesn't start fires is no less a reason for not packing empty bottles out to civilization, though.

Making a minimum impact when you're enjoying the outdoors isn't just down to not leaving rubbish or trying not to cause a major conflagration. It's leaving everything as you find it, whether it's down to closing a farm gate behind you in the Yorkshire Dales or not hacking lumps off a tree in Nepal just because you want to build a fire.

Some would argue that the bright, unnatural colours of modern outdoors clothing contribute an unwanted visual pollution. Certainly you'll fare a lot better at something like birdwatching with subdued colours. For me, it's a matter of taste. Whatever colours they're wearing, people are a transitory part of the countryside and I'd much rather see them behaving responsibly as far as real environmental impact is concerned. Two or three backpackers with electric blue rucksacks and rainbow coloured clothing might stand out on a hillside, but that's all. Twenty or thirty in a group – and that's not out of the ordinary by any means – and it wouldn't matter whether everyone was wearing army DPM and camouflage face cream, the real effects of their

Birch backpackers.

passing are likely to be much more lasting.

The minimum impact approach isn't really so difficult. It's simply a matter of common sense and a realization that increasing numbers are taking to the outdoors – all of whom should be keen not to spoil it for anyone else. If the most effective form of conservation is for no one to go at all, then isn't the next best thing to make everyone else think you haven't?

CLOTHING CARE

This is not a problem on day walks or short trips, but you do need to think about how you're likely to cope with cleaning clothes on longer ventures out into the wilds. The last thing you want to do is pollute some pretty mountain stream with soapy lather, so if your clothes are starting to take on an unbearable niff, either rinse them out in the water or do the soaping and rinsing well away from the stream. I remember being told that weighting your clothes with stones and leaving them on the stream bed for a while was quite a good idea. Naturally I put this advice to the test. It seemed to work quite well, at least until I saw the trousers I'd weighted down in a Himalayan river in India starting to roll downstream!

WATER

Treatment

'Don't drink the water!' It always used to be the favourite piece of advice for hardened holiday-makers setting out for their annual fortnight sprawling naked on some Mediterranean beach in a 'do or fry' attempt to acquire skin cancer. But whatever apprehensions, real or imagined, people may have had about contracting some unspeakable bug from a Torremolinos tap, it does pay to think about the quality of your water supply, whether it comes out of said tap or you fish it straight out of a stream. There are times when I wish I'd given the subject closer attention, particularly when I've discovered a dead sheep or other rotting animal upstream of my campsite after several hours of uninhibited use. Still, it does give the morning cuppa a little extra body, I suppose . . .

If you suspect the local water supply, and are either boiling or purifying the tap water, it follows that you shouldn't take any drinks with ice made from tap water. Freezing does *not* purify the water! And, of course, you should use treated water for washing food and for cleaning your teeth. It's just as easy to pick up a bug by swilling dodgy water around your mouth for a few seconds.

The simplest effective method of giving bacteria, flukes, cysts and viruses a really hard time is to boil the water for at least five minutes. Note, however, that as you increase altitude, atmospheric pressure decreases and boiling temperatures lower. The upshot of this is that if you boil your water for five minutes at, say, 12 000ft (3660m) it will only have boiled at around 100°C, not necessarily enough to ensure all the bugs have died. Experts recommend that for every 1000ft (300m) above sea level, you should add on an extra minute's boiling time.

It's likely, too, that if you're in that sort of situation, fuel for your stove will be a critical weight factor, so you don't really want to use it all on massive boil-ups. Alternatively, it may be that you don't

want to travel with the necessary flame-thrower secreted about your luggage. The answer is to treat the water with purifying agents such as chlorine (Puritabs), iodine (Potable Aqua) or silver (Micropur).

If you use tablets, it's best to filter the water first or, if you can, let it stand overnight to give suspended particles a chance to settle out. Even in the clinical, germ-free wilderness of Iceland, I've found unfiltered glacial water to be one of the finest laxatives available. Where the chance of bugs is that much higher, tablets should be left in the water as long as possible before you start drinking. I'm not particularly bothered by the taste of chlorine-based pills, but I accept that some might be. The other types are a bit more tolerable in this respect.

Don't leave it until your tongue is trailing along the ground before you treat your water. Chlorine tablets like Puritabs kill off bacteria and, despite the anxieties of some, they can dispose of amoebic cysts, provided the tablet is left in the water as long as possible before drinking – at least an hour. Iodine tablets, or two to three drops of tincture of iodine in your water, will disinfect it and again, should be allowed to stand before drinking.

The other alternative for travellers is a portable filter which does all jobs in one. Ones using disposable cartridges tend to be based on activated carbon, which have the added advantage of removing chemical compounds which might give the water a nasty taste. Such filters vary from the one-person 'Survival Straw' and passive filters such as the H²OK and Pre-Mac Travel Well, which use gravity to trickle filtered water into mug or bottle, to

The MSR Waterworks, America's state of the art water purifier for backpackers.

pump-operated filters like the MSR Waterworks and Pre-Mac Trekker Travel Well, with relatively high outputs.

The disadvantage with carbon filters is that their flow rate decreases the more they're used, so it's best to carry a spare cartridge. For group use, it's still hard to find an equal to the Swiss Katadyn filter, a favourite with Red Cross workers for over 50 years. It uses a porous ceramic filter which can be cleaned in the field when it becomes clogged.

Storage

So you've filtered, boiled or treated your water. Unless you have a system which can treat water as and when you need it – assuming there's a reasonable incidence of streams, ponds or taps – you'll undoubtedly find it most convenient to carry some with you. Cheap polythene bottles might look OK at first glance, but my experience with them is that the tops tend to leak and it's all too easy for them to split. It's a watertight case for spending a little extra money!

The aluminium bottles made by the Swiss company Sigg are as good as you can get – completely seamless, with screw tops incorporating a pourer, sealed with a neoprene rubber washer. My two Sigg bottles are smothered in dents after 15 years' hard use and they're still perfectly serviceable. They're handy too for holding water just off the stove after a good boil. The German company Markill also makes good aluminium bottles with secure tops, as does Camping Gaz. Make sure you get a bottle which is lacquered inside, though. Ones without, more generally used for carrying fuel, can impart a nasty metallic taste to the water. You don't want to filter it again, do you?

Alternatively, you could look at the American Nalgene containers – available in a range of sizes and made from an almost indestructible nylon, also with guaranteed leak-free tops. The only drawback with all such sturdy containers is that, empty or full, they take up the same amount of room – a fair point if space in your luggage is at a premium.

The way round this is to use a collapsible container such as Field and Trek's water bag or one of the range of Liquipak flexible containers, the smaller models of which are designed to attach to a belt or rucksack harness. The F&T Water Bag uses a double-skinned polythene bag in a smaller nylon fabric bag, with an unusual but very effective spigot to control water flow. It holds 2 gallons (9l), but crumples down to the size of a tennis ball when not in use.

Liquipak's impressive range of water carriers – everything from a 1¾-pint (1-l) personal water

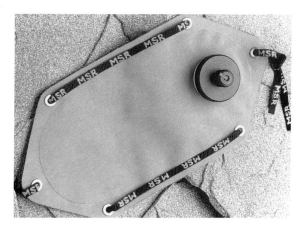

The Dromedary, a flexible water bag made to mate up with the MSR Waterworks filter.

pack to a 12-pint (7-l) water carrying rucksack – uses the same principle, this time with a Mylar/aluminium laminate inner not unlike the sort of silver plastic, flexible containers often found in wine boxes. I've used the small model strapped to one shoulder strap of my rucksack and, with just a quarter turn to open the water valve, I found it quite easy to take a good slurp without even having to stop walking.

The latest in high-tech drinking aids is the CamelBak, from America. It's a flexible container in a padded outer sheath which also has straps and buckles so you can wear it on your back on its own like a mini-rucksack. But the difference is that it has a delivery tube which you can clip on your clothes with the end near your mouth and a valve which opens by gripping between your teeth, so you can have a drink as and when you want without stopping!

How you store your water depends on where you are. The traditional way of keeping water cool in desert conditions is to use a canvas bottle or bag. Water seeps slowly through to the outer surface and, if you remember your school physics lessons, keeps the bulk of the water cool by evaporation. Otherwise, packing your water in the depths of your rucksack will keep it insulated from the worst ravages of the sun.

At the other end of the scale, water can be a little tricky to pour out of its container if you've allowed it to turn into nasty cold lumps, and indeed, can even damage some flexible containers. Keeping it in the tent inside a rucksack or spare clothing overnight is usually sufficient, but in extreme cold, you may need to share some of your space inside the sleeping bag!

CHAPTER 8

A Scrambler's Tale

Along the Dinosaur's Back

by Bill O'Connor

THERE ARE FEW MOUNTAINS that can disturb a scrambler's thoughts as much as the shattered piles of rocks that form the Welsh mountain mass of Tryfan and the Glyders – Fach and Fawr. Three thousanders all, they form a plexus of peaks in a semi-circle above Llyn Ogwen.

Whether you approach up the over-deepened trench of the Nant Ffrancon valley along Telford's road from Bethesda, or across the wider plain from Capel Curig, the panorama is equally stunning. They stand, a stark skyline of jutting rocks, like the carcass of a prehistoric beast whose flesh has sunk and withered to the bone. Now exposed, the massive vertebrae make up the bulk of triple-headed Tryfan, whose summit skull boasts a pair of tusks, bleached by weather and polished by the bold leaps of countless mountaineers.

For my money, the ideal day to traverse Tryfan and the Glyders is not a cloudless, blue sky sort of day, but one when there's a promise of better things, and the hills are covered in fair weather cumulus or wreathed in mist. Clouds give scale to mountains, and mystery to an unfolding route: offering a conundrum to be solved by skill and navigation. It was on such a day that I last traversed the 'Ogwen Horseshoe'.

We parked the car in the layby beneath the milestone Buttress, the prominent crag at the toe of the North Ridge of Tryfan. It is a crag criss-crossed by classic routes which has been more or less neglected by modern 'hard-men', but nevertheless sports some fine lines in the lower grades. Well protected, they are ideal for the aspiring scrambler who wants to learn the rock climber's craft. Our scramble meandered through the chaos of boulders on the left of the sunless Milestone Buttress. Leaving the path to find more difficulty among the outcrops, we climbed between terraces of billowing heather on slaty fangs of rock, then traversing leftwards (more to find the sun than difficulty) we emerged at a milk-white terrace of quartz and the

junction of a trilogy of paths. There was our own, a second that ascended the North Ridge direct, and another that rose from the well-marked Heather Terrace raking the East Face.

Ahead, the North Ridge of Tryfan arched like the spine of a massive beast, its buttresses like backbones separated by terraces of heather and flattish, quartz-veined ledges. Above a huge 'quartzy terrace', sadly littered by unnecessary cairns, several paths take lines of less resistance where it's possible to walk without scrambling towards the summit; indeed it can be good sport to see how far you can get without using your hands. But the dedicated walker will be attracted more by the endless possibilities on either side, where steps of jagged, compact rock lead, by devious means, upwards. Eventually walker and scrambler alike are forced on to the west flank of the mountain as the ridge and East Face become too precipitous.

Route-finding is never difficult – after all the aim is to keep to the ridge wherever possible. Having never taken the same route twice, it's obviously climbable almost anywhere so that skill or the lack of it will dictate the line. Some options inevitably lead to an impasse, when a retreat to easier ground becomes the sensible move. But then the safe scrambler has in mind the age old adage 'Don't climb up what you can't climb down.'

Near the top, after a well-marked notch between the north and central buttresses, the route choice narrows down to scrambling over bare rocks. Well provisioned with holds, veined with quartz, there is a final defiant surge to the summit boulder field. There, two rocks, that from below look for all the world like tiny figures, stand petrified on the summit; they are known as Adam and Eve. It's custom for the cautious to climb and touch their tops while the boldest leap or stride between the two.

The scramble continues over the craggy back of Tryfan to its southern summit with a descent down the long, rocky ridge to Bwlch Tryfan 700ft (213m) below. In poor weather the easiest options are to the right on the west side of the ridge, but the scrambler will want to find a way down the steeper steps of the true line. At the bwlch (pass) between Tryfan and Glyder Fach, a dry stone wall provides a marker dividing east from west, which at the low point is breached by the 'miner's track' that runs between 'Oggy Cot' and the Pen-y-Gwryd – it must have been a long hard hike in all weathers for the miners on their way to the barracks on Snowdon. Today it offers a quick and safe descent to the A5 via Llyn Bochlwyd.

For those whom the summit siren calls, the path again leads upwards with the fingery wall pointing the way towards the delights of the aptly named 'Bristly Ridge'. The walkers' path climbs on the east side of the wall up a broad gully of loose scree, whereas the scramblers' option climbs direct. Once again an eye for a line dictates the route through impressive scenery; a rocky ridge bristling with pinnacles, seamed by gullies and isolated by fresh air on three sides. Once again the options are numerous, the holds invariably good, although in places the steps are certainly steep. The 'Bristly' is a good place for scramblers to practise their ropework, as there are plenty of natural anchors for belaying.

The climbing up the ridge is delightful, and the ambience quite different from Tryfan. When at last the real scrambling runs out, shattered rock and scree lead quickly to the bouldery summit of Glyder Fach. But the day is still far from over. In mist it's easy to go astray between the Glyders' tops. The 'Castle of the Winds', an aptly named outcrop of jutting rocks is the next marker. In winter, decorated with frost flowers, it can appear out of cloud like a fairytale Bavarian castle. The path soon leads to the higher Glyder Fawr, and the massive pile of stones that form its summit.

The Ogwen Horseshoe continues on north-west, skirting high above the great rock slabs of Cwm Idwal before descending down a seemingly endless scree slope to the pool of Llyn Cwn. Ahead there are options.

Those tempted by the fleshpots of Ogwen and the delights of the café will descend a diagonal ramp of boulders and scree beneath vegetated cliffs and the dripping black recess of Twll Du, the Devil's Kitchen, a veritable cauldron on a misty, wet day. It's an impressive way down and leads below the huge slabs of Idwal – which are climbed by Faith, Hope and Charity and the help of sticky rubber!

Those with the legs for it will want to climb the long slope beyond Llyn Cwn to the top of shapely Y-Garn and descend to Cwm Idwal via the fine ridge extending eastwards towards Ogwen. The ridge forms the cwm that encloses hidden Llyn

Clyd. The ridge is a perfect place to sit and watch the world far below. My old geography master at school, himself called Idwal, once told me a tale about Llyn Idwal – about the prince whose name it bears, and how birds, because of some great, past sadness, will never fly across the lake. I remember as a lad being moved by this tale, and because of it remember clearly the lesson about glaciation, cwm formation and deposition of moraines being taught at the time. But I have to say, having watched from the eyrie of the ridge, 'gulls have no respect for myth and legend.'

THE ART OF SCRAMBLING

Defining the gentle art of scrambling is no easy thing. On a simple level it may be right to assume you can define it in terms of a mountaineering continuum, at one end of which is walking, pure and simple, while at the other end, the extreme end, if you like, is technical climbing on snow, rock and ice. Somewhere in the middle of this imaginary progression is scrambling; it begins where walking ends and ends where climbing begins. The problem, as ever, is coming to an agreement about where these lines are to be drawn.

Like much else in the mountains, the perception of difficulty and danger is a personal thing. Experience, skill, fitness and indeed personality help us make judgements about what is possible.

When I first became interested in mountains I was given a book by Edward Whymper, *Scrambles in the Alps 1860–69*; it had a big influence on me. Whymper orchestrated and took part in the first ascent of the Matterhorn in 1865. Today, most people reading that book would probably argue that Whymper should have called it, *Climbs in the Alps*, and that his routes on the Matterhorn, Pelvoux or Grandes Jorasses are far too difficult or dangerous to be called 'scrambling'. I don't agree. I believe and have always felt that rock scrambling offers the greatest freedom and sense of adventure in the hills. I also believe that it is potentially among the most dangerous of the 'games climbers play', and therein lies much of the satisfaction.

Perhaps one of the most enjoyable elements of scrambling is continuous movement over awkward ground. Unlike walking, scrambling terrain makes you use your hands and feet, and, most important of all, your head! Not as another point of contact you understand, but the brain must be engaged before you 'pass go', if you are going to find the best

Scrambling with the aid of a short length of fixed cable on Erlspitze, in Austria's Karwendal Mountains.

rope work and protecting themselves, in the same way as a rock climber. Personally I feel happier with Whymper and the Alpine analogy than with comparisons with pure rock climbing. Let me explain.

At the time when Whymper was climbing, during the second half of the nineteenth century, Alpinists were still making first ascents. They were concerned with finding the easiest and safest way to their chosen summit. Equipment was basic and so were rope techniques. Climbers invariably climbed with guides. Most of the time they moved together, following the line chosen by the guide. Often they were unroped. When roped they invariably moved together with a short distance between them. On more difficult sections, they stopped, the guide would go ahead, find a safe stance and bring the others up, protecting them with a rope from above. In those days they had a rule: 'The leader never falls'. It seems to me that this is a mirror image, apart from the guide, of modern scrambling.

Victorian mountaineers also had another rule. They didn't climb up what they couldn't climb down. It makes a lot of sense, although learning how to set up and use abseiling techniques should also be part of the ambitious scrambler's repertoire.

RABBIT'S TROD – WHERE EAGLES FEAR . . .

A. F. Mummery, the legendary mountaineer whom many regard as 'the father of modern climbing', once said:

A man may love climbing and care naught for mountain scenery; he may love scenery and hate climbing; or he may equally be devoted to both. Those who are most attracted by mountains are those who, to the fullest extent, possess both these sources of enjoyment – those who can combine the fun and frolic of a splendid sport with the indefinable delight of lovely form, tone and colouring.

Those words for me are the essence of scrambling – in many ways the purest form of mountain pursuit. The finest scrambles are invariably an exhilarating challenge – always demanding skill and concentration, and free-flowing movement, without, for the most part, the need to resort to the rope. But mountain scramblers are twice blessed, for their playgrounds are set among the most profound scenery the hills have to offer: the airy ridges, steep

line up a complex, broken buttress or avoid a soaking in some gill-filled gorge.

Most people who enjoy the hills find scrambling quite natural, particularly the young. It's enjoyable hopping from boulder to boulder or playing among the rocks. Frictioning up rough slab or pulling on 'jugs' up a steep wall are essential skills in the scrambler's repertoire. Unlike the technical rock climber who uses ropes all the time, is belayed by a partner and protects himself using a variety of gadgets, the scrambler invariably climbs without protection. Even when climbing with friends, the scrambler is, to all intents and purposes, soloing and the consequences of a fall are therefore serious. Of course, there are times on more difficult and dangerous scrambles, if conditions or companions demand it, when a rope is called for and should be used. It's then that the scramblers must know about buttresses and deep gills. It was Ruskin who remarked that mountaineers regarded the hills simply as 'greased poles' – but he, romantic that he was, was never a mountain scrambler.

However, it's hard at times to know where scrambling ends and rock climbing begins. It could, of course, be argued, quite legitimately, that climbing begins when safe movement depends on the rope, the need to belay and the necessity of moving one at a time. But then, like beauty, difficulty and danger are in the eye and mind of the beholder.

Take, for instance, Gillercombe, and the fine buttress which bears that name above Seathwaite at the head of Borrowdale, in England's Lake District. Like much of the valley it was neglected by climbers until the early part of the twentieth century. Bentley Beetham, an Everest pioneer and the champion of early scrambles and climbs around Borrowdale, recalled in the 1953 *Fell and Rock* guidebook to the area, 'that in the 18th Century a long, strong rope was kept in Borrowdale, by subscription, for the purpose of letting men down into the rocks to take the nests and young of eagles'.

Today, there are no eagles left on Gillercombe, more's the pity, but if eagles have long since shunned the place . . . there is, thanks to Beetham's exploration, a place where rabbits can safely tread. For all intents and purposes Gillercombe Buttress may not appear as scrambling terrain, but therein lies the joy of scrambling, and the reward for having an eye for a line and route-finding skill.

The farm at Seathwaite is the starting point of many a lakeland jaunt – paths lead off towards Glaramara, Great End, Scafell and the Gables – Green and Great. For scramblers, intent on the Gables, but wanting a change from the well-marked route to Styhead Tarn and the 'climbers' traverse' behind Napes Needle should look no further than the path into Gillercombe and Green Gable. The walkers' path skirts the cascading falls of Sour Milk Gill on the left, but those looking for sport should traverse quickly into the stream and find a way up its secluded, rocky right-hand side.

Now it has always been a general rule that in bad weather a walker trying to descend to the valley should avoid following unknown mountain streams – made dangerous through slippery rocks and unseen waterfalls. Whereas for the scrambler, looking to gain high ground, these are the very places that can offer the most enjoyable route – which is the point of this tale.

The scramble up Sour Milk Gill rises, as the river falls, in a series of steps – the way hugs a rocky line between waterfalls and the grassy fellside. The rock is sound and rough, except in a dry spell when water-worn slabs, egg-shell smooth, are revealed,

If I were you, I'd stick to walking. Renowned fell-runner Hugh Symonds demonstrating the light-footed approach to seeing the mountains.

glistening and naked. After heavy rain the ambiance of this and other gills is powerful and often scary. The thundering fury of a river in spate, and the feel of spray as you scramble from hold to ledge, add a new dimension to the game – the scramblers' equivalent of an Alpine Grand Course.

But there's more to it than that – if only Ruskin had known, for the scrambler is privy to the mountain's secrets; whirlpool hollows, water-worn over aeons, are now botanical gems filled with ferns, mosses and Arctic Alpines – hidden from general view they become the preserve of those who are willing to climb the 'greasy pole'. Low down, the route lies concealed beneath a canopy of red-berried rowan, silver birch and deep green holly, their roots providing jug-handled security on several steep steps. Last time there I shared my lunch with a brazen chaffinch who watched my pilgrim's progress without alarm, hopping from boulder to branch he stayed by my side until the last tree.

Route-finding on the flank of Sour Milk Gill is never difficult, and what's more it's a good place to learn your craft. There are plenty of choices, some of them tricky balance moves over deep pools, but invariably exits and options exist with a traverse into easier ground. Higher up, a large waterfall next to an isolated pinnacle is best turned on the left by a slab with incut holds.

The angle relents once the hanging hollow of Gillercombe is reached, then the way leads over a meadow of water-filled sphagnum and springy bog cotton towards the obvious buttress below Brandreth, marked on its right-hand side by a scree-filled chute. It was here that Bentley Beetham trod and found a way up the right-hand side of the buttress; a route that for most people will define the line between scrambling and rock climbing.

His route, called Rabbit's Trod, and its many variations, offers a splendid scramble to the top of the crag. Followed exactly it provides over 700ft (213m) of climbing at a moderate standard – much of it up gentle slabs, where most opt for the security of a rope. But the same slabs and knobbly rock steps offer alternative lines – avoiding the awkward bits – usually by easier variations on the right. After the relative confines of the gill, the open, slabby atmosphere of the buttress provides a fine contrast.

Making for an obvious notch on the crest of the right-hand skyline, the way now curls round the north end of the buttress. On the right, the scree shoot provides the easiest option, for those whose nerves are shot – it leads easily up or down! But the purist will want to stay close to the edge, savouring the exposure on the left. A series of steep steps and slabs lead upwards towards two chimneys, set one above the other. The second is the technical crux of the route, but is easily turned on the right for those wanting to leave the rope uncoiled. Easy slabs of clean, but well-scratched rock now lead comfortably to the summit cairns where once eagles surely perched. If the rope is out and you're enjoying the situation, a traverse round to the left provides a final, airy pitch close to the top of the classic climb of Gillercombe Buttress – good scrambling.

From the top of the crag the Gables beckon – and why not when a fine, open ridge of springy turf leads towards Gillercombe Head and a steady climb to Green Gable, Windy Gap and Great . . .

Getting to grips with some easy boulders provides useful practice for scrambling.

SCRAMBLING COUNTRY

Unlike the rock climber, whose preferred habitat is pristine mountain crags, sea cliffs, outcrops and, increasingly, indoor climbing walls, the scrambler has no such constrictions. The joy of scrambling is variety, length and discovery.

Mountains, of course, offer endless possibilities and a chance for discovery. There are scrambling guidebooks covering the most popular areas. They describe the classic, known routes, sometimes downgraded climbs of the last century; the lines the pioneers chose for interest and difficulty. The rocky ridges are obvious: Snowdon via Crib Goch or Helvelyn via Striding Edge are fine examples of easier, airy scrambles. On routes like these the experienced walker with a head for heights should have no real problem. There are a few awkward steps where you need to use your hands, but much of the way is little more than exposed walking, calling for care and a bit of nerve.

Watercourses also provide scrambling country. Often hidden, these deep, waterfall-filled gorges can provide a unique experience. Dungeon Gill and Ashness Gill in the Lake District are two well-known classics. Then there are the buttresses. The scrambler in Britain can find climbs up broken, rocky hillsides that are all but Alpine in length. The south-east face of Ill Crag in the Esk Valley offers 1300ft (396m) of vertical scrambling. In Scotland there are countless mountains that offer far more. Perhaps the most exciting thing about scrambling is the chance of discovery. There are so many possibilities for finding your own way. If you have the experience, skills and judgement, there's plenty left to do. Even if it has been climbed before, the chances are, if it's off the beaten track, you'll not notice that others have been before you.

It's not just the mountains that offer great scrambling. Britain's rocky cliff line provides endless possibilities for sea-level scrambling. But beware – just as the mountains have the added objective danger of weather, the coast has the threat of the sea. Take care with the tides and freak waves.

Just as rock climbs are graded for difficulty, so too are scrambles. Generally speaking, guidebooks have adopted three grades of difficulty for scrambles.

Grade 1: These are fairly straightforward rough or exposed walks, with some difficult steps where you need to use hands and feet. Route-finding is usually obvious with considerable choice. Ropes are not usually required. Escape or retreat is invariably easy.

Grade 2: Things get harder. The scrambling is more difficult and continuous. A rope may be required, and route-finding becomes more important to find the best line. Escape becomes more difficult.

Grade 3: A combination of exposure, increased difficulty and route-finding make this the hardest grade. The scrambles are usually more sustained than Grade 2 routes. A rope is usually advisable, even for rock climbers. Escape or retreat becomes even more difficult.

It should be obvious that all of these grades can be affected adversely by weather conditions. Strong winds on exposed ridges, heavy rain in a watercourse, or both on a greasy buttress may make them unpleasant or impossible. But judgement is part of the scrambler's skill, which comes of course with experience, and in gaining that lies pleasure.

In winter conditions, of course, scrambles become far more difficult undertakings, and in many cases serious climbs. Watercourses freeze up to form steep ice climbs. Cornices form on ridges, and buttresses under snow and ice can provide the most difficult and serious undertakings of all. They require other skills and equipment, and can no longer be considered scrambles. Of course, being

winter doesn't mean they are always under winter conditions. This is particularly true south of Scotland. Certainly in the Lake District I've enjoyed scrambling right through the year, particularly so during recent mild winters.

BLAVEN – CLACH GLAS TRAVERSE – THE FINEST SCRAMBLE IN BRITAIN

Like a bird on the wing, the tiny plane bucked on the thermals over the Hebridean Sea. Staffa, the Summer Isles and the myriad small islands of the west were set below us – granite gems in an azure ocean.

The call had come from Ronnie Faux the day before to get ourselves to Carlisle airport. It was mid-week, and we had two days free, with the weather fair and set to hold. A vast high was languishing over Scotland, so it was time to head for Skye, Britain's fairest isle and finest mountains. Our sights were set on the Clach Glas – Bla Bheinn (Blaven) traverse, arguably the best scramble in the land.

Through the headset I could hear Ronnie calling Skye airport, a small strip beside the sea at Broadford.

'Alfa Yankee Victor Mike calling Skye – over.' The message repeated several times got no reply, so we read the chart and lined up for the approach. Circling low the concrete runway appeared, shrouded thinly by sea mist; the wind sock drooped like a proverbial lead balloon. We taxied to a low shed which serves as control tower at Skye International and a short, red-haired, ruddy-complexioned man waddled over to greet us.

'Haloo to you – it's a grand day right enough. Would you be stopping the night?'

In the shed, Ronnie explained that he had had difficulty contacting the tower, and that he wasn't even able to pick up the signal of the navigation beacon.

'Ach well, right enough', said Donald McDonald, for that was his name. 'That's because we havenae got the radio – aye, and as for the beacon, you would nay get that either – for I havenae switched it on!'

By the time we had eaten lunch in Broadford and taken the taxi to Loch Slapin, it was well after noon. Across the loch, whose waters were stained turquoise by outwash from the Torrin marble

Scrambling requires a bit more fitness, agility, and a head for heights – but it's fun!

along the sharp crest, grasping warm, rough rock and admiring the ruddy tops of the rounded Red Cuillin. This scramble is full of surprises, and looked all the while as though it would need the rope, which, as it turned out, stayed safely coiled in the bottom of the sack the whole day.

From the col, a short, steep wall gave access to a sharp ridge whose pinnacles could be climbed direct or turned more easily on the right. With perfect visibility, route-finding was no problem, although in cloud the descent from some of the pinnacles would be trying, while in wet or winter conditions, despite good grip on the rough-textured gabbro, it would become a major undertaking.

Ahead, as we balanced the bristling arête, rose the formidable tower of Clach Glas. As shapely as the Matterhorn, it appears the preserve of the 'rockjock', but stands as a glorious impostor as its first ascentionists proved. Like the ridge, the options for the scrambler narrow down until a stone shoot provides an exit left and a slanting rocky gully then leads back right, with interest, to a small skyline notch, and the key to the final problem. We padded up a steep, rough rock slab on the left, turning a bulge until, a few giant rock steps later, we plonked down on the airy summit of Clach Glas.

Pure space was everywhere, and the sun shone high above the saw-tooth ridge of the Cuillins. We agreed it was as far to go on as it was to go back, and there was time enough left in the day to do either. In any case, of days like this you must drink deeply. Moderation had no place here – we were heady by now, and longed to get drunk!

But the descent from Clach Glas is no place for an unsteady head. A steep little slab angled like a rooftop leads to the edge of all things, and in turn gives way to a crest of broken rocks. Looking back, the arete and the pinnacle look impossibly difficult, and not at all the place for an unroped scrambler; indeed in any other conditions we would have opted for the security of the rope. Ahead, another sharp drop was soon scaled, first right and then left down a ramp on large holds, which at long last gave way to what on this ridge are the verdant pastures of the Clach Glas/Bla Bheinn bealach – which proved a splendid place from which to view the majestic scene. This commodious plot, called the 'putting green' by earlier visitors, is surrounded by great amphitheatres of naked rock, Alpine in scale and without equal in the kingdom.

By now of course it was quite late in the day, and the east Loch Slapin side of the ridge was in deep shadow. In front of us rose an imposing ridge leading to the bulk of Bla Bheinn, which looked and proved the sting in the tail. An awkward step and a

quarry, the serrated skyline of Bla Bheinn and Clach Glas rose inky blue against a clear sky.

It was late, right enough, as we left the layby near the Dunaiche Burn. With the infamous ennui of the islands taking hold, we wandered up Skye's northern bank, past thundering falls towards Choire a Caisse. Skirting a deep gorge in the Allt na Dunaiche, we traversed the flank of Sgurr nan Each, intent on simply gaining the scree and climbing to the deep-cut notch between it and the black gabbro ridge leading to Clach Glas.

By the time we had sweated to the col, for it was hot, the air, the exercise and the magnificent view towards Ruadh Stac and the fangs of the Black Cuillin had combined to lift our spirits and flagging feet. There was time enough, we agreed, to push on to the Clach Glas summit. It was proving a rare day indeed; dressed in shorts and T-shirts, we scrambled rightwards traverse followed, with easy ground leading in turn to a stone shoot giving access to a wide, square-cut chimney. Climbing from its shadowy recesses we emerged into blinding sunlight, with the last of the difficulties behind us.

We trooped upwards, back into shadow following an obvious line on a path of large boulders on the north-east slope of this great blue hill to the sunlit summit. From there we continued along the line of shadow and light to the southern peak of Blavein. It was getting late, and the sun would soon be casting fingers of light between the main Cuillin peaks. It was obvious that we wouldn't make it to the pub for last orders, but then no one was in the mood for going down. We sat on the summit looking out at the bay of Camus Fhionnairigh, the island of Soay and the purple haze of the sea.

We played with the idea of bivouacking on Bla Bheinn. The nights are so short in the far north, and in any case it was warm, right enough. In the end we followed the Camasunary Ridge to the south for a while before dropping south-east towards the col and Fionn-choire at the head of Coire Uaigneich, which would lead us to the Dunaiche burn and the shores of Loch Slapin.

GEAR FOR SCRAMBLERS

In most respects, the scrambler wears the same basic clothing as the hill walker or rock climber, climbing on a high crag. Ideally, clothing should be neat fitting, yet allowing a wide range of movement. By and large, scrambling is more dynamic than walking. You should have enough layers to keep you warm throughout the day, so if you are in the mountains, take note of the weather forecast.

Footwear can be critical on more difficult scrambles. If you are mountain scrambling, you need a comfortable boot that you can walk in and enjoy a full day on the hills. However, most scramblers benefit from having a slightly stiffer boot which lets you stand on smaller holds and edges. Many scramblers carry a pair of specialist climbing rubbers for use on more difficult routes. These lightweight, tight fitting, sticky-soled boots allow you to use the smallest holds, to smear and use friction. They are a delight to climb in, a very different experience. But be warned – in the wet, on greasy rock they are difficult, and for walking they are impossible.

Serious scrambling calls for a rope. Don't compromise and go for a short, thin, lightweight one. If you need to belay, you need to do it properly. That becomes apparent when someone falls off. A full weight or single rope is what you want, which means a 10.5 or 11mm nylon rope which meets the UIAA specification. You will also need a couple of slings and karabiners, and ideally a small selection of 'nuts' – and I don't mean the edible kind! Above all, you need to know how to use your rope.

So before you venture on to difficult ground, practise the techniques somewhere safe. Get some instruction from someone with experience or from a mountain guide. In confined gills or gullies it makes sense to wear a crash helmet. Many experienced mountaineers enjoy scrambling because of the freedom of movement it allows. They solo, don't take a rope and don't wear a crash helmet. At the end of the day that's part of the 'freedom of the hills', an individual decision. I began this chapter on scrambling by mentioning Edward Whymper who, after a lifetime of adventure and scrambling around the world, died of old age in Chamonix, at the foot of the mountains he loved. Let me end with some words of advice from him, taken from *Scrambles in the Alps*.

. . . There have been joys too great to be described in words, and there have been griefs upon which I have not dared to dwell; and with these in mind I say, Climb if you will, but remember that courage and strength are nought without prudence, and that a momentary negligence may destroy the happiness of a lifetime. Do nothing in haste; look well to each step: and from the beginning think what may be the end.

CHAPTER 9

Above the Snow Line
Winter techniques and equipment

by Graham Thompson

A CHILL IS IN THE AIR, the trees are bare, the days are short and your mind turns to . . . winter backpacking! OK, so it's cold and the weather isn't always the kindest. But the hills are quiet, the air cool and clean, the snow hides eroded tourist footpaths and the winter arena opens up a whole new world of adventure.

But it's not all fun-filled wonder. Winter backpacking is a serious proposition, with little leeway for errors. A winter backpack, whether it be for a day or a week, needs the correct equipment, careful planning, and well-practised skill and experience. Oh, and plenty of good luck with the weather helps as well!

CLOTHING

To help enjoy the day you'll need to wear plenty of clothes. In summer you may be lucky enough to get by with your army surplus turn-downs, high heels and jeans. But in winter your clothing can be a life saver.

Layering system

Modern clothing uses the layering principle, comprising three basic layers: the base layer, mid-layer and outer layer.

The base layer consists of a 'wicking' material often known as thermal underwear (garments that transport sweat away from your skin to the outer layer of the garment). The garments are worn to keep the surface of the skin dry, so they are close fitting. They come in various thicknesses or weights, and for winter a slightly thicker or heavier fabric is required. Alternatively you could wear two thin layers. The main fabrics to look out for are Polartec 100, polypropylene, polyester and chlorofibre.

Good clothing provides essential protection in demanding conditions, such as on this mountaineering trip in the Karakorum.

The mid-layer provides the main insulation. Those pretty-coloured fleeces that are worn mainly in the pub in summer are just the thing for cold winter walking. There are plenty of designs, and it's worth looking for a practical design with plenty of pockets for your compass and gloves etc. Many mid-layer garments are made from Polartec 110, 200, 300 and polyester.

Getting togged out in waterproofs can be fun, especially when the fabric is one of the modern breathables, such as this one put together by Craghoppers.

If it's really cold, you may need to carry an extra insulation layer to supplement your basic mid-layer garment. Some designs fit over one another more easily than others, so take care when you make your purchase. These extra insulation layers can either be another fleece, or a pullover filled with down or synthetic insulation.

The outer layer is a good waterproof. Basically this can be the same jacket as you use in summer, although some designs are better suited to winter backpacking – large cargo pockets with storm flaps, a big wired hood that fits over your woolly hat and a snow skirt inside the jacket make life a little more pleasant in winter. If your budget allows, choose a breathable jacket made of Gore-Tex, Sympatex or similar material.

Salopettes

One of the problems with conventional clothing is that you can get a chill at the base of your spine when you bend over or if your jacket rides up. In the summer this isn't a serious problem, but in winter it gets pretty uncomfortable, especially if some snow or ice gets down your back.

That's where salopettes come in. They are like a baby romper suit with a high waist and bib to protect your body from chills and spills in the snow. They're designed for active walkers, cross-country skiers and mountaineers, making them ideal for the winter backpacker. There are many different designs, some allowing more easy access than others for calls of nature!

Salopettes are designed as mid-layers or outer layers. Materials include polyester, Polartec 200 and Ultrafleece for mid-layers, and Gore-Tex or Sympatex for outer shell designs.

Berghaus Ascent salopettes – lightweight fleece to provide warmth and freedom of movement.

Heads, hands and feet

Hats

Anything between 25 to 70 per cent of your body heat escapes through your head, so if you're feeling chilly, put a hat on. Hats come in all shapes, sizes and colours. Basically they all do the same job, but some are better than others. A woolly hat or balaclava is fine, but these days high-tech fleece, thermal and breathable hats have revolutionized the bonce-cozy.

Some designs incorporate long ear flaps which are superb in driving winds. A peaked cap keeps spindrift at bay, while a thermal or fleece balaclava keeps your neck and the sides of your face warm. Some fleeces have a sewn-in fleece hood which is very useful because it seals the neck from spindrift.

Gloves

Once your body temperature begins to lower, your brain lets your fingers and feet get cold, so that the blood supply can concentrate on keeping your body core warm. In summer you can get by with a pair of thin, synthetic gloves. In winter that's fine for fiddling with the controls on your camera and unwrapping a Kit-Kat, but a pair of mitts is required for extra protection. The Dachstein mitt, made of 100 per cent wool, has a legendary reputation for

The pick is a specialised one for ice climbing, but the Extrem Mitts will keep any fingers nice and warm.

durability and warmth. Modern equivalents use Gore-Tex breathable shells with pile or fleece linings.

Socks

Chilly tootsies are frequent in winter, but a little added insulation can help. Two pairs of socks instead of one is the first step. Use the same layering principle to make the most of this combination. A thin, thermal sock made of polypropylene wicks sweat away from the skin and acts as a base layer. While loopstitch socks trap air for insulation and act as the mid-layer, your boots form the outer, waterproof layer.

PUTTING YOUR BEST FOOT FORWARD

Winter boots

Boots for winter walking need to withstand wet snow and step kicking, take a crampon and grip snow slopes. The boots are generally more substantial than bendy summer boots, and are collectively categorized as four-season boots.

Soles

A winter boot needs a substantial tread to grip soft snow. The traditional Vibram sole is the well-established standard. The edges of the boot sole will be used for edging, so they need to be firm and square. The heel too is best if it is square so that steep slopes can be safely descended, even on firm snow. (Some people find that the stepped grip on some cut-away heels perform wholly unsatisfactorily on snow).

Midsoles

Winter boots need to be stiff from front to back if crampons are to be fitted. The minimum degree of stiffness is given by half-length steel shanks on traditional leather boots or by special injection-moulded midsoles on modern boots. Fully flexible boots will work loose from many models of crampon.

Winter boots also need good edging grip when traversing firm snow on steep slopes. So a boot should have very little torsional (twisting) flex. A fully flexible boot will roll off its edge and send the wearer glissading down the mountain.

Uppers

Winter boots need to withstand wet snow for long periods, so they are made of thicker, one-piece

OK, I'll carry the rucksack.

Always get your pal to dash off to do the dramatic pose – it saves energy!

Clive Tully on the Kuari Pass, Garwhal Himalaya, India.

Austerdal valley in Norway.

Trekking in the Garwhal Himalaya in India. A brolly can be pretty useful for keeping the sun at bay.

Austerdalsbreen Glacier, Norway.

The Canadian Rockies, a trail walker's paradise.

The advantages of trailwalking: the superb view from the Crib Goch.

Forests and rivers in Finnish Lapland.

Wild camp in the Rondane Mountains, Norway.

Nanga Parbat

SCARPA Manta and Alp boots with Vibram M4 sole units capable of taking "step-in" crampons.

leather, or even plastic. The uppers need to be stiff to withstand the impact of kicking steps and so they don't collapse under the pressure of crampon straps.

Leather or plastic?

Plastic boots fulfil all the requirements of a winter boot, with the bonus of an insulating inner boot, to keep your feet toastie warm and dry. The drawbacks are that they are less comfortable than well broken-in leather boots, being heavy, cumbersome and clumsy on rocks. However, they perform superbly on snow, and step-in crampons can be used. They are very durable, and provide bombproof protection for your feet from the wet and cold.

Gaiters

There's no doubt about it, a lump of ice in your boot is none too comfortable. To stop snow or ice getting in, wear a pair of gaiters. In summer you can get by without gaiters, but in winter this is a recipe for cold and soggy feet.

The most comfortable are made from breathable materials, while the most durable are made of canvas or tough nylon. The Yeti design that totally encloses the boot is superb, and gives the best protection when walking in deep snow. The weak points on conventional gaiters are the ties which go under the boot. These eventually break if made

of cord. Consider gaiters that have a nylon tape or a wire trace, which is more durable in any conditions.

GETTING A GRIP

Crampons

In the early days of nailed boots, crampons were hardly used. The nails gripped the ice and step-cutting was used to handle any tough situation. However, with modern Vibram soles, crampons are essential kit for any winter walking expedition into the mountains.

Walk into an outdoors shop, and you'll be faced with rigid, flexible and articulated crampons, with anything between 4 and 12 points. Then there are step-in bindings or strap bindings. Confused? Well, it's not that complicated really, because most of the more technical designs are for ice climbing rather than winter walking.

Rain or snow, the Yeti gaiter shines through whatever the conditions. Shown here is the Yeti Extrem, winter mountaineering with crampons for snow and ice.

How many points?

For winter walking, standard crampons with 8, 10 or 12 points are needed. The 8-point designs, without the extra front points, are pure walking crampons. They're suitable for more flexible boots and are fine for walking on flat terrain.

Many models today include the extra 2 front points, which are used for front pointing up steep slopes, making either 10 or 12 points in total. On flat terrain, the front points aren't used, but they don't get in the way either, so there's no disadvantage in having them. Crampons with the extra front points can be used for climbing graded steep ice climbs and winter gullies.

Rigid, flexible or articulated?

Crampons are either rigid, flexible or articulated. Rigid crampons are designed for extreme ice climbing, when only the front points are used. They need to be used on boots constructed with a fully stiffened sole. They can be used for walking, but they are less comfortable than flexible or articulated designs, and exert more stress on the metal.

For winter backpacking, take a look at flexi and articulated crampons. Flexi crampons are intended for use with more flexible boots. They consist of a solid toe and heel plate connected by a 1in (3cm) wide sheet of steel, thin enough to bend and provide the flex.

In theory, flexi crampons can be used on boots of any stiffness. However, the strap bindings will tend to restrict circulation on boots with soft uppers. Their suitability for tackling steep snow slopes is governed by the stiffness of the boot. If flexi crampons are used on stiff boots, then steep slopes can be tackled. If used on bendy boots, stick to flat snow and ice.

Articulated crampons are similar to flexi crampons except that the sheet of springy steel is replaced by a stiff, hinged bar. They can be used with fully stiffened boots or three-quarter shank boots. If worn on more flexible boots, there is a danger they might snap.

Getting them to fit

Crampons must be adjusted to fit the boot with a light spring-fit. The boots should just stay on without the straps being fitted. It's worth taking your own boots along to the shop to check the adjustment and fit of the crampons before making your purchase.

To fit them on to the boot, lay them on some flat ground so that all the straps and buckles lie outside the metal framework. The buckles should be to the outside of the feet when fitted – that should sort out which is the left and right crampon.

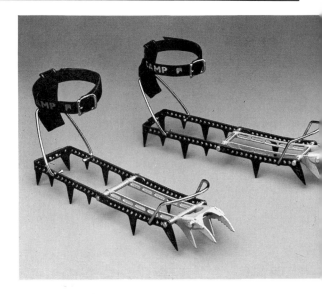

If you have to ask how much they are, you can't afford them. Probably the most expensive crampons in the world. Camp-Lowe titanium Footfangs, 16 point crampons with step-in bindings retailing at just under £200.

Fastening

There are two main methods of lacing up all those straps and buckles. The traditional style is most often used, where the straps link rings on posts around the outside of the crampon. The alternative is the French style, using an extra ring which sits over the top of the boot. On the French style, the ring must be located in the correct place and this means that the crampons cannot easily be used on different types of boot – even choosing to wear gaiters can affect the fit. But their advantage is that they are quick and easy to fit.

On fully stiffened plastic (and some leather) boots, step-in bindings can be used to fasten the crampons. These are similar to ski bindings and require that the boots have a thick welt (lip which protrudes from where the upper attaches to the sole) at the toe and heel. These bindings are very quick and easy to fit.

Maintenance

When the points become blunt, sharpen them. On the downward facing points, use a file along the narrow edges of the metal, not the broad faces. The front points should be sharpened to the same shape as a chisel by filing from the top downwards. But note that if the points are too keen, they will blunt more easily.

Nuts and bolts should be checked regularly, as should areas of possible metal fatigue such as attachment posts, hinges and the side bars of rigid crampons.

Bits and bobs

Plastic sole plates are worth checking out. They can be attached to the underside of the boots when crampons are fitted, to reduce balling up (when snow clogs the sole of the boot between the spikes of the crampons). However, they are another item to fit as your fingers begin to freeze, so are best suited to walks which require wearing crampons for long periods.

Rubber spike protectors are very useful when stowing your crampons inside your rucksack. They're available as complete mouldings with legs and feet like a toy rubber octopus. They fit over the spikes and prevent them tearing your rucksack or your hands when grappling for your sandwiches. You can also get crampon bags which are very good, and make packing and unpacking your crampons far less dangerous to your fingers.

TAKE YOUR PICK

Ice axes or ski poles?

Walkers mainly need something to help them keep balance. They've been using the ice axe shafts for years, but more recently, there has been a shift towards using one or even two ski poles.

Ski poles

Ski poles help prevent a slip for a walker in the same way as they do for a skier. Walkers' poles suitable for winter need to be adjustable in length and able to be fitted with a snow basket.

The problem with a ski or walker's pole is that if you do slip, it's 'tally-ho' all the way to the bottom – fine if there's a gentle run-out, but not so funny if you slip on a steep slope with a 500ft drop at the end. For steep terrain, when a slip could send you glissading all the way back to the car park, an ice axe is essential.

Ice axes

There are as many types of ice axe on the market as there are crampons or fleeces! But in the same way that many crampons are designed for serious ice climbing, many ice axes are too. The axes with drooped or banana-shaped picks and short shafts are for the climbers. For winter walking we need a more general ice axe with a longer shaft and a shallower angled pick.

The shaft

Traditional ice axes are made with ash shafts. These days alloy shafts are the norm, with a long rubber grip near the spike. The shaft is generally a flattened oval shape in cross-section to give a secure grip.

The length of the shaft required depends on your height. For walking, you need a shaft which reaches the ground on gentle slopes, but is not too unwieldy on steep slopes or when ice axe braking. Walking axes are available from 55 to 85cm.

In general, if you hold the axe by its head at your side, the spike should be 2 to 3in (5 to 8cm) above the ground. However, some walkers prefer a slightly shorter axe, because this allows for easier ice axe braking, while others argue that with a longer shaft, a serious slip is less likely.

The head

The head of the ice axe has an adze on one end and a pick on the other. The more expensive models tend to have a one-piece drop-forged head, while the less expensive will have an adze welded to the pick. Either has a satisfactory performance, although the one-piece drop forged head may feel more comfortable in the hand.

For general walking, the degree of angle or curve on the pick should not be too great, otherwise it will 'grab' when used for self-arrest and be torn from your hands. A gentle curve is required to be sufficient for self-arrest, while still being useful for other pick work – front-pointing steeper slopes and step cutting, for example.

The adze is used mainly for cutting steps and clearing the snow, like a shovel. The shape is not too important, although a flat angle is better, so avoid the drooped adzes of climbing axes. A larger adze is more efficient at clearing snow when digging an emergency snow hole, but a little unwieldy when cutting steps.

The spike

At the opposite end of the shaft to the head, the main function of the spike is to provide a sharp point so that the shaft can be driven into the snow. As long as it will do this, its actual form doesn't matter.

The wrist loop

Some axes come fitted with a short wrist loop, attached to a ring which slides up and down the shaft, allowing you to grab either head or shaft. The disadvantage with using a loop around the wrist comes when you realize the axe is usually carried in the uphill hand. When zig-zagging up steep slopes, it is necessary to change hands at each turn and change the wrist loop. In practice this is time consuming and interrupts the flow of movement. Also, if control of the axe is lost during self-arrest, the falling walker will probably end up with some nasty battle scars. However, if the loop is allowed to dangle freely it can snag on a rock or a crampon. If you don't wear the wrist loop, it should be securely wrapped around the head and shaft. Alternative methods include a removable wrist loop, which can be put away when not in use.

Some walkers prefer a lanyard of webbing tape, about the same length as the shaft, tied through the hole in the axe's head. The other end has a wrist loop long enough for the axe to be held in one hand while the wrist loop is in the other. Whichever method you choose, it's often useful to have an axe holster at your waist into which the axe can be slotted conveniently when walking on easy terrain.

Keep the rubber protectors on the head and the spike – that way you'll protect the back of your car, the train seats and your mates from serious injury. It's also illegal not to have protectors on the spikes in some Alpine countries.

MORE PROTECTION

Helmets

A helmet does have its place in winter mountain walking. The start of a thaw can often loosen rocks and cornices, which can be dangerous if you happen to be somewhere underneath. And if you slip, a head injury is very likely, particularly if you lose control of the ice axe.

Ropes

A rope is very useful when approaching a summit cairn perched near a cornice or negotiating the rim of a plateau in a white-out. If you misjudge the edge, you'll surely find the cornice with dire consequences. If roped together, the back person can belay the brave front person as the front person approaches the edge. A 45m long, 9mm diameter nylon rope is all that is required.

But note that ridges in winter are very serious mountaineering expeditions. A rope, along with experience in winter belaying techniques is required, and this is where winter walking becomes winter mountaineering.

CAMPING GEAR

In general, all your summer camping equipment will be of use in winter. But remember that weather conditions are generally worse and less predictable. You'll need extra clothing, bigger sleeping bags and a bigger rucksack to carry it all in.

Rucksacks

Your average summer rucksack will suffice for most winter walks. However, there are a few features that come in handy when winter walking. An ice axe loop is probably the most useful feature to check for. Most sacks have one, although some more technical sacks have two (obviously two loops are needed by climbers using two axes). A loop will be fitted near the base of the sack to hold the head of an axe, while towards the lid a buckle and strap holds the shaft in place.

The capacity for winter walking needs to be slightly greater than in summer. Extra fleeces, hats,

The Cyclops Expedition – big carrying capacity with minimal weight.

gloves and crampons take up a lot of space. I find 35l rucksacks a little small, and prefer 40l for a day walk in winter. Similarly winter tents and sleeping bags are larger, so expect to use 65l as the minimum. I prefer a 75l rucksack.

Depending on your mode of travel, you may need equipment attachment straps on the sides. These are very useful for skiers, allowing them to stow their skis on the sides of the rucksack. But for winter backpacking, they're also useful for holding a rope, ski poles, ice axes, snow stakes and Karrimats. Straps on the top of the rucksack lid are useful for attaching crampons, but make sure you use spike protectors or expect a few scars during your trip. Many walkers prefer to stow their crampons inside the rucksack anyway.

The design of some rucksacks incorporates a snow lock, a drawcord-fastened extension to the rucksack opening, which prevents spindrift from creeping in when walking all day in wind-driven snow.

Not all rucksacks have side pockets. This Ice Star is a 40 litre sack aimed at climbers and scramblers.

Tents

If you camp in the valley on official sites, you can probably get by with your standard tent. However, wild camping on exposed winter sites requires something designed for wild conditions. Traditionally the best tents for wild winter weather are the 'A'-frame ridge tents exemplified by the Vango Force 10. But modern dome tents are also capable of taking a rough beating.

A free-standing geodesic design has the advantage of a higher space to weight ratio, and requires fewer pegging points – useful when the ground has frozen. One feature particularly useful in winter is a valance (an extra skirt of material extending from the base of the fly). Dump snow or rocks on it to keep the drifts at bay while providing extra security during storms.

Instead of conventional round wire pegs, snow stakes or dead-men (alloy plates) are preferred in deep snow. Alternatively, you could use a few spare stuff sacks filled with snow, buried with the guy line secured around its middle. Stuff sacks have the advantage of weighing very little with minimal packed size. Unfortunately, many modern tents incorporate glass-fibre poles. Give these a wide berth. Low temperatures make them brittle and prone to snapping.

Camping in the snow demands good quality equipment.

During a blizzard, you won't want to cook your freeze-dried spag Bol outside, so go for a tent with a large or extended bell end. Also consider the living space in the tent. Remember in winter that the dark bit is pretty long. So you're going to be stuck in your nylon cocoon for around 15 hours a day with the possibility of a blizzard raging outside.

Sleeping bags

Extra insulation is the order of the night. You need a bag that can cope with temperatures down to 14 or 5°F (−10 or −15°C), generally expressed as a four-season bag. You may be able to get by with using your summer bag plus extra clothes or a liner, but a four-season bag is more comfortable.

The choice between synthetic or down filling is far easier in winter. Down is lighter and less bulky than synthetic materials, and therefore wins easily. A hood with drawstring and/or neck baffle is essential to keep the warmth in.

Insulation mat

Whatever sleeping bag you have, insulation from frozen ground is essential. Thinner three-season, closed-cell foam mats such as the Karrimat are adequate, but the thicker four-season type is better. If money is in plenty, then a Thermarest is the most comfortable bed you're going to find for winter backpacking.

Stoves

Many stoves are affected by the cold, so some care is required when choosing your model. Also you'll probably be cooking inside the tent, so a not-too-volatile fuel is required which doesn't flare up during lighting. Finally, you need your fuel to be cheap and efficient, because you'll have to use plenty if you end up melting snow for your water supply.

White gas is one choice, but its volatile nature means that great care is required in its use. Paraffin is safer but it is messy to use and can flare up during lighting. Methylated spirit has low heat output and is expensive. The best choice is a butane/propane mix, which works well in freezing temperatures and below. The cartridges are also sealed when not in use, making them easier to deal with when empty.

Bits and bobs

A vacuum flask is pretty useful when you stop for a break on a windswept, ice-cold summit to admire the view. Despite their extra size and weight, the

Down-filled sleeping bags still provide the best warmth for weight. These ones are Mountain Equipment's Iceline and Snowline.

modern, stainless steel flasks are superb. The old-fashioned glass ones are fine, but even when wrapped with a piece of foam mat, they soon break.

If you're heading for serious snow, you'll find a snow shovel very useful. Digging snow holes, making a clearing for your tent or digging your tent out of the snow is far easier with a shovel. It can be stowed on the outside of your rucksack with equipment straps.

TIME SPENT PLANNING IS NEVER WASTED

Unfortunately the winter day has only a few daylight hours, so it's wise to plan to get out early. Make your sandwiches the night before, check the time of sunrise and set an alarm clock. For the more experienced, extra hours can be snatched by setting out with head torches before sunrise. This also has the advantage of reducing avalanche risk, because the snow will be more stable before the warm morning light has hit it.

The Trangia – Sweden's best-selling meths burner with integral windshield. It packs together with its own cookset.

Winter route-planning

To estimate the time to complete your walk, use Naismith's Rule. The modern equivalent is:

Time to complete walk = 1 hour per 3 miles (5km), plus 1 minute per 33ft (10m) climbed.

But this is only an estimate. Your fitness, the weather and the condition of the snow will drastically affect this time. In reality, your walking can vary from 0.9mph (1.5kph) to 4mph (6kph) depending on the terrain you're crossing. In winter a good average is 2mph (4kph).

While planning your route, make a note of escape routes, which in winter's changeable weather will probably be needed. Deep snow, difficult terrain or plain bad weather can all affect the time to cover a walk, so a quick exit may be required towards the end.

Before completing the plan, make a final check on the weather. Mountain forecasts give avalanche conditions as well as general weather, which is very useful, particularly when you're visiting a new area. Even a local weather forecast can be wrong and, in the mountains, they are often inaccurate. Keep an eye on the sky and try to get in tune with the weather as it develops through the day.

Leave a message

It is even more important in winter than it is in summer to leave a route description with someone before your departure. White-outs, avalanches or simple slips can leave you lost, injured or buried in snow. At worst, leave a message in the window of your car, so the traffic warden can find out why you've been double parked for so long on a bank holiday weekend!

STEER CLEAR

The white stuff which makes winter days so special is also the winter backpacker's main enemy. The snow floats down to the earth in millions of tiny crystals, settles and the crystals bond together. The bond between the crystals of a layer of snow which fell at the same time is better than the cohesion between the fresh layer and the base layer. This difference in bonding produces the snow's inherent instability.

For winter backpacking the instability of snow is of prime importance, for snow is what we travel on and live in. So how can the winter backpacker minimize the dangers?

Avalanche awareness

The best way to avoid an avalanche is to avoid the mountains, but that isn't an option for the winter backpacker. Instead, learn as much about avalanche protection as possible. For the winter walker, avalanche awareness is as important as navigation, but it takes practice and experience to master.

Avalanche awareness begins with the weather. In the same way that the weather changes hour by hour, so the avalanche danger changes quickly. There are three main weather factors to pay attention to; precipitation, wind and freezing level.

Precipitation is important because it can saturate existing snow, possibly resulting in wet snow avalanches or cornice collapse.

Wind speeds of over 15mph (24kph) can dump snow into corries and on to lee slopes, while cornices can also form. This transportation of snow to form windslabs can also occur in otherwise clear weather. To help judge the effect of the wind, look out for snow plumes which indicate that snow is drifting on to leeward slopes, forming windslab, a very hazardous form of snow.

The freezing level greatly affects avalanche risk. Continuous cold temperatures will maintain an unstable snowpack, while sub-zero conditions may even increase the instability. Warm temperatures near or just above freezing will tend to allow the snow to settle, thereby increasing stability. However, a rapid rise in temperature may cause the snow to melt, with the possibility of cornice collapse and wet snow avalanches.

Clearly it's all pretty complicated, and there are no hard and fast rules regarding the effects of weather on avalanche risk. But generally, if you have two of these factors together then avalanche risk is high.

Digging a snow pit

One method for checking the condition of the snow pack is to dig a snow pit to assess the layers of snow, noting the differences between them and the bond between them. Discontinuity between layers affects the snow stability.

Isolate a column on three sides approximately 30cm square and dig down to a stable layer of névé (firmly packed snow) or ground. Then cut down the fourth side (usually the back) of the column, as far as the depth of your shovel. To check the layers

Saunders Spacepacker Plus in an idyllic setting in Norwegian mountains.

of snow, pull (don't lever) on the back of the column, with a snow shovel. If you don't have a snow shovel, use your hands to pull on the snow layers. If you do this, make the back of the column the same depth and width as your hands.

Repeat the cycle until all the layers have been identified and assess your results subjectively. A very easy shear means that the layer is unstable. A difficult shear means that the layer is stable. Because of local variations, you should do a few tests to assess the situation. Remember to fill in all your snow pits afterwards.

Assessing the terrain

Once you've assessed the conditions of the snow pit, you then need to assess the risk, which is related to the lie of the land as much as the snow-pack.

The following points should be considered when assessing terrain.

1 Avalanches are most common on slopes of 30 to 45°.
2 Lee slopes are where most of the windslab accumulations are greatest, and where cornices will form.
3 Open slopes are ideal for forming large areas of windslab.
4 Convexities on a slope create greater stress on the snow pack.
5 During thaw conditions, a slope with large boulders and trees will anchor the snowpack, making full-depth avalanches less likely.
6 Look out for the following avalanche warning signs: recent avalanche debris; large snowballs rolling down the slope; sudden collapse of snow underfoot; hollow feeling and creaking noises; cracks in the snow; and mini slabs released.
7 The deeper the snow, the greater the danger. Snowfall in excess of 0.7in (2cm) an hour can lead to avalanche risk. Fresh snow remains unstable for at least 36 hours.

During your planning, assess the route for avalanche risk. If possible, stick to ridges and plateaux. When there is an unstable snowpack, steer clear of lee slopes, convex slopes, steep slopes, open slopes and areas where snow has accumulated. If you need to decide whether or not to cross an avalanche slope, always choose the safer alternative.

Crossing suspect slopes

The day will come when it really is impossible to find an alternative to a suspect snow slope, in which case some precautions must be taken.

Get out early: Snow is more stable before the morning light begins to warm the bonding between the snow crystals.

Stay high: When crossing a dangerous slope stay high above the slope.

Straight up: If you must ascend a dangerous slope, go straight up and down. Don't traverse back and forth across it.

Convex slopes: Snow covering convex slopes is under tension and is therefore more likely to fracture, resulting in an avalanche.

Rock outcrops: Take advantage of rock outcrops and slight ridges, where snow build-up will be less and the rocks will stabilize the snow pack.

One at a time: Expose only one member of the party to a potential risk at a time. Other members of the party should watch for any movement in the snow. Do not rope up unless good belays are available.

Batten down the hatches: Before crossing the slope, zip up your hood, and put on extra clothes, hat and gloves. A scarf around the mouth will stop snow getting inside your mouth and lungs. Put on your helmet if you have one. If you're avalanched, snow will get everywhere and it may be some time before you are found.

Cliffs: Before crossing the slope, check for any steep cliffs and try to make your crossing well away from vertical drops.

Loosen rucksack: Loosen the straps on your rucksack, and undo the waist belt and chest strap.

Transceivers and avalanche cord: An avalanche transceiver or a long cord, if carried by a party, makes finding a buried victim very easy.

Be prepared: Assess the escape routes in case you are avalanched and note your position on the slope.

If caught in an avalanche

This is like telling someone how to swim before they have entered the water, then leaving them to get on with it. However, some idea of how to survive is better than none at all.

1 Shout out to attract your fellow walkers to your predicament.
2 If near the fracture line, drive your axe in, and you may be able to step off it, or at least delay your fall and let some of it pass down the slope before you rather than after you.
3 If swept away, try to stay on the surface by using a swimming motion and roll like a log from danger.
4 Keep your mouth closed if you go under.

5 If you go under, try to push yourself to the top before you stop moving. Use your hands to make a breathing space for your mouth, then push them to the top as you come to rest.
6 If buried, rest and stay calm. If you're able to move freely, it may be possible to dig yourself out.

If you witness an avalanche:

1 Try to keep the victim in sight.
2 Once the avalanche is over, check for further danger.
3 If safe, check the victim and offer first aid.

If the victim is buried:

4 Mark the place where you last saw the victim.
5 Make a quick search of the area where the victim may have landed.
6 Do not desert the victim and go for help. After 30 minutes the buried victim has only a 50 per cent chance of surviving.
7 Probe the area systematically with anything at your disposal.
8 If still unfound, send someone for help, while the other members of the party continue to probe the area.

Cornices

Cornices are those beautiful waves of overhanging snow that are built up by the wind on the lee side of a ridge. They can be as dangerous as they are beautiful. Stay well away from them, because if the cornice fractures, it will break well behind the crest, taking you with it.

Take care of your eyes, particularly in the mountains, where reflected glare is intense. Mountain glasses shield your eyes from harmful ultra-violet.

Ridges

Some of the finest summer walking is found on the great mountain ridges of Crib Goch (Snowdonia), Striding Edge (Lake District) and the Aonach Eagach (Scotland). But under snow these routes can become serious mountaineering expeditions. The level of difficulty depends on the snowfall, but even after light snow, a narrow ridge becomes slippery underfoot. Under deep snow, full winter mountaineering equipment is required, including ropes and belaying equipment. If in doubt on a ridge, turning back is the safest option.

Hypothermia

Hypothermia, or exposure, is one of the main dangers to the winter backpacker. It is caused by the loss of heat from the body core. When the body becomes chilled, it begins to reduce circulation to the skin and extremities in favour of keeping the vital organs at the correct temperature. A fall in the temperature of the body core leads to mental deterioration, loss of muscular control which leads to unconsciousness and finally death.

To guard against hypothermia, the walker needs to ensure that the vital organs are kept at the correct temperature. Therefore do not plan a walk that

High camp in the Karakorum.

will make you over-tired. Wear warm/waterproof clothing at all times and take a spare, warm layer, because it's always cooler on the summit than it is down in the valley. Eat and drink plenty of high-energy foods, so the body has a high reserve of fuel at all times.

Frostbite

Frostbite is rare in Britain. Closely related to exposure, it occurs when the body starts to shut off blood circulation to the extremities in order to retain heat in the central core, thus allowing skin tissues to freeze in cold temperatures. Frostbite usually occurs in abnormally low temperatures such as may be experienced during a high-level winter bivouac. Superficial frostbite is best treated by applying body warmth. Do not rub the patient, because this can cause a too rapid warming effect. If the frostbite is serious, the victim must receive medical help quickly.

To prevent frostbite, keep the body core warm as well as the extremities, avoiding tight-fitting boots and clothing which can limit circulation.

WINTER WALKING SKILLS

Walking on snow with an axe

The axe can stay on the sack until the ground steepens to the point where a slip would be fatal. But don't leave it on the sack too long. Many accidents begin as a simple slip, but result in an avoidable fall. If in doubt, get the axe out.

Flat or gentle slopes

Carry the axe by its head, on the uphill side of the body. The pick should point back, with the thumb under the adze, the palm over the head and the fingers around it. In this position, the axe is held ready to use in self-arrest. A wrist loop adds to security, but is not essential. When walking, plant the shaft into the snow for balance and security, while the feet kick steps.

If you're traversing, kick the sides of the boot into the slope. If heading directly up a slope, kick the toe in. If heading down, then dig the heels in.

Moderate snow slopes

On moderate slopes, the axe can be held in the brace position – with the uphill hand holding the shaft, which is in the snow on the uphill side, while the downhill hand holds the head across the body. However, this is not the most secure technique, and it is safer to keep the ice axe on the uphill side at all times. To do this when zig-zagging up a slope, change hands each time you change direction.

Steep slopes

As the slope steepens, it may become impossible to traverse. This is when you should face the slope head on and kick steps. Plant the shaft of the ice axe in the snow, with one hand holding the head, until at least half of the shaft is buried. The axe now provides security while the feet are replanted higher up the slope. If it is impossible to get the shaft to penetrate half way, use a two-handed grip, with the second hand holding the shaft just above the snow.

Descending snow slopes

Don't underestimate the descent of a snow slope. At the end of the day, when your legs are tired and you're feeling rather pleased with yourself, it's all to easy to tumble and find yourself wishing you'd practised your self-arrest technique earlier on.

Steep slopes
On firm snow, face the slope, thrust the shaft of the axe as far below as you feel comfortable. Then kick

steps with your feet straight down. As soon as the angle eases, turn sideways and begin to traverse the slope in a diagonal line, keeping the axe on the uphill side. Kick either the toes, sides or heels of your boots into the slope to suit the angle.

Moderate slopes
Face down the slope and plant the shaft just ahead of your feet every two or three steps. Walk stiff-legged into the slope, digging in your heels and lean out so that all your body weight is over the balls of your feet.

Easy slopes
Simply dig your heels in as you stride down the slope, keeping the axe in the walking position or in the self-arrest position. Remember to keep the weight over your feet to prevent a tumble.

Self arrest

Apart from posing on the fells, the main use of an ice axe is for self-arrest – stopping your unfortunate slip turning into a slide to the base of the mountain.

As soon as snow starts to appear on the hills, get out and practise your self-arrest technique. Find a gentle concave slope with a good run-out clear from boulders and cliffs. Dig a seat in the snow to act as a launching pad, then throw yourself down the slope – head first, feet first, on your back and on your front.

While practising, take off your crampons and rucksack, because both of these complicate the procedure. To protect your bonce from a bounce off the ice axe, wear a helmet. Alternatively, if you're new to winter walking, invest in a winter walking course, where the techniques can be learned under qualified instruction.

To stop a slide, the pick of the axe needs to be embedded in the slope. The axe is held in the braking position, with one hand holding the head at chest height with the palm over the top, and the thumb under the adze. The other hand grips the shaft near the spike. To be prepared for this position, walk with the adze pointing forward.

Feet first, on your back

Bend at the knees and hips while rolling over on to your front, keeping your feet clear off the ground. The important thing to remember is to roll towards the hand holding the head of the axe. If you don't, the spike will catch the slope and may tear the axe from your hands.

Dig the pick into the snow, with a steady pressure from your body through your shoulder. Once again, a sudden application could tear the axe from your hands.

Head first, on your front

The first thing to do is to turn the body around. Reach out as far as possible, with the hand holding the head of the axe. Plunge it into the slope and allow your body to swing about the pivot. Bend your knees to keep your feet off the ground. Once the turn is complete, lift the axe, pull the head under your shoulder and dig the pick gently into the slope once again.

Head first, on your back

First thing to do is to turn your body. Keeping the feet clear of the snow, reach out to the side on which you're holding the head of the axe. Dig the pick in to form a pivot. As you swing round, bring your legs below you and roll on to your chest. Reposition the axe under your shoulder for self-arrest.

Glissading

One of the quickest ways off the mountain is a controlled bum-slide. Although glissading can be fun, it is also very dangerous, and should only be attempted where there is a clearly visible run-out, free of avalanche danger, boulders and other obstacles.

To be ready for an emergency, the axe should be held in the self-arrest position. The technique then is to sit in the snow, controlling your speed with your feet and the spike of the axe, which is trailing alongside you. When you become really proficient you can do a standing glissade, which is like skiing on your boots.

Step-cutting

Step-cutting is a dying craft, since most walkers rely on their trusty spiked crampons for crossing ice flows, but once mastered it can save a great deal of hassle and time when you're faced with only a small splash of ice.

The basic full step is cut by first making two slashes with the pick in the shape of a 'V'. The middle of the 'V' is then chopped out with the adze, starting at the point of the 'V' and working up.

In firm snow it's possible to use a single blow from the adze to cut a slash step. Hold the axe near the spike on the shaft and swing the axe in an arc so that the adze cuts a step a few inches deep. The step needs to be just wide enough and long enough to take the side of the boot. With practice, this method allows a good rhythm to be developed, and a series of steps can be cut much quicker than full steps.

Walking with crampons

Crampons transform your grip on snow or ice, but on the wrong feet, they can also transform your walk into a series of trips and near misses. Keep your feet about hip distance apart, to avoid tripping on your gaiters. Your feet should remain as flat as possible, so that all the spikes are in contact with the ice. As the slope steepens, flex your ankles and bend your knees. Hold the ice axe on the uphill side and make zig-zagging traverses of a slope to relieve strain on the ankles.

When traversing, flex your ankles or point your feet down the slope to keep all points of the crampon in contact with the slope. Use the ice axe for support on the uphill side. At first it's worth practising walking up and down some ice slopes before getting yourself into a situation where a slip could be fatal.

Front pointing

Once the slopes start to become really steep, the front points can be used. Attack the slope head on, and kick your front points into the snow or ice. The soles of the boots should be tilted slightly up from the horizontal, planted about hip distance apart.

To gain security from the ice axe, use one of three techniques. First, hold the axe in the braking grip, with one hand on the head and one on the shaft, and dig the pick into the slope just above your head. Alternatively, use the pick like a dagger, with your hand over the head, digging the pick in just below chest level. Finally, try swinging the axe while holding the shaft near the spike, so the pick digs in well above your head. A wrist loop is essential for this option.

Descending ice/snow slopes

The problem when descending in crampons is that it is difficult to plant the axe for security and that kicking the front points in is difficult. Therefore, turn sideways as soon as possible and descend in a diagonal line.

Steep slopes

Follow a diagonal line. Hold the axe in the braking position and dig the pick into the slope at about head height. Face out, keeping all the downward points of the crampons in contact with the slope.

Moderate slopes

Follow a more direct line and bend the knees to keep the weight over the downward points of the crampons. Use either the same axe position as before, or dig the spike in while holding the axe in the braking position.

Easy slopes

On less steep slopes, the pick can be planted while the shaft is used as a hand rail and your weight is kept over the crampons.

Balling up

Crampons aren't perfect, and they don't suit all types of snow. In damp snow your crampons may become balled up, when snow clogs between the points. If left unattended, the soles of your boots will soon resemble giant ice cubes fresh from the freezer. Regularly give your boots a firm tap with the ice axe to dislodge the snow.

WINTER NAVIGATION

During a winter walk, particularly on the high mountains, the clouds can blow in quickly. Within seconds the white snow of terra firma becomes indistinguishable from the fluffy white clouds above. This is known as a white-out. In these conditions the ill-prepared walker can quickly become confused and disorientated. Cairns, old footprints and even the edge of the mountain become indistinguishable, making the task of walking from point A to point B a difficult and possibly dangerous proposition. The only method of safe navigation through a white-out is accurate use of map, compass and distance-estimating techniques such as timing and pacing.

Staying on course

To give yourself the best possible chance of setting the compass correctly and accurately, find some shelter or turn away from the wind to avoid the spindrift. It can be worthwhile to calculate useful bearings at base level before they are even required. For example, the summit of Ben Nevis requires careful navigation in a white-out. The required bearings can be calculated and recorded in comfort and warmth the night before. If the cloud comes in, the correct bearings can be transferred to the compass, thereby eliminating some of the errors that can be made in the confusion of a white-out.

Ooops, where's the compass?

Once you've set the compass you don't want to lose it down the mountain. Tie it on to your jacket chest pocket zip puller, if you have one. That way it's safely stored, but accessible, and it won't matter if

When is a watch not a watch? When it tells the altitude and air pressure as well – pretty useful for mountain walking. This one's the Casio BM-500WJ-IV weather station watch.

you drop it during a raging blizzard. A spare map and compass in your rucksack is worth taking.

How far, so far

Pacing techniques are used to estimate your distance. But remember that in deep snow or ice the number of paces taken to walk 100yd will be different from the number taken on firm soil or rock in summer. Take the opportunity early in the winter season to check your pacings over various distances on different winter terrains. A small table can then be written as an *aide-mémoire* – although you might remember the figures today, you'll be thankful when the blizzard is raging and you're trying to remember how many paces you take while wading through knee-deep snow.

Another method of estimating distance is by timing. Accurate timing is difficult, but does provide a useful guide to the length of a day's walk. Timings for various distances over different winter terrains need to be calculated in advance and noted.

Onward and upward

You've checked your bearing, you've calculated the number of paces required and you have an estimate of how long it's going to take to reach a feature. The time has now come to walk into the white-out.

Complete concentration is essential – not as easy as it sounds when spindrift is blowing around your face. A pair of goggles is useful, and complete faith in your compass is essential.

To hold the course, try and sight a line along a ground feature such as a rock peeking through the snow, or a hump or hollow in the surface. But if nothing can be seen, then stick rigidly to the compass bearing using leap-frogging techniques and back bearings. If there are two or three of you, the other members of the group can be used as direction markers, but if you're going solo all you can do is concentrate on the compass. The solo walker can roughly check the direction walked by taking a back-bearing along the line of footprints left in the snow.

For more on navigation, see Chapter 5.

BENIGHTMENT

You're lost, the night is rolling in and there's no hope of finding safety in the valley. Your only chance of survival in winter is to find some form of shelter.

Limited shelter can be gained from a boulder or beside a large snowdrift, but for the most comfort, make your own shelter. Once again, it's your multi-pointed winter tool, the trusty ice axe, that will prove its worth as you construct a shelter. If you've brought along a snow shovel, you can be warm and cozy even quicker, but an ice axe will suffice.

It's possible to dig a snow shelter in 30 minutes, although a bit of pre-season practice is advised, unless you enjoy learning the skills when cold, tired and fighting for your life!

Shelters in a snowdrift

The easiest shelter to build is one dug into a large snow slope (leave igloos to the Eskimos). Before making like a mole, wrap up well with waterproofs, because snow gets everywhere and you don't want to risk a chill from wet gear. Start near the top of the snowdrift, so that the dug-out snow falls down the slope. Burrow directly into the snow making a hole which is about shoulder width. Once well into the drift, dig upwards.

The final shelter should be egg-shaped. You should be able to sit up, with your feet in the cold air at the bottom, and your head and chest in the warm air at the top. To prevent suffocation, push

your ice axe through the side to make an air hole. A final block of snow can be placed in the entrance once you're cozy inside. When the basic shelter is finished you can be your own architect, making as many rooms as you have ever dreamed of. Indeed, many high-altitude mountaineers have kept digging their snow hole bigger and bigger all night, just to keep warm.

Shelters on flat ground

When benighted on a plateau, you'll need to dig straight down through the snow pack. First, dig a pit long and wide enough to lie in. Then dig blocks of snow to form a roof over the pit. The roof blocks need to be thick enough so they don't collapse, but thin enough so that they can be carried to the site. Clearly it's worth some pre-season practise.

Due to the difficulty of finding a perfect snowdrift or quality of snow on the plateau, a combination of the two types of shelter will often be required. Whichever type of shelter you build, remember to mark its position from above, so others don't crash in unexpectedly.

Your own body heat will keep the inside of the shelter warm, but insulation needs to be provided between your body and the ground. Sit on your rucksack or spare clothes for insulation. If you've brought along a Gore-Tex bivvy bag and a sleeping bag, you can make your benightment very comfortable and maybe even enjoyable!

WINTER CAMPING

Winter camping is often only performed out of necessity. Foul weather usually buffets and batters the tent almost to the point of submission. However, given good weather, it can be a wonderful experience which you'll never forget. Morning may bring a sunrise, the light glistening on the ice-encrusted mountain plateau. An early start will lead the winter backpacker over untrodden snow slopes for the most perfect of mountain days.

Picking a pitch

If you're going to be in any mood to catch the sunrise, you'll want plenty of beauty sleep during the night, so a comfortable pitch is essential. A site should provide protection from prevailing winds and the ground should be as flat as possible. It needs to be well drained, and safe from potential dangers such as flooding or avalanche.

A nearby water supply is very useful, so it's worth planning ahead to find a pitch near a stream or lake. Trees provide some protection against the wind, although a big avalanche will easily flatten them. Try not to pitch your tent directly beneath them. During a thaw, the tree may dump snow on to your tent. In windy conditions, branches can break off and bombard your tent with much unwanted firewood.

If you want to keep warm overnight (of course you do), avoid pitching in hollows, because cold air sinks, chilling the parts your insulation doesn't quite reach.

Keeping the tent up

Getting the pegs to hold the tent down can be a problem in winter. If the ground has frozen rock hard, use boulders and rocks. This is where a tent with a valance comes into its own. Boulders can be placed along the valance and around the pegs. The guy lines can also be tied to boulders or logs if necessary. Place the boulders carefully, because in a wind, the sawing action of the guy line over a rock can fray and break through it very quickly. Remember to put all those rocks and boulders back where you found them after striking the tent in the morning though – the aim is to leave no trace of your presence.

On deep snow stamp out a flat surface, with channels for guy lines. Pegs can then be buried horizontally in the snow. Once the temperature drops to freezing point overnight, the pegs will be secure. Keep your ice axe handy to dig them out in the morning though! It's worth carrying dead-men, dead-boys or stakes for regular camping in deep snow. These alloy plates, once buried in the ground correctly, are far superior to pegs. Ice axes and skis also make very good guying points. Alternatively, take some extra stuff sacks. Filled with snow, buried with guy lines around their middles, they form very effective anchors. If your tent has a valance, pile snow on it to hold the tent down and prevent drafts whipping about inside.

Water, water everywhere?

Water will be one of your main concerns. If you can camp near clean, running water, then collect some before settling into your tent. A large, collapsible water bag is ideal for this. If there's no readily available water supply, then you'll have to use your stove to melt snow. This is a slow process and uses a lot of fuel, so it's worth making the most of your supply once collected. If you're in any doubt about the quality of the water, boil it for ten minutes, then

A signal flare can be pretty useful in survival situations.

use Puritabs or iodine solution, which kills most known germs dead.

Once you've collected your supply of water, you can bury the container in the snow to prevent it from freezing as easily: snow is a good insulator and a bottle of water buried down to 12in (30cm) below the surface should remain unfrozen overnight.

You're going to need a minimum of 5 pints (3l) of water a day, a lot if you have to melt water to produce it! If your urine is running dark yellow, you're not drinking enough. Take measures immediately to increase your intake, but try to avoid gulping large quantities of ice-cold water, because it will chill you quickly.

Cold comforts

Keeping warm and dry is very important in winter. British weather dictates that it will probably rain as much as it snows, so the chances are that you'll be soaked to the skin by nightfall. As soon as the tent is pitched, change into your dry clothes or get straight into your sleeping bag. A plastic bin liner is useful for storing your wet clothes overnight.

Rather than sitting around getting cold, do your cooking from the comfort of your sleeping bag, and eat and drink plenty. This will make you feel more comfortable, even while a blizzard rages outside. The heat from the stove will warm the air inside the tent, adding to your comfort.

Before sleeping, leave the stove ready to make your early morning cuppa. It will save time and energy in the morning. When you wake to a cold, crisp winter morning, you can stretch an arm from your sleeping bag to light the stove, then snuggle down until the water boils. Also, the heat from the stove will begin to defrost the inside of the tent.

Night lights

Finally, don't forget your head torch, candle or gas lantern – and a good book. Nights are long in winter, so they're ideal for reading or planning the next day's walk.

CHAPTER **10**

Whoops!

Safety in the Mountains

by Clive Tully

IF YOU TAKE CARE, use common sense, and your navigation is up to scratch, you shouldn't come to any harm. But things do go wrong; the weather changes, you or someone else in your party becomes tired and a lapse of concentration puts you off-route. It's so easy for a catalogue of factors to build up and conspire against you.

It's almost inevitable that, at some stage, you're going to be presented with the possibility of illness or injury while you're out walking or trekking, and of course it's Murphy's Law that it'll happen at the furthest point you can possibly be from civilization. I've had one or two close calls myself, like the time a fierce gust of wind picked me up on the summit of Beinn Bheoill, in Scotland, and neatly deposited me on rough, stony ground on my left knee. Fortunately, I came away with nothing worse than a slight bruise. It would have been a different story if I'd broken my leg.

And although the national press loves to sensationalize the occasional fatal accidents which happen in the hills (while paying scant regard to the daily carnage on Britain's roads), the majority of fatalities aren't due to falls or hypothermia, but heart attacks, perhaps brought on by a touch of over-exertion.

How you cater for each and every eventuality is beyond the scope of this book, but I would recommend looking at the courses on offer at places like Plas y Brenin in Wales and Glenmore Lodge in Inverness-shire, because, above all else, they instil a sense of confidence. Not only do you learn how to keep yourself out of mischief, you can also pick up more advanced techniques like river crossing – handy for Scotland, certainly, and even more useful once you start going further afield. And once you have the confidence to deal with whatever Murphy decides to sling at you, you'll find yourself able to be a little more adventurous.

USEFUL KIT

There's no substitute for knowledge, common sense and a positive attitude in an emergency situation. But you can cope with a lot of the likely problems to befall a hillwalker in trouble if you've prepared for the worst with some useful items of equipment. I'm not recommending the 'survivalist' approach, so don't think you need to equip yourself with snares and vicious knives. You'd have to be stranded for days on end for food even to enter the survival equation.

Your most important priority in a survival situation is to protect yourself. Get yourself into a position where you're unlikely to be bombarded by falling rocks or trees, and preferably somewhere as sheltered as possible from the weather. Hypothermia is your biggest danger, and the most effective means of keeping it at arm's length is your own portable shelter – a survival bag. If you're travelling in a group, the lightweight nylon shelters, such as the Karrimor Instructor's Survival Unit, are superb. Essentially a large nylon tube with drawcords at top and bottom, it can accommodate a group of half a dozen or so, and it warms up surprisingly quickly.

Otherwise, you should have an individual survival bag, made from 500-gauge polythene, usually orange, obtained for a couple of pounds from an outdoors shop. There are lighter weight bags on the market, vacuum-packed to the size of a packet of cigarettes, but I don't recommend them and neither does the British Mountaineering Council (BMC).

And you can also buy space blankets, which I would dearly like to see off the market. These aluminized mylar foil blankets promise much but deliver little, and a blanket isn't much use to you on a gale-swept hillside. How do you keep it wrapped

around you? And its claim of reflecting body heat is totally misleading. A reflective coating reflects radiant heat, which at the most amounts to 10 per cent of your total heat loss. The majority of your heat loss is down to convection, and evaporation of water from your skin and clothes.

In an emergency situation, the 500-gauge survival bag is robust enough not to collapse around you in the wind, and, when pulled over your head so the opening is at your feet, you can sit down on your rucksack, insulated from the ground, with a polythene bubble protecting you from the elements. You'd be surprised just how quickly it warms up inside, and in winter, I recommend taking a long-life candle (and a lighter) which you can use to warm up the inside even quicker (also providing a comforting light for you, and a useful glow to help the mountain rescue spot you in the dark). And when hypothermia is a real possibility, breathing warm air does you far more good than any amount of extra clothing.

FIRST AID KITS

Not all the casualties in the hills are fatal, thank heavens, so it makes pretty good sense to carry a first-aid kit with you. One old stalwart of the British outdoors press told me he had been mountaineering for 40 years, and never carried a first-aid kit in his rucksack. This 'seat of the pants' approach isn't what I'd recommend for mere mortals, however.

But having a basic first-aid kit with you is only part of the story. It's also rather important to know how to use it. It may not take a Mastermind champion to work out which way to put on a sticking plaster, but if your first-aid kit is worth its salt, it'll also carry one or two large bandages to deal with broken limbs or sprains. Do you know what to do with those?

Of all the first-aid kits I've come across in the last few years, the distinctive yellow Gregson Pack is the most ideally suited for British hill walkers. Not only does it contain everything you need to deal with fractures, burns, sprains, cuts and grazes, but also the unique and almost indestructible packaging includes instructions which tell you exactly what you need to do, when you need to do it!

Past criticisms of first-aid kits have always been that with what most have in them, you could assemble the lot yourself for a fraction of the cost. All well and good, provided you do actually take the trouble, and you know what you ought to have in your kit. The Gregson Pack takes it all a stage further, though. The instructions for the various areas are sealed into the package, so you have what you need in front of you, completely waterproof. And unlike one or two first-aid kits I've laid eyes on in the past, the instructions aren't in the sort of vague language used by those who aren't absolutely sure – it's all culled from authoritative sources such as the BMC and Royal Society for the Prevention of Accidents (RoSPA).

The most common mild affliction for walkers is the blister, although happily, modern boot and, yes, even sock technology has meant that a new pair of boots doesn't require the traditional agonizing period of breaking in. A better fit and greater comfort means fewer blisters. When they do happen, usually in hot weather when your feet perspire, softening the skin, there are really just two choices. Either you pack it in or you carry on.

If you're doing a long backpack, and you're miles from anywhere, you carry on. And while my advice of lancing the blister is not strictly favoured by the medical profession on the grounds that it introduces the possibility of infection, their notion of treating it gently with a plaster is formed on the basis that you do pack it in and don't carry on! Sterilize your needle by holding it in a flame beforehand, and then gently push the point in at the edge of the blister, at the same time using a clean tissue to exert a gentle pressure on it. It may take more than one lancing to get all the fluid out. Once that's done, put a plaster over the spot, grit your teeth and start walking.

There are plenty of products for such complaints in Spenco's range of sports medical kits – Second Skin, a jelly-like dressing for burns, blisters and other sore spots, Biosoft Skinpad, an adhesive, padded dressing designed to stop blisters forming and, inevitably, the Blister Kit, which contains a

---

A good first aid kit is an essential item for your rucksack, and this is one of the best – the Gregson Pack.

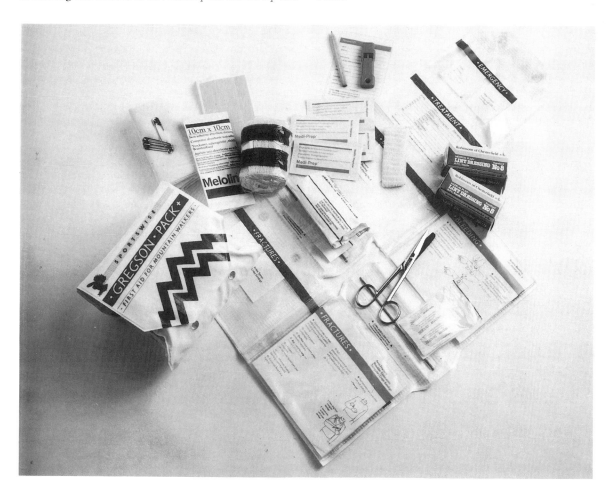

comprehensive set of dressings and pads for the real connoisseur. Another good one is Compeed, a Danish sports dressing distributed in the UK by Sorbothane, the people who make shock absorbing footbeds for all manner of sports footwear. Again, its primary role is in protecting against further abrasion once a sore spot begins to develop.

Another useful product to augment a basic first-aid kit is Stop Hemo. It's a wound dressing made from calcium alginate (derived from seaweed), which promotes extremely fast blood clotting. It's been used in major surgery for nearly 40 years, but only recently has it been possible to manufacture calcium alginate dressings for general use at an affordable price. The Stop Hemo pack, available from most chemists, contains four plasters and two swabs.

Immobilizing sprains and fractures comes down to your own ingenuity, particularly if you don't have a first-aid kit, and the best way to find out a bit more is to do a first-aid course. St John Ambulance do a good basic course, although some of the advice given may need a slightly different interpretation for hill walking, trekking or adventure travel. What you'll also be taught, and have the opportunity to practise, is the basic ABC of life support, essential if you're to save someone whose heart has stopped and/or has stopped breathing (it's called CPR these days – cardio-pulmonary resuscitation). Apart from St John, there are also several outdoors centres which offer mountain first-aid courses – all valuable knowledge to give that useful extra dimension to your first-aid kit if you have to use it in earnest.

When you get into the realms of travelling abroad, it's even more important to make sure you augment your first-aid kit with those useful additional items like indigestion tablets and antihistamine tablets, to turn it into a general medical kit as well. It goes without saying that if you're taking any particular prescription, or you're in an area which requires anti-malarials, you should have those with you at all times. Expeditions going into remote places generally have someone medically qualified to administer prescription-only drugs, but if you're travelling independently, it would pay to consult the Expeditionary Advisory Centre (see Useful Addresses) for further information.

Anti-diarrhoeal pills, such as Lomotil and Imodium, are powerful constipating drugs, and best used only if finding a loo or any other useful spot is going to be awkward. It is best by far to stick to simple rehydration. Take plenty of fluid, made into an electrolyte solution by using any of such products that are made for athletes. You can buy special rehydration sachets such as Dioralyte from chemists, or you can make your own by mixing a

teaspoon of salt with a tablespoon of sugar into a pint of water. These remedies are also much more effective than water on its own if you suffer from dehydration as a result of heat exhaustion.

Losing fillings from your teeth, or having a crown break off, can be enough to leave anyone feeling down in the mouth, and if it happens abroad or somewhere remote, it can really mess up your plans. Dentanurse is a kit specially designed to cope with such problems. The kit contains tubes of zinc oxide filling and a hardening agent laced with oil of cloves, a non-fogging adjustable mirror, probe, spatula and mixing tray. It also includes a sterile needle for use if you do have to pay a visit to a dentist where hygiene is suspect. Mind you, if I was that worried, I'd take the extra pain and trouble to find somewhere reliable, since I'd still be uncertain about the drill bit. You can also buy more comprehensive collections of needles, usually under such names as Aids/Hepatitis B avoidance kits.

Another useful kit to look at is a snake bite extractor. It's a vacuum device, designed to remove venom from snake bites without the highly dangerous trauma caused by gung-ho practices involving razor blades, sucking and spitting. But while I haven't so far had the pleasure of putting the device to work on snake bites, I have used it with great success on insect bites and stings. Certainly the effect it had on a bee sting on one of my travelling companions was quite dramatic. The extractor sucked out the poison successfully, instantly removing the pain too.

Improvisation is often the key to effective first aid, but a good medical kit will always make a difference. So don't do like my journalist friend and go unprepared. You just might not be so lucky!

FIRST AID

So what kind of thing do you need to know? It's a good idea to acquaint yourself with the basic elements of first aid – better still to go on a mountain first-aid course, since some of the things you pick up on a typical St John Ambulance course aren't quite so relevant out in the mountains.

If you're presented with an unconscious accident victim, the ABC of life support is still a good rule of thumb – airway, breathing and circulation. Check first of all that the airway is open and that there are no obstructions – vomit, dentures, snow. If the patient isn't breathing, you must do the breathing

Hope you never have to meet this lot in earnest.
Members of the Search and Rescue Dog Association.

for that person. Hold the patient's nose, seal your mouth over the patient's mouth and blow until you see the rib-cage rise. At the same time, check for a pulse. Don't mess about trying to get one at the wrist. The neck is the best place. If you rest your fingers across the Adam's apple and then let the tips slip down into the cleft at the side, you'll pick up any pulse that's going. If the patient's heart has stopped beating, you'll have to restart it by using cardiac massage – using the heel of the palm, and with your other hand on top, press down on the sternum and release. Do this four or five times, and alternate with the breathing if there's just you. If there's someone else with you, one can do the heart and one can do lungs.

Once the patient is breathing again, place in the recovery position, on the patient's front with head to one side to keep the airway open and prevent any possibility of choking if the patient vomits. The arm and leg on that side are hitched up at right angles to prevent the patient rolling over.

If you suspect spinal injuries, the patient should not be moved. However, you must temper that against the situation you happen to be in. If there was the imminent danger, say, of rockfall if you remained where you were, then you would have to

risk it. But if at all possible, stay put, erecting the tent if you have one over the patient to provide some shelter.

Bleeding

Major wounds must receive immediate attention. If you have your Gregson Pack, you have everything you need to handle the situation. Otherwise, you must improvise, which includes using spare bandages. Don't tie tourniquets – they're recognized as being extremely dangerous. Put pressure on the wound itself and bind bandages over until the blood stops coming through. Don't let the patient bleed freely while you root about in your rucksack. If it comes to it, stick your fist into the wound. The aim is to control the bleeding with no delays. And by the same token, don't be too fussy about clinical cleanliness. Speed is of the essence.

Once you have stabilized a life-threatening condition, you must take stock of your situation and decide on your next move. Do you go for help, wait for a mountain rescue search party or try to attract someone else's attention? How you react depends very much on what kind of terrain you're in, the proximity of the nearest point of civilization, the number of people in your party (and of course their own condition).

Broken bones

It's usually possible to make temporary splints for broken limbs. Arms can be bound with a triangular bandage, or you can improvise with a spare pair of trousers or jacket. An injured leg can be immobilized with such things as a Karrimat, tent pole or ice axe. If there's nothing else to hand, tie the injured leg to the good one, using spare clothing between the two for padding.

Shock

Any kind of trauma is likely to be accompanied by shock. The pulse is fast but weak, and the breathing becomes shallow. In a mountain situation, you need to treat the patient as a hypothermia victim, who needs protection against heat loss as quickly as possible.

Hypothermia

Apart from being something to which any accident victim is open, hypothermia is a threat to any walker who gets cold and tired. The initial signs may be slurred speech, repeated stumbling, shivering or uncharacteristic behaviour. One person I saw on his way with hypothermia became quite aggressive. On the other hand, the time I got it, I became very quiet and uncommunicative. Apathy, loss of co-ordination – both are signs of the onset of hypothermia.

As the body loses heat, it shuts down circulation to preserve the remaining warm blood around the vital body organs. Any means of artificial heating to the exterior of the body could have a harmful effect – the blood vessels dilate around the warmed area, allowing cooled blood to flow through the heart. Breathing warmed air is best, which is why a candle inside a survival bag can make such a tremendous difference.

This is the stage to act. Don't bash on, because the person concerned will almost certainly collapse, and then you really do have a problem. Administer a hot drink if you can and find some shelter. If you have a tent, put it up and get your patient in a sleeping bag as quickly as possible, preferably with someone else to provide some shared body warmth. Failing that, get your patient into a survival bag – not stretched out as though you were in a sleeping bag. Cut a corner off the closed end of the bag to provide a 2-in (5-cm) diameter air hole, then pull the bag over the head, sitting down on a rucksack to provide insulation.

Advanced hypothermia
Whilst the patient is still shivering, the problem is serious. Once the patient stops shivering, things are getting worse. Pulse and respiration will be weak, and the patient will slip into unconsciousness. Further loss of body heat leads to coma and death. But don't even give up at this stage. A patient can be apparently dead from hypothermia, and still be able to revive, since the body's vital functions slow down to the point where you would be unable to detect them.

When it's too hot

Heat exhaustion can be a real problem in hot conditions and is made all the worse if you're exerting yourself. If you don't keep up an adequate intake of water, you'll sweat and sweat till your head aches and you feel faint or dizzy. Get into the shade, rest and drink – preferably an electrolyte solution such as you'd use for rehydration after a bout of diarrhoea.

Once you're at the point where you're no longer sweating, and the skin goes hot and dry, you now have the more serious condition of heatstroke. The answer is to cool the patient, either by wrapping in cold, wet cloth, or by fanning the patient until his temperature drops.

In both instances, prevention is far easier than the cure. Keep up your water intake. As a general rule of thumb, you should be consuming 1 pint of water for every 10°F per 24 hours. So if it's 80°F (26°C), you need a gallon (4.5l) of water every day.

Incidentally, some people have the mistaken idea that salt is the answer for hot conditions. Admittedly, a pinch of salt along with some sugar in your water will make it more effectively absorbed, but on no account take salt tablets or salt on its own. Dehydration makes your blood thicker and taking extra salt will make it thicker still.

Burns

This is not likely to happen to you on a day walk unless you happen to fall into a volcano, but it's always a possibility for backpackers. But if you do manage to burn yourself on a stove or hot pan, you have the best treatment to hand, assuming you've camped close to your water supply. You can reduce the pain and minimize tissue damage by dunking the burned part into cold water as soon as possible. Keep it immersed for at least ten minutes. Then apply a clean dressing (there's a special burns dressing in the Gregson Pack), and head off to the nearest doctor's surgery if it looks nasty.

BENIGHTMENT

If you did the proper thing before you set off, you would have left a note of your route with someone responsible, charged with notifying the police if you don't reappear. Always make sure your responsible link with civilization is informed when you complete the walk – which reminds me of the time I was with a group in Snowdonia in Wales. I'd decided to climb Crib Goch and on round to the summit of Snowdon, while the others decided to take a more gentle stroll up the Pyg track. I met them still going up as I was on my way down, and by 7 o'clock in the evening, I'd had a drink and was expecting to see them back at the campsite. Two hours later they still hadn't appeared and I'd actually already contacted the police to let them know I was getting worried.

Of course, you've guessed it. They'd actually finished their walk, and headed off to the pub without thinking they might have been missed, or that the mountain rescue might have been sent out on a wild goose chase!

You don't have to become incapacitated by an injury to be faced with the prospect of an unexpected night out under the stars. It may be that your navigation fouled up, or your plans really had you trying to bite off more than you could chew. If you're equipped with a torch, you're warm and dry, in good spirit, and you know where you are, you may decide to bash on even though the sun has gone down.

Provided you know what you're doing, that's fine – it can even be pretty exhilarating. I quite enjoy setting off for a four- or five-hour walk in the late afternoon – as everyone else is coming off the hills, I'm claiming them for myself! And there are magical moments to be had watching the fiery glow of sunset from a summit.

But if you've pushed yourself too far, the worst thing you can do is try to bash on, because that's the way which leads to accidents. If you have a survival bag, you should be able to protect yourself. You may not be overly comfortable, but you will last out the night.

Try and find a sheltered spot, sit on your rucksack to insulate yourself from the ground, with the survival bag pulled over your head. Sliding into it like a sleeping bag is fine if you happen to have a sleeping mat, but since day walkers wouldn't normally carry such a thing, it's best with the bag over your head, and about 2in (50cm) of one corner on the closed end cut off to provide sufficient ventilation.

Put on all your spare clothing, put on hat and gloves, and pull your hood over your head. You could end up so cozy, you decide to take up this kind of primitive bivvy as an extension to your normal walking activities!

Benightment in winter conditions is covered in Chapter 9.

ATTRACTING ATTENTION

Whistle

A perry whistle will do, but the Canadian Fox 40 is the loudest you'll get anywhere. The international distress signal is six blasts, followed by a pause of a minute, then repeated. The answer to the signal is three blasts.

Torch

At night, you can switch the torch on and off to flash the international distress signal described above.

Flares

It's possible to get mini-flares which can be fired into the air. But since you're unlikely to have an inexhaustible supply, make sure you fire them off when you're fairly positive there's someone around to see them.

Strobes

You can get all sorts of natty little gadgets which emit pulses of light visible from considerable distances. Strobes are probably a bit excess to requirements for a day walk, unless you like loading yourself down with gear, but could be useful on longer trips.

Talented flare for survival.

Heliograph

During daylight a heliograph, a small mirror with a hole in the centre, can be used to flash sunlight at someone in the distance – even to an aircraft. Look through the hole from the back of the mirror, and sight it on the point you want to flash at. Useful as a shaving mirror, too!

Building a fire

Depends on where you are, and your circumstances. If you happen to be stranded somewhere like Alaska, with your only hope of maybe attracting attention from an aircraft, a fire might be a useful signalling tool – kept with damp foliage to make smoke by day and plenty of dry wood to make it burn bright by night. But unless you've swotted up on the ways of the backwoodsman, you'll probably find this a bit more difficult than you think.

INSURANCE

You're out walking somewhere when, quite by chance, you slip over and break your leg. It's something that could happen to any of us, and which indeed happens frequently throughout the year. On a footpath not that far removed from civilization, it's relatively easy for your companions to find a telephone and get an ambulance to pick you up. Now picture the same scenario somewhere more remote. This time, it's a mountain rescue job which could involve a stretcher evacuation, or even a ride in an RAF search and rescue helicopter.

The same little slip could happen while you're abroad. What happens then? If you're in an EC country, you're entitled to medical attention under reciprocal agreements with the UK, provided you're in possession of form E111 (provided by your local DSS), which will reimburse all or part of your medical expenses, depending on which country you're in. Mind you, I'm not so sure it's such a brilliant idea relying solely on form E111. What it doesn't guarantee is the very best medical treatment money can buy. Frankly, I'd be a bit apprehensive if I were hospitalized in one or two EC countries without the back-up of insurance! There's also the problem that form E111 doesn't cover any extra expense you might be put to as a result of being hospitalized in a foreign country.

If mountain rescue services are involved, there's a fair chance you'll be presented with a bill. If you weren't insured, you might wish they'd left you to your fate, because in areas like the Alps, the going rate for a rescue can be anything up to £10 per minute! Indeed, there are many places in the world, including the Himalaya, where a helicopter won't even take off unless they have definite proof that you're insured.

The good news is that, provided you're walking or trekking, standard travel insurance, available from your local travel agent at very reasonable rates, will cover you quite adequately. The only time you need to pay extra is if you're taking part in some sort of winter sport, like skiing, and even here, they never usually charge more than double the standard rate. Travel insurance specifically excludes technical climbing, in other words, where ropes and equipment are involved, but it is possible to cover yourself at not too great a cost through one or two specialist companies.

The levels of cover offered by travel insurance differ from one policy to another, so it's worth checking the small print. Medical expenses cover needs to be adequate for what might possibly be involved. For instance, a serious medical problem while you're trekking in the Himalaya or Andes won't necessarily just involve a helicopter evacuation to a hospital.

Given the standard of some medical treatment around the world, it's essential your cover can pay the cost of an air ambulance repatriation flight if necessary. As such, you ought to be looking at policies with a medical expenses sum insured of £1 million. One or two policies even offer unlimited medical sums insured. Most importantly, your policy needs a 24 hour emergency telephone service, so if you do fall ill or injure yourself, and need speedy repatriation, they can set the wheels in motion straight away.

Travel insurance usually includes personal accident cover, paying a sum for death or specified degrees of disablement, and a fairly substantial sum to cover your legal liability to third parties. Of course, it's much more likely that any claim on travel insurance will be of the more mundane variety – loss or damage to money or personal effects, but check that the sum insured is adequate for your needs. It may be that they limit their liability to a maximum sum per single article, typically £100 or £150.

If you're carrying high-value things such as a camera, watch or tape recorder, be sure the limit for any one item will actually buy you a replacement. Those sorts of items may best be covered by the all risks section of your household contents policy. If you take that route, it's worth checking the geographical limits specified in your contents policy. You may have to pay a very small extra premium if you're travelling outside Europe.

If the worst happens, and you're unlucky enough to have something pinched, make sure you report it to the local police within 24 hours, and retain a copy of your statement. Without it, the insurance company is unlikely to entertain your claim.

Any insurance policy always has a list of exclusions – items or events where the underwriters won't pay up after you've suffered a loss. The standard ones include any damage caused by war, riots, supersonic bangs and anything to do with nuclear contamination. They also include the mundane and more likely things such as wear and tear, mildew, damage by moths or vermin and losses where items have been confiscated by police or customs.

The cost of travel insurance is a modest price to pay for peace of mind. One thing is certain – it's fatal to think that misfortune won't happen to you. So, wouldn't you rather be prepared for it, just in case it does?

CHAPTER 11

The Walker and the Law

by Hugh Westacott

JUST AS A LEARNER DRIVER is required to have some knowledge of the law before driving a vehicle on the public highways, so should a walker have some understanding of the legal aspects of walking. Not only will such knowledge expand walkers' horizons and allow them to plan routes with confidence, it will also prevent them incurring the wrath of landowners, and enable them to enjoy their walking knowing that they are entitled to be where they are. It should be noted that a public path (sometimes referred to as a right of way) is a public highway and receives the same protection in law as a road. Wherever the term 'public highway' is used without qualification in Acts of Parliament, then that law also applies to public paths.

This chapter is designed to give the trail walker sufficient information to provide a working knowledge of the law governing rights of way and access in the United Kingdom, and some helpful information about the legal position overseas. It does not pretend to be exhaustive, and readers who wish to pursue the subject in more detail should obtain copies of the books mentioned in the text.

There are also matters of behaviour that may not necessarily be governed by legislation, which every trail walker worth the dressing on his boots would regard as deeply offensive. Obvious examples are dropping litter, lighting fires, damage to property and picking wild flowers. The Country Code, although published by the English Countryside Commission, is applicable to trail walking anywhere.

1 Enjoy the countryside and respect its life and work.
2 Guard against all risks of fire.
3 Fasten all gates.
4 Keep your dogs under close control.
5 Keep to public paths across farmland.
6 Use gates and stiles to cross fences, hedges and walls.
7 Leave livestock, crops and machinery alone.
8 Take your litter home.
9 Protect wild life, wild plants and trees.
10 Take special care on country roads.
11 Make no unnecessary noise.

The Country Code suffers from the ambiguities and vagueness inherent in all succinct codes of conduct that are so easily learned parrot-fashion. For example, if 'Fasten all gates' is intended to mean 'Close all gates', then the instruction is incorrect because gates are sometimes deliberately left open by farmers as part of their system of farm management. 'Keep to public paths across farmland' implies that it is permissible to walk anywhere in open country, although in most parts of England and Wales, the walker commits a trespass if deviating from the right of way, unless an access agreement has been negotiated.

THE UNITED KINGDOM

Unfortunately, the law covering rights of way and access in the United Kingdom is not uniform and has to be described separately under the headings England and Wales, Scotland, and Northern Ireland. It should be noted, in particular, that the position in Scotland differs markedly from that of England and Wales.

England and Wales

The laws governing rights of way in England and Wales are quite specific and should be strictly adhered to. It is a rigid system, and changes to routes can only be made by due legal process. A public path may be obstructed for years, even built upon, but it remains a public highway until the necessary legal steps are taken to close or divert it. If a house is built on a right of way, then, theoretically, the trail walker is entitled to walk through the living rooms of the house or climb over the roof!

Rights of way fall into one of the four categories that define who may use them.

1   A footpath is defined in the Wildlife and Countryside Act, 1981 as '. . . a highway over which the public have the right of way on foot only, other than such a highway at the side of the road.' This definition precludes the use of footpaths by horse riders and cyclists, except with the express permission of the landowner, and always providing that there is no local authority by-law prohibiting riders and cyclists.
2   A bridleway is defined by the Wildlife and Countryside Act 1981 as 'A highway over which the public have the following, but no other, rights of way, that is to say, a right of way on foot and a right of way on horseback or leading a horse, with or without a right to drive animals of any description along the highway.' (Note that section 30 the Countryside Act 1968 allows the riding of bicycles on bridleways providing that they give way to horse riders and pedestrians. The local authority has the power to make by-laws prohibiting the riding of bicycles on any particular highway.)
3   A 'byway open to all traffic', often referred to colloquially as a BOAT, is defined in the Wildlife and Countryside Act 1981 as 'a highway over which the public have a right of way for vehicular and all other kinds of traffic, but is used by the public mainly for the purpose for which footpaths and bridleways are so used.' Under the terms of earlier legislation, byways open to all traffic were known as 'roads used as public paths' (RUPPS).
4   A road used as a public path, known colloquially as a 'RUPP', is defined in the National Parks and Access to the Countryside Act 1949 as '. . . a highway, other than a public path, used by the public mainly for the purposes for which footpaths and bridleways are so used.' Under the Wildlife and Countryside Act 1981 every RUPP must be reclassified either as a byway open to all traffic, or as a bridleway, or as a footpath.

Many trail walkers like to be accompanied by their dog. Statute law makes no mention of dogs on rights of way, but the judgment *R v Matthias* in 1861 held that a landowner could remove from a public path '. . . anything . . . except such things as are usual accompaniments of a large class of foot passengers, being so small and light, as neither to be a

Alan Hinkes, in "bush-whacking" mode!

nuisance to other passengers nor injurious to the soil.' Although this particular case was about a perambulator, the principle enunciated would seem to apply to dogs. Section 1(2)(c) of the Dogs (Protection of Livestock) Act 1953 forbids the owner of a dog to allow it to be at large in a field or enclosure where there are sheep (maximum penalty £200). Section 1(2) of the same Act makes it an offence to allow a dog to attack or chase livestock, and section 9 of the Animals Act 1971 gives farmers the right to shoot dogs found chasing livestock.

The official record of rights of way is known as the 'definitive map'. It is maintained by the highway authority (most usually county councils, but by the district councils of former metropolitan counties and by London boroughs) and shows all public paths within its jurisdiction. If a path is shown on the definitive map, that is conclusive evidence in law that it is a right of way at the time the map was made, and may only be diverted or extinguished by due legal process. The definitive map may be seen at highway authority offices, but is normally only consulted by local footpath secretaries, and others interested in preserving and maintaining rights of way. Most trail walkers rely on the Pathfinder and Landranger Ordnance Survey maps on which public paths are printed in distinctive colours. Highway authorities inform the Ordnance Survey of changes to the path network and, by means of computerized mapping techniques, these revisions are incorporated whenever the map is reprinted.

The Ordnance Survey is meticulous in recording the status of public paths on its Landranger and Pathfinder maps, but it is often difficult to determine whether the so-called 'white roads' – minor lanes and driveways – are public highways. As a rule of thumb guide, if a 'white road' serves as the only link between two public paths, it is likely that the road may be used by the general public.

In the context of walking, trespass means to pass illegally and without permission on to another's property. Trespass is not a criminal offence (notices stating that trespassers will be prosecuted are a meaningless bluff), but a civil tort, and the injured party can either obtain an injunction against the offender, or sue for damages, even though no provable harm has been done. Landowners and tenants can require trespassers to leave their property or return to the right of way, and may use reasonable force to compel them to do so. In practice, it is most unlikely that an action would result from unintentional trespass because of the cost involved. Providing that walkers keep to the right of way, then they cannot be held to be trespassing.

The highway authority owns the surface of rights of way (this is a philosophical concept only, as the landowner owns everything beneath the surface), and is responsible for asserting the rights of the public to the use and enjoyment of public paths, and to prevent their stopping up or obstruction.

The highway authority is mainly responsible for extinguishing (closing) or diverting public paths and normally only puts the necessary legal procedures into operation at the request of the landowner. Extinguishments are rarely justified except in unusual cases, such as where there are parallel routes around a field, enabling one to be dispensed without loss of amenity. Diversions are sometimes necessary to enable development to take place and still preserve the path network. Orders for diversion and extinguishment have to be advertised, and most of those that are opposed are decided by the courts.

Obstructions are not permitted on rights of way.

A farmer has no more right to string barbed wire across a public path than to erect a fence across a public road. Landowners must keep gates and stiles in good condition, and can claim up to 25 per cent of the cost of new structures from the highway authority. Under the provisions of the common law, members of the public have the right to remove as much of the obstruction as is necessary to allow passage. However, this right should only be exercised by local people fully conversant with the facts. It would be most unwise for a trail walker in unfamiliar country, relying solely on the evidence of an Ordnance Survey map, to remove an apparent obstruction, because the path might have been diverted after the map was printed.

Although technically not an obstruction, there are few obstacles more daunting to the trail walker than a deep, wet, ploughed field. Legislation introduced in 1991 has placed more stringent obligations on the ploughing of public paths. It is illegal to plough headland paths – paths that follow the edge of the field – except in those rare circumstances where a common law right to plough them exists. If a right of way that crosses fields is disturbed, for example by ploughing or harrowing, the surface must be restored within 24 hours (or two weeks if the soil has been disturbed previously that season). Restored cross-field footpaths must be at least 1m wide; cross-field bridleways must be at least 2m wide; headland footpaths must be at least 1.5m wide; and headland bridleways at least 3m wide. All restored paths must be clearly visible on the ground.

Crops, with the exception of grass, must be prevented from growing or falling over the line of the path.

If a farmer fails to comply with the law, the highway authority has the right to restore the line of the path after giving the landowner 24 hours' notice, and to charge the landowner for any costs incurred. Offenders may be prosecuted by the highway authority.

The maintenance of bridges is normally the responsibility of the highway authority unless they are owned by another body such as British Rail or British Waterways.

Highway authorities have a statutory duty to signpost public paths where they leave roads. They are not obliged to waymark rights of way, although in practice many do, especially where a legal diversion has been made from the original route. Bodies such as National Parks and the National Trust frequently waymark routes. Sometimes voluntary

Approach to Blencathra, Lake District.

societies such as ramblers' organizations undertake waymarking activities, but they have to obtain permission from both the landowner and the highway authority. One of the most remarkable examples of waymarking by a non-statutory body is to be found in the Chilterns. After many years' patient negotiation and hard work, the Chiltern Society has succeeded in waymarking almost every one of the many hundreds of miles of public path in this popular Area of Outstanding Natural Beauty.

Bulls may, under certain conditions, be pastured in fields crossed by rights of way. Under section 59 of the Wildlife and Countryside Act 1981 and section 44(1) of the Countryside (Scotland) Act 1967, farmers may pasture beef breed bulls that are accompanied by cows or heifers in fields crossed by rights of way. However, it is illegal to pasture bulls more than ten months old of a recognized dairy breed such as Ayrshire, British Friesian, British Holstein, Dairy Shorthorn, Guernsey, Jersey and Kerry in fields crossed by rights of way.

It is always illegal to keep an animal, including a bull, known to be dangerous in a field crossed by a right of way.

Access

From the above outline it can be seen that the law in England and Wales is straightforward and readily understood, but there is a grey area known as access. This concept may best be described as the roaming at will away from rights of way – access – on uncultivated land. Access is usually, though not universally, understood to apply to mountains and moorland; beyond the limits of cultivation and enclosure which is often referred to as 'open country'. Unless an access agreement has been negotiated, there is no legal right to roam at will on mountain and moorland, although the custom is hallowed by tradition in some parts of England and Wales, notably in the Lake District.

Although there is no general right of access to open country, some authorities, notably the Peak National Park, have negotiated access agreements with landowners. Under these arrangements, members of the public may gain entry to access land at designated places and then roam at will. The boundaries of areas subject to access agreements are usually indicated on the Ordnance Survey's Outdoor Leisure maps. The National Trust, which owns huge tracts of countryside, normally allows the public access to its land situated in open country.

Contrary to popular belief, common land always has an owner, and there is no general right to roam. Common land gets its name because over the centuries certain individuals have obtained particular rights in common such as the grazing of cattle, the extraction of timber etc. Only about 20 per cent of common land is subject to a right of access.

There is no general right to camp without seeking the permission of the landowner. Notices forbidding camping, such as frequently appear on National Trust land, must always be respected, but the discreet backpacker who camps overnight in an isolated spot away from prying eyes is unlikely to be challenged. If the backpacker follows the splendid American maxim of minimum impact, he will leave no trace of his campsite, and the landowner will never know that there had been an uninvited guest. In some areas, notably the Lake District, the practice of wild camping in open country is tolerated.

The best treatise on the legal aspects of trail walking in England and Wales is *Rights of Way: a Guide to Law and Practice* by John Riddall and John Trevelyan (Ramblers' Association/Open spaces Society, 1992, 2nd edn). Also try *Garner's Rights of Way* by J. F. Garner (Longman, 1989, 5th edn).

Scotland

In Scotland, there is comparatively little public emphasis on legal rights to walk. There is a widespread belief in the Scottish psyche, unsupported by legal sanction, that there is a moral right for everyone to enjoy the hills. It is also understood by Scottish trail walkers that the quid pro quo is sympathy, understanding and consideration for the legitimate interests of landowners. In order to appreciate this delicate relationship, it should be understood that Scotland has a tiny population of only five million people, most of whom live in the Central Lowlands belt. Much of the rest of Scotland is predominantly hilly, with great tracts of wild upland country on which the tramp of walkers' feet has, as yet, made little impact, except in a few especially popular areas, and on popular Munros and sections of 'official' paths. There are indications, however, especially where some of the great estates are purchased by foreigners unfamiliar with the Scottish tradition of access, that this mutual tolerance is under strain.

Trespassing is not in itself a criminal offence, and an aggrieved party cannot raise an interdict (sue) for trespass. The only remedy open to the landowner is to require the trespasser to leave the property or return to the right of way. Thus it can be seen that the considerate walker has nothing to fear from trespassing in Scotland, which is yet another reason why it is usually possible to walk any path shown on the map, and why in open country there is a tradition of access.

Providing that they respect sporting interests and avoid areas in the hunting season where grouse-shooting (12 August to 31 October), and deer-stalking and hind-culling (August to February), is taking place, trail walkers have tremendous freedom to roam. Information on where shooting and stalking is taking place may be obtained locally from the factor's (estate manager's) office, post offices, police stations, public houses, hotels, tourist offices and Youth Hostels. Trail walkers exploring Scotland during the hunting season should always make sure that their proposed route will not conflict with sporting interests. Whatever your private views of deer-stalking may be, you must appreciate its importance to the Scottish economy, and understand that you will be imperilling the freedom to roam if you do not behave considerately. The addresses and telephone numbers of landowners, factors and keepers in the Highlands may be obtained from *Heading for the Scottish Hills*, compiled by the Mountaineering Council of Scotland and the Scottish Landowners' Federation, Scottish Mountaineering Club, 1992.

There is no general right to camp, but wild camping in open country by backpackers is generally tolerated.

The Scottish Rights of Way Society Ltd have erected signposts on many of the major rights of way, but waymarking is virtually non-existent as it is considered alien to the Scottish walking tradition. It is significant that there are only three official long-distance paths in Scotland, and one, the Speyside Way, is unlikely ever to be opened along its planned length. The concept of long-distance paths has caused unease among many Scottish trail walkers, as they fear their existence may be used as an excuse for curtailing the tradition of access.

The law relating to rights of way in Scotland is more flexible and dynamically responsive to change than is the law in England and Wales, giving the trail walker considerably more freedom to roam north of the border. The majority of Scotland's rights of way came into existence under the provisions of the common law, although there is some legislation. The planning authority has the responsibility of asserting and protecting the public's enjoyment of rights of way, and may keep registers of rights of way. The Ordnance Survey does not show rights of way on its maps of Scotland, but, in practice, paths depicted on Ordnance Survey maps may be used by trail walkers.

A footpath is defined in the Countryside (Scotland) Act, 1967 and the Town and Country Planning (Scotland) Act 1972 as 'A way over which the public have the following but not other rights of way, that is to say, a right of way on foot with or

Negotiating a stile in Langdale.

without a right of way on pedal cycles.'

A bridleway is defined in the Countryside (Scotland) Act 1967 and the Town and Country Planning (Scotland) Act 1972 as 'A way on which the public have the following but no other rights of way, that is to say, a right of way on foot and a right of way on horseback or leading a horse with or without a right to drive animals of any description along that way.'

A right of way is deemed to have been created if the following conditions are met:

1 the route must link one public place with another;
2 the route must be reasonably well defined;
3 the route must have been used by the general public, without seeking the express or implied permission of the landowner, for at least 20 years.

Rights of way may be closed if the landowner can demonstrate that the route has fallen into disuse for a period of 20 years. Minor diversions may be made to the route providing that the public acquiesce. Alternatively, the landowner can apply to the planning authority for permission to make an official diversion.

Camping isn't always about big views from the tent. Spacepacker Plus in the forests of Finnish Lapland.

Section 43 of the Countryside (Scotland) Act 1967 permits a landowner to plough a right of way for agricultural purposes, providing that the landowner gives notice to the planning authority beforehand and reinstates the surface of the path. The common law allows the public to continue to use a right of way that has been ploughed.

Bulls may, under certain conditions, be pastured in fields crossed by rights of way. Under section 44(1) of the Countryside (Scotland) Act 1967, farmers may pasture beef breed bulls that are accompanied by cows or heifers in fields crossed by rights of way. However, it is illegal to pasture bulls more than ten-months old of a recognized dairy breed such as Ayrshire, British Friesian, British Holstein, Dairy Shorthorn, Guernsey, Jersey and Kerry in fields crossed by rights of way.

The best treatise dealing with Scottish rights of way is *Rights of Way: a Guide to the Law in Scotland* by A. E. Anton, published by the Scottish Rights of Way Society Ltd, 10/12 Sunnyside, Edinburgh EH7 5RA, 1991, 2nd edn.

Northern Ireland

There is little legislation relating to rights of way in Northern Ireland. The Access to the Countryside (Northern Ireland) Order 1983 places responsibility on district councils to map and keep open rights of way, and to create new ones where necessary. It also gives district councils the power to close rights of way where they are no longer needed. Under common law, certain individuals, families and those engaged in a particular pursuit such as the extraction of timber or turf may have the right of passage in particular circumstances, but such considerations do not normally apply to the walker.

Walkers, if they keep away from the vicinity of large towns where, over the years, friction may have developed between 'townies' and farmers, are unlikely to encounter any difficulties using paths and tracks shown on maps published by the Ordnance Survey for Northern Ireland. There is a dense network of lanes and minor roads on which motor traffic is sparse, but comparatively few field or mountain paths except in Mourne.

THE LAW OUTSIDE THE UNITED KINGDOM

It is clearly impossible in one brief chapter to give a comprehensive account of the law relating to rights of way worldwide, but it is possible to make some general and helpful observations. Readers intending to walk abroad are recommended to obtain suitable guidebooks.

Europe

In most European countries rights of way have legal protection. Many countries such as France, Switzerland, Austria, Germany, Belgium, Denmark, Sweden, Norway and Luxembourg have a long-established tradition of walking, and have networks of well-waymarked paths. Sweden and Norway have a law known as *allemansratten* (every man's right) that allows the trail walker to wander at will and to camp anywhere, except in a private garden, for one night without the need to seek permission. Mediterranean countries also have numerous mule-tracks and unsurfaced minor roads that make excellent walking routes. All European countries have developed long-distance paths, and some have been linked to European international long-distance paths, known as E-routes, that criss-cross the continent from end to end.

The New World

In the United States, Canada, Australia and New Zealand, there is no equivalent of our local path network. There is splendid walking in all these countries, but the trail walker usually has to visit one of the numerous state and national parks to find a system of well-maintained trails. There is usually a park reception office where maps and advice can be obtained. In some of these countries there is a 'nanny' culture that Britons may find irksome. For example, there may be an entry fee to the park, the number of visitors is sometimes restricted and permits are often required for backpacking trips. Nevertheless, visitors should be aware that many of these parks are uninhabited, distances can be immense, water can be scarce and the wildlife may pose hazards. Visitors who get lost may never be seen again. Many national parks in the western United States and Canada are closed during the winter.

The Third World

In the more remote mountainous areas of Third World countries, there are paths and tracks that are vital communication links between villages, and these are often available to trail walkers. Most trail walkers will prefer to explore Third World countries with the help of a tour company, but the really determined and adventurous should seek local advice on suitable routes.

CHAPTER 12

Keeping Track

Diary, photos, video

by Clive Tully

Keeping a diary can be electronic. The Microwriter AgendA, a palmtop computer on which part of this book was written!

IT'S NICE TO REMEMBER your travels in some way, if only to have something to browse over and reminisce about of a winter's evening. And there are certainly plenty of ways you can do it. One of the easiest is to keep a diary. I know some ardent Munro-baggers who keep a record of every mountain they climb. With over 270 Munros, even a cursory paragraph about your exploits on each one would add up to a fairly hefty tome, but for all that it would be a personal record quite unlike anyone else's.

I always keep a diary when I travel, jotting down everything from the obvious things like where I went and when, to my impressions and observations about people I met on the way. Mind you, for a writer, it's pretty much the kind of stuff that keeps me going, anyway. If you're moving with the times, and have progressed beyond scribbling furtively in dog-eared note-books, you might like to try a palm-

top computer. My constant companion on most trips is a Microwriter AgendA. It has an unusual layout of 'microwriting' keys quite unlike a typewriter keyboard, which allows you to write one-handed. And apart from keeping my diary on it, it also has diary and database functions, and word processing which has enabled me to knock out newspaper features while languishing in my tent in the wilds. Another comparable palmtop is the Psion 3.

Are you an artist of any kind? Simple drawings can be dashed off fairly quickly, maybe even to illustrate a diary. Of course, once you progress to anything more elaborate, like a painting, you may decide it's easier to work at home from some kind of reference – probably a photograph.

AUDIO CASSETTE

The advent of the personal stereo has its down-side when you're stuck in a railway carriage listening to the irritating chatter from some mindless zombie's Walkman turned up too loud. But for backpackers, a small audio cassette recorder makes an interesting way of keeping track of your expeditions.

It can be fun doing your own little personal *Down your Way* recording and, if you have a camera as well, you can even experiment with a little multi-media. One of my favourites is a group of school-children I recorded singing in a remote village in Northern India. It still brings a lump to the throat even now when I look at my colour slides and play the tape.

Like video, power may be a problem, though one or two models are available now which are solar powered, and it's also possible to buy small, light-weight solar chargers to keep your NiCads charged up.

VIDEO

In just a few short years, video cameras have trans-formed from huge unwieldy lumps barely able to fit in a rucksack, to tiny compact machines which sit in the palm of your hand and which take up no more space than many SLR cameras. And the fact that they're so small and light means they could easily come along on a backpacking trip. The only drawback is available power supply for recharging batteries. But you can get round it to an extent if you take spare battery packs with you.

Unless you're a real video freak, and you want to take one of the all-singing and dancing models with zoom lens and in-camera editing facilities, I'd go for the smallest and lightest, which, like the smallest of 35mm stills cameras, has a fixed focal length lens. OK, so you can't zoom in on a subject, but you can still walk towards it to get a closer viewpoint. Quite a few mountaineering expeditions filming docu-mentaries have used little camcorders like this for the high-altitude stuff, where a heavier machine would be too much of a burden, so you can be sure the quality is good.

CAMERAS – THE COMPACT CHOICE

Taking photographs is as personal in terms of levels of interest as walking itself. It's something you can take very seriously, and spend time and money to develop (sorry) or, with a more casual approach, you can get by with simple records of your travels and adventures. That's not to say you should ignore 35mm SLRs if you're a really keen photographer. But unless you limit yourself to one camera body with one or two lenses, it's easy to cripple yourself with extra pack weight. The compact camera makes an ideal choice for the walker who wants some-thing uncomplicated with which to take decent snaps.

For one thing, it's eminently suitable for anyone looking for low weight and bulk – most will fit com-fortably into a shirt pocket, although for protection against the weather and the inevitable knocks and scrapes, you may well choose to store your camera in a padded pouch. For another, the majority of compacts are virtually idiot-proof. That's not intended as an unkindness to the photographer, simply to say that provided you know how to com-pose your picture, the camera will deliver a good shot every time. Recent years have seen tremen-dous advances in compact cameras, and you now have a mind-boggling choice of all singing and dancing models, with flashing lights, bleepers – I'm sure some of the little devils even talk to you!

Even with photography at this level, you have to decide exactly what you need from a camera. If all you want is a very basic job to supply you with postcard-size prints, then you could choose from

The Nikon RF10, an easy to use compact camera for the fast-moving walker.

the range of 110 cameras. They vary from folding models to disc cameras and their fixed focus lenses deliver reasonable results. The drawback with 110 cameras is that the choice of film is limited compared to 35mm, and that because the negative area is that much smaller, picture quality is not so good. Indeed, if you want any decent-sized enlargements of your pictures, then we really have to talk about 35mm cameras.

You can get 35mm film for colour and black and white prints, colour slides and different film speeds to allow for variations in lighting. So, straight away, you have a lot more scope. The smaller and more basic 35mm compacts have fixed focal length lenses – that is, they don't zoom and you can't remove the lens to slot on another of a different focal length as you can with an SLR. Compacts usually have a wider angle lens than standard SLRs, most commonly 35mm. Moderately wide angle lenses like these are eminently suited to landscape and 'point and shoot' photography, because for any given focusing distance, the depth of field is far greater. The advantage is that focusing tends not to be that critical.

But spend a little more money and you can fix yourself up with a compact with built-in motorized zoom, giving you a choice of focal lengths, usually between 35 and 70mm, or thereabouts.

The most basic cameras require you to guess the distance between the camera and the subject, which you then set on the lens focusing ring. Others are a little more sophisticated, with a rangefinder focusing system where you can actually see when the subject is properly focused. In practice, if you have the lens on any compact set to F8 or smaller, you can virtually forget about focusing. I've had sharp results from several 'grab' shots where I've either forgotten or not had time to focus.

The vast majority of compacts these days don't just have automatic exposure, but autofocusing as well. But just as it's possible for certain lighting conditions to fool an auto-exposure camera into delivering an incorrectly exposed photograph, it's also possible for an autofocus to be fooled, usually when your subject happens to be off-centre in the frame of your shot.

The larger compacts are the ones which go for 100 per cent idiot proofing, with programmed automatic exposure, autofocus, autoflash in low light and autowind. Some don't even let you load the film yourself, you just drop a cassette into the camera and the autowind takes it on to the first frame. While the non-photographers among us may welcome so many electronic helping hands, such facilities come at a price. With built-in electric

motors and larger batteries required to drive them, these cameras are heading towards the weight and bulk of some of the smaller SLRs.

A good many photographers with flashy SLRs and braces of lenses look down their noses at compacts, be they of the pocket variety or the slightly larger autofocus jobs, yet it's interesting to note that a good many Fleet Street photographers have a compact stashed away in their gadget bags. That has to say something for the quality of picture they produce. My reasons for having such a camera are the same as any other walker or backpacker's – it's small and light, and just the job for a good, sharp picture with the minimum of fuss.

Pictures of what?

Composing a picture comes naturally to some. To others, it's a skill that needs to be worked on. Rules, of course, are made to be broken, but if you use the standard rule of thirds as your start point, you can at least produce an acceptable composition. If you divide your picture area into three, both horizontally and vertically, you have two sets of parallel lines crossing each other. The idea is to compose your shot so that the points of interest fall on one of those points of intersection. So it could be that if you choose to place some perspiring, hairy backpacker into your picture to add foreground interest and scale, you'd place him or her to the left or right, along one of those imaginary lines.

And getting a strong foreground is a great way of adding depth to your picture. Your subject may be a range of distant hills, with a valley in between. Take the shot standing up and you'll end up with a disappointing photograph. On the other hand, if you get down low and perhaps put some boulders, flowers or the aforementioned perspiring, hairy backpacker in the foreground, and already the picture takes on depth and interest.

Once you've mastered that, you need to think about lighting. The way a subject is lit is, in some situations, almost more important than the subject itself. You may have a really interesting subject, in a devastating composition, but if the light that's hitting it doesn't suit the picture, it won't work. Note that I said 'doesn't suit'. Many people are put off taking photographs the moment the sun goes behind a cloud, when in fact you may be able to take all sorts of shots. Admittedly it won't be anywhere near as bright, but you will have a virtually

Too hot to walk? Cool off in a waterfall, like this one in New Hampshire.

shadowless diffused lighting that can be very effective, and which actually renders colours more naturally. There are two main aspects you should consider when you take your photograph – the quality of the light and the direction of the light, particularly in relation to your viewpoint.

Light changes with the weather, the time of day and the time of year. The light of early morning produces long shadows, picking out even the tiniest bumps in the landscape. While the setting sun will do this as well, morning light is crisper and generally with more of a yellow tinge, as the lower temperature and humidity of the night will have left the air clear. The light at dusk still produces interesting shadows, but because the air temperature will be warmer, and there is likely to be a higher concentration of dust and pollution in the air, the shadows will be slightly more diffused and the colour more orangey/red. The thing that characterizes a low sun more than anything is its warmth of colour. That warm, orange glow makes even the starkest subject come to life.

It's possible to buy filters which remove the slight colour casts caused by different colour temperatures – various grades of orange balance up cool light and shades of blue are used to bring warm light back to 'normal'. I can't recommend it. You might render your subject more accurately, but it's a lot more trouble fiddling around with filters for this sort of thing and your landscapes would look uniform. Why transform the warm glow of a sunset or the bluish look caused by a heavily overcast sky? No, stick with what you have and regard it as another element in a creative picture.

When it comes to filters, the only essential one, especially when you're in a mountain environment, is a skylight or ultra-violet filter. Ultra-violet light is invisible to the human eye, but its effects can be seen on colour film, especially in pictures of distant views and where there is some haze in the sky. Without this filter you may get some loss of definition, and shadow areas may come out with a blue fluorescence.

The direction of the light in relation to the subject, and your viewpoint, plays an important part in the photograph. A high midday sun will give very little shadow in a landscape, although what shadows there are will be very intense, as the sun is much brighter. You'll also get high colour saturation and high contrast. What most people might regard as normal lighting would be front lighting, with the sun illuminating your subject from somewhere above and behind you. It can certainly be regarded as safe as far as exposure is concerned, as even the most elementary metering system will give an accurate exposure from this type of lighting.

If you stick to this, you'll rarely get a bad picture. On the other hand, you can add much more interest to your photographs by deliberately exploiting different types of lighting.

A low sun will give the characteristic long shadows and warm colour temperature, but you must be more careful about where you stand. If the sun is behind you in line with your subject, your own shadow may intrude into the picture. If you can't change position, try to get yourself as low as possible. This will shorten your shadow and may be enough to keep it out of the shot.

Light coming from one side makes for some very pleasing effects and, of course, as you move it further round in front of you in relation to your subject, you come into the realms of back lighting. Here, the sun is still out of your picture, but the shadows are now falling towards you. This type of lighting produces spectacular effects when reflected in water, ice or snow, and also looks very good with trees in the picture, where the light glows through the leaves. Exposure needs a little more care here. If you're using a camera with manual control, it's best to meter off the grass or whatever is in the middle foreground. Automatics may tend to underexpose this type of scene, so it's best to use your exposure compensation setting, which will generally give a half or a full stop overexposure. Failing this, you can alter your film speed setting to make the camera overexpose.

The easiest way is to divide your current film speed by two and set that on your camera. In effect, if you were using 100 ISO film, and you set it to 50 ISO, you're telling your camera to expose for a less sensitive film – in fact, halving the ISO is equivalent to overexposing one F stop. (Similarly you could underexpose one stop by doubling your film speed.) Do remember to reset your camera after the shot, though – otherwise the rest of your pictures will be wrongly exposed!

With a very low angle of light, or a low viewpoint, you can take some interesting *contre jour* shots. This is where you position the sun behind your subject, so that you just get a silhouette. If any part of the light source shows through, either around the edge of the subject or through leaves in a tree, you will get some flaring, caused by the light scattering inside the lens. Modern lenses with multi-coating tend to produce striking effects which can actually enhance the picture. The effect depends on the aperture and length of exposure. Small apertures make a multi-pointed star shape; the flare with larger apertures tends to go into a more circular patch.

With standard to wide-angle lenses, the more off-centre the light source is, the more likely it is

Afternoon tea – on trek in Nepal.

that you'll get iris flare, another startling effect, where a line of coloured 'ghost' hexagonal diaphragm shapes appear across the picture. The number of 'ghosts' that appear depends on the number of elements in your lens and they may be different colours depending on the individual type of multi-coating. Don't attempt these shots with non-reflex cameras if the sun is very powerful. Strong sunlight could burn a hole in the shutter and, with your viewfinder slightly off the lens axis, it would be difficult to predict the effect anyway. Similarly, it's not a good idea trying this sort of thing on an SLR with a powerful telephoto, unless you have some spare eyes!

Using the light source itself as part of the composition can produce stunning shots and sunsets are the obvious examples here. Sunsets nearly always provide magnificent opportunities for photographs and you don't have to worry about burning shutters or retinas, since the power of the sun is much diminished when it gets this low. Some of the most spectacular sunsets come at the end of a day of bad weather, when the sun sinks below the level of the cloud and suddenly the whole sky is alight! Don't be put off if it's a little misty. The light may be weaker, but you can get a beautiful watercolour effect, with the whole picture taking on an orangey-yellow glow. Sunsets over water are particularly attractive, as you can capture the reflection as well.

The main thing to remember, whether you're shooting a sunset over land or water, is not to get carried away too much with the euphoria of that fiery sky. If you have no other elements in your picture, the chances are you'll be disappointed. Try and place yourself so you have a good foreground – some trees, boats, a tent or a lone figure – something that will look good in silhouette. If you photograph a back-lit subject with a view to getting the exposure on the subject correct, it will be at the expense of an overexposed background. For this reason, I generally take the nominal exposure metered by the camera as the best one. This way, the sky is rendered in its full glory and the foreground elements are fairly dark or silhouetted. If in doubt with any type of back-lighting, the best thing to do is shoot a variety of different exposures – at the very least, one normally, and one overexposed.

The chances are you'll end up with two versions, both of which will be good for different reasons.

So, what about when the sun disappears altogether? It's not the photographic disaster you might think. With an overcast sky, the level of light is obviously a good deal less, but it does provide an even, diffused lighting which can be quite appealing in the right situation. Dull lighting tends to lower contrast, and it is this which most people pick out as the reason why their photographs lack depth and intensity. The way around this is to go for much bolder compositions. The rendition of colours is much more subtle in this type of lighting, as it is unaffected by light reflected from surrounding objects – fields, buildings, even the sky.

Even the fact that it might be raining shouldn't deter you from taking photographs. Again, it's likely that the level of light will be much reduced, and you have the movement of the rain itself to contend with. As I tend to use fairly slow films, I'm always near the limit for hand-held shots, with very slow shutter speeds. This blurs all the rain to the point where the picture hardly shows the drops themselves, although you would see their effect in puddles and the wet sheen on the ground.

With faster films, you can use faster shutter speeds, which tend to freeze the movement of raindrops in the middle distance, although the ones closer to the camera will appear more blurred. Stormy weather often produces very quick changes in light, which can be quite subtle or very dramatic. If you have your camera near to hand in a weatherproof bag or pouch, you can be ready to take advantage of those brief splashes of moody light when they spear through the clouds.

Finally, a mention about films themselves. The range is quite vast these days, from very slow ones, which I tend to favour, to high-speed films which can freeze subjects even in dim light. Slow films generally have higher contrast than high-speed ones, which is the reason I prefer them, especially when it's dull. The drawback is that you often need very steady hands or a tripod. If you're forced to do a hand-held exposure at a slow shutter speed, it helps to wedge yourself, or the camera, up against an immovable object. Problems can occur with very fast films when it's really sunny, when even the fastest shutter speed and the smallest aperture is still too much for a correct exposure. Once you've settled on a film you like, it's best to stick to it. That way you'll get to know how the film performs in different situations, and the next time a certain type of lighting crops up, you'll know what sort of effect you're likely to get on film.

PROTECTION

Even a humble notepad needs a little protection on a backpacking trip. Unless you're using waterproof paper, it's best to ensure the pad is always stored away in a plastic bag to guard against the ravages of damp. Electronic devices need proper protection, too, both from possible damp and from knocks, and would benefit from the kind of protection available for cameras.

It's amazing that people spend hundreds of pounds on sophisticated cameras, but quite often neglect to provide proper protection. It has to be worth spending at least 10 per cent of the camera's value on a decent bag or pouch. Several companies make padded camera pouches from the same robust materials used in rucksacks, though few offer as many models to fit the majority of camera/lens combinations as Camera Care Systems. Their extensive range includes not just pouches which can be attached to a rucksack hip belt, but larger bags to take cameras, lenses and other photographic accessories.

CHAPTER **13**

The Armchair Mountaineer

by Alan Hinkes

In climbing mountains, danger is a present and constant element, not remote as in other sports. It is always with us, behind the veil of pleasant circumstance, and we can be at grips with it almost before we are aware.

SO WROTE Geoffrey Winthrop Young, in his classic *Mountaincraft* manual in the 1920s.

I heard a rumble like a hundred horses' hooves which immediately turned into a roaring thunder like a Tornado jet taking off. My mind, wondering what it was, seemed naïvely and metaphorically to open for a micro-second like a startled child's mouth.

Immediately, with the logical brain of an accountant, I realized what it was and what the consequences would be. I had guessed correctly. It was an avalanche of rock boulders. It was heading for me and I was going to die!

As the fusillade crashed and exploded around me, I clung on to my ice axe trying to shrink into my helmet, as rocks battered on and bounced off it. Massive blocks the size of deep freezers smashed into the snow and ice next to me, showering me with shrapnel as I cowered helplessly.

It was like standing on an open battlefield, being bombed with shells. I knew any moment that a big block was going to land on me and squash me like a beetle. I would be swept down the slope by the sheer force of the smaller cascading rocks pounding me. I was helpless, cowering, clinging to my ice axe, waiting for the end.

Miraculously, all the big blocks missed me and my helmet saved me from the smaller chunks. The bombardment lasted about 15 seconds and then, mercifully, it stopped. Hardly believing my luck, and aware that it could be a temporary respite, I climbed down the slope, gasping, to collapse in the relative safety of a rock rib and relieve my bursting, fear-stretched bladder.

This incident happened to me in 1992 on Nanga Parbat, the world's ninth-highest mountain, some-

times called the 'Killer Mountain'. Having climbed up to over 25 000ft (7000m) on an acclimatization reconnaissance, I was on relatively easy terrain, crossing a wide snow and ice gully at 16 500ft (5100m) and was descending back to base camp for a rest before the final push.

The mountain was in bad condition due to the warm weather loosening rocks from the frost-shattered slopes above. After that narrow escape I decided that the objective rockfall danger was too great at that time, and I returned home, leaving the mountain for another year.

Some say that the risk is too great and that Himalayan mountaineers have a 'death wish'. I know my fellow mountaineers along with me have no such desire to die! We all love life and perhaps love it more from being 'close to the edge'. Many have families, and my daughter Fiona does not want me to die either. But why risk it as I must?

I am regularly asked, 'Why do you do it?' Can I reply 'Because it's there' as Mallory did? Why do soccer players play soccer? OK, it's not as dangerous, but why do Formula One racing car drivers do what they do?

Eric Shipton, the man famed for the celebrated photograph of the 'Yeti' footprint, said it was impossible to provide an entirely satisfactory explanation for any recreation. Perhaps more so for mountaineering with its inherent danger.

The predominant motive in any human activity varies according to the temperament of the individual. Mountaineering provides good exercise in pleasant surroundings, a sense of satisfaction in overcoming difficulties, the joy, akin to dancing, controlled rhythmic movement, a stimulating contact with danger, a wreath of beautiful scenery and a release from the tiresome restrictions of modern life.

When I began fell walking as a young teenager, it was an exciting challenge and adventure in the hills. I knew the risks of being caught out in poor weather without the correct equipment, and the dangers of bad navigation skills. I was confident enough in my map techniques not to get lost, and was also sensible enough to carry waterproof clothing and an emergency heavy-duty polybag, so death never seriously crossed my mind. I had practised sleeping out on the moors in a polybag on survival courses, and I knew I could suffer a night in the open.

I aspired to climb the big, rocky ridges on the Scottish mountains, and I felt that a knowledge of rock climbing would be useful to help me scramble on the bigger hills. So I learned to rock climb. It was hell at first. It was winter, and the bitterly cold sandstone rock chilled my fingers to the bone. I got 'heat aches' in my fingers – the excruciating pain when the blood starts flowing again as your hands warm up.

Nevertheless, I soon got hooked on rock climbing, and the potential for serious injury and death became greater. But again, I was confident in my climbing ability to be sure that it would never happen to me! (Well it didn't anyway!)

I only really began to understand that people died in the hills when I spent summer seasons in Chamonix – the 'Death Valley' as some continental newspapers call it. Luckily, though, I was spared some of the exceedingly shocking experiences of several climbing friends – bodies falling, screaming past them down mountain faces, and stumbling on gruesome remains. Some climbing friends did get killed in the Alps, and I became more aware of the objective dangers of avalanche and storms. The Alps are serious, not friendly and forgiving like the British hills can be – if you're lucky.

In the Himalaya I am more aware of the death risk than ever before. Some of the best British mountaineers have been killed here. A lot of base camps have memorial stones and frozen, desiccated, semi-mummified corpses are sometimes found, providing a horrific reminder of the risks. The two British mountaineers who climbed K2 in 1986 (making the first British ascent) never returned from the 'shoulder camp site' at 26 000ft (8000m). They perished along with several others in a major storm. No Briton has climbed K2 since.

There are only 14 separate mountains over 26 000ft (8000m) in the world. All are in Asia, in the Himalaya and Karakoram ranges. This great mountain chain stretches for 1550 miles (2500km) from Pakistan and Sinkiang province of China in the west, through India, Nepal and Tibet to Bhutan in the east.

Everest, the highest, at 29 028ft (8848m) was first climbed in May 1953 by Edmund Hilary and

Where'd that hill go to? Backpacker contemplating disappearing into the mist.

Sherpa Tenzing Norgay, with an expedition led by Colonel John Hunt, now Lord Hunt. They approached the mountain through Nepal. From base camp they climbed through the dangerous Khumbu ice fall – an area of tottering seracs (ice cliffs) into the western cwm, on to the South Col and up the ridge to the top.

The first attempts on Everest were from the Northern Tibet side by British mountaineers in the 1920s. Everest became known as a British mountain, and in the pre-Second World War years, seven British expeditions attempted to conquer it.

The first reconnaissance attempt was in 1921. This expedition successfully discovered a route to the North Col at 23 000ft (7000m). It included George Leigh Mallory, who was to become synonymous with Everest attempts in the early 1920s. Some would say he became obsessed with Everest. Mallory was the man who quipped 'because it's there' when asked why he wanted to climb Everest. Was he being cynical? Was he fed up with people asking why? Why not indeed if it is there – does a man need a reason?

Mallory was somewhat of an enigma. He hated Tibet and he thought Lhasa was a fetid, squalid place. In those days, to reach Everest involved a long sea voyage to the Indian sub-continent, a train journey over part of the country and then an arduous overland trek crossing the Himalaya range north of Darjeeling to reach Tibet. Nowadays it is a flight to Kathmandu in Nepal, or Lhasa in Tibet, before a relatively short trek to base camp. On the Nepal side it takes seven to ten days to trek to base camp – on the Tibetan northern side, it is now possible to drive in 4×4 vehicles to the base camp road head, near to the old Rongbuk Monastery at 16 000ft (5000m). This road (more like a track) was built by the Chinese in the 1960s for their ascent of the mountain.

Mallory devoted years of his life to Everest, if only with the time spent travelling there and back!

In 1922, the attempt was equipped with experimental open-circuit oxygen apparatus. An easier route was found to the North Col via the East Rongbuk glacier. Mallory, Norton and Sommervell reached 26 984ft (8225m) without bottled oxygen, and Finch 27 296ft (8320m) with an experimental oxygen set. On the 1924 attempt, Norton reached 28 116ft (8570m), 900ft (274m) from the top, without oxygen. Then a summit bid was mounted by Mallory and Andrew Irvine. They were last sighted by fellow team member Noel Odell. He was at 26 082ft (7950m) and believed he saw them during a brief clearing in the cloud at the 'second step' at 28 215ft (8600m).

There was a sudden clearing of the atmosphere above me, and I saw the whole summit ridge and the final peak of Everest unveiled. I noticed far away on the snow slope leading up to what seemed to me to be the last step but one from the base of the final pyramid, a tiny object moving and approaching the rock step. A second object followed, and the first climbed to the top of the step.

They were never seen again. Did they reach the top, 790ft (240m) higher to perish on the descent? It remains a mountaineering mystery. It was 1933

before another expedition was mounted. On this attempt, an ice axe was found near the first step, which could only have belonged to Mallory or Irvine.

I have been up to over 25 000ft (7600m) on the North ridge, and most of it is a scramble, akin to a Welsh mountain ridge in winter. However, the second step is a difficult *mauvais pas*. The Chinese had to fix a 30ft (9m) ladder up the right side to help their team to the top in the 1960s. If Odell saw Mallory and Irvine on the second step, perhaps one of them fell and pulled the other one with him. There are possibly easier variations to the step – Reinhold Messner avoided it on his solo ascent. I would like to think that Mallory and Irvine made it to the top and disappeared on the descent. I am sure it would have been possible if the weather and atmospheric conditions were favourable – Mallory certainly deserved the prize of the top.

After a few more attempts, the Second World War interrupted matters. No one had climbed higher than Norton.

If Everest became a 'British Mountain' in the 1920s and 1930s, another giant, eight-thousander Nanga Parbat, 26 658ft (8125m), became a 'German Mountain'. It's the ninth-highest mountain in the world and has earned a reputation as one of the most difficult. It was first attempted by a British expedition in 1895, one of the first to the Himalayan eight-thousanders. The celebrated Alpine climber A. F. Mummery led an attempt on its north-west face. Along with two Gurkhas, he disappeared without trace, probably engulfed in an avalanche, becoming Nanga Parbat's first mountaineering victim.

In the 1930s, while the British attempts continued on Everest, German and Austrian expeditions were mounted to Nanga Parbat. On two attempts in 1934 and 1937, 26 people were killed and Nanga Parbat became known as the 'killer mountain'. It was eventually climbed in July 1953, six weeks after the first ascent of Everest, by the heroic Austrian mountaineer Hermann Buhl. He made an epic solo push to the top and back, and was lucky to survive. The weather was kind to him when he had to bivouac out in the open, but he suffered terrible frostbite and later amputations. It has become one of the greatest and perhaps most extraordinary achievements of mountaineering and endurance, recounted in his book *Nanga Parbat Pilgrimage*. Or was it madness? Did he miscalculate and push too hard, too far and was lucky to survive? To me, no mountain is worth a toe or a finger.

The first eight-thousander to be climbed was Annapurna in 1950, by the French mountaineers Maurice Herzog and Louis Lachenal. They had a terrible ordeal on the descent and suffered badly with frostbite. Herzog had fingers and toes amputated, and Lachenal lost all his toes.

Annapurna was climbed in 1950 without supplementary (bottled) oxygen. The ascent of Everest in 1953 used supplementary oxygen. But it was not climbed 'without oxygen' until May 1978, by Italian mountaineer Reinhold Messner and Austrian Peter Habeler. Messner went back to make the first solo ascent of Everest in 1980. Then in October 1986, Messner became the first person to climb all 14 eight-thousanders. The Polish mountaineer Jerzy Kukuczka followed Messner's achievement in 1987. No one else has yet climbed all 14 eight-thousanders.

It's a hard act to follow! There may be 277 Munros in Scotland, but they're a lot more accessible, have a lot less objective danger and a lot of thicker air to breathe!

THE 8000M PEAKS

Mount Everest	8848m	(29 028ft)
K2	8611m	(28 250ft)
Kangchenjunga	8598m	(28 208ft)
Lhotse	8511m	(27 922ft)
Makalu	8481m	(27 824ft)
Dhaulagiri	8167m	(26 794ft)
Manaslu	8163m	(26 781ft)
Cho Oyu	8153m	(26 748ft)
Nanga Parbat	8125m	(26 656ft)
Annapurna	8091m	(26 544ft)
Gasherbrum I	8068m	(26 469ft)
Broad Peak	8047m	(26 400ft)
Shisha Pangma	8046m	(26 397ft)
Gasherbrum II	8035m	(26 361ft)

All of these mountains have an 'easy' route to the top, a route that is not too technically difficult. It would be possible even for a fit, motivated and well-acclimatized 'scrambler' to ascend these peaks with a qualified UIAGM mountain guide, such as a British mountain guide (BMG). The main problems would be Everest, which is probably Scottish grade 2 or 3 standard, but at nearly 30 000ft rather than 3000ft, as on a Scottish Munro in winter, it is a different prospect. Jumbo jets fly at this height, and the air temperature is usually no warmer than –13°F (–25°C), often –40°F (–40°C). Just moving and surviving is an arduous task, while anything 'energetic' is virtually impossible. Movement is usually a few steps at a time, with a rest in between and big gasps for air.

The other big problem would be cash. The peak fees for Everest are high and climbing in Antarctica is equally as expensive.

As when I began fell walking, I feel I know the risks, and am confident in my skills and experience. The Himalaya offers exciting challenges – and arguably the ultimate test. If you do not come back from a mountain, you've failed. You can always withdraw from an attempt and try another year. Mountains do not go away – they do get more expensive to climb, though! Peak fees are increased every year, Everest from Nepal topping the list at US$50,000 for up to five climbers.

No rescue team or helicopter is going to help you on a 26 000ft (8000m) peak. You might as well be on the moon, since helicopters have an altitude ceiling of 21 300ft (6500m). A 26 000ft (8000m) peak is an unforgiving environment. Above 25 000ft (7500m) is the 'death zone', a zone where the human body rapidly deteriorates. There are the high-altitude problems of cerebral and pulmonary oedema, a build-up of fluid in the brain and lungs. Once contracted they are rapid killers and the only treatment is descent – not always possible in a

SEVEN SUMMITS

Some mountaineers dream of climbing the 'seven summits' – the highest mountains of each of the seven continental land areas. They are:

Everest	Asia	29 028ft (8848m)	Nepal/Tibet
Aconcagua	South America	22 835ft (6960m)	Argentina/Chile
Denali (Mt McKinley)	North America	22 322ft (6194m)	Alaska, USA
Carstenz Pyramid	Australasia	16 532ft (5039m)	New Guinea
Kilimanjaro	Africa	19,340ft (5895m)	Tanzania
Elbruz	Europe	18,481ft (5632m)	Georgia, CIS
Vinson	Antarctica	16 860ft (5139m)	Antarctic

storm or over difficult and avalanche-prone ground. The cold, too, is more intense, and the body is more susceptible to exposure and frostbite due to lack of oxygen at such altitudes.

Preventing dehydration is a big problem. Obtaining fluid is a tiresome process of melting snow and ice. If enough fluid is not drunk, the blood becomes thicker and more sluggish, and the chance of contracting frostbite or even a thrombosis becomes greater.

I have felt fear, but I do not climb to get scared. I climb for the feeling of achievement and well-being, using my acquired skill and experience to overcome difficulties. Epics can (and will) happen though, and I have had a few.

One such occasion was on a mountain called 'White Sail' or 'Dharmsura' in the Indian Kulu Himalaya. It is a 21 000ft (6400m) peak, and I was attempting an unclimbed route on its 3500ft (1060m) west face.

Two of us set off with three days' food and gas to melt snow for water, hoping for a rapid ascent before the weather broke. Carrying any more food would have slowed us down – our rucksacks were 44lb (20kg) as it was when we set off over unknown terrain. No one had even attempted this route before, and it proved difficult to climb.

This is what backpacking is all about – putting your feet up at the end of a hard day in the hills.

A thin veneer of ice (verglas) and snow covering the steep rock made climbing difficult. After two bivouacs, sleeping on sloping ledges, a violent storm broke. We were trapped in blizzard-like storms for two days on a sloping ledge with only our sleeping bags and a bivouac sack to protect us. We had not carried a tent, because it would have been too heavy, and there were no ledges big enough to erect one anyway.

The ledge measured about 2m by 1m – we kept our climbing harnesses on and tied ourselves on to the rock with ropes. It was like trying to sleep on a sloping coffee table in a blizzard.

Surviving became an arduous task. We made water by holding a small gas stove between my legs, balancing the pan of melting snow delicately on top. Our fuel cartridges were nearly finished, so we could only make lukewarm water and, anyway, we had nothing left to cook. We couldn't climb on at the height of the storm and, weakening by the hour, we realized death was a real possibility.

Our sleeping bags, sodden during the day, froze

at night. Trapped on this tiny eyrie at over 20 000ft (6000m) we were slipping, dazed, into a stupor of stiffness and cold. We didn't panic, just experienced a controlled terror. What good would panicking do anyway?

We talked of our loved ones. My daughter was just 18 months old. I wondered what she would think when she was older if I perished. I owed it to her to live. Would my body ever be found?

We decided to get on with the job and make an attempt to climb up. We were less than 1000ft (300m) from the summit. Going back down would involve some difficult traverses, whereas I'd been to the top the year before, and knew an easier route down. Anything would be better than starving and freezing to death, as snowfall and sibilant spindrift buried us.

We were alone! We had got ourselves into this – we had to get ourselves out. But we had full confidence in one another and we climbed on autopilot together, understanding and giving succour to each other. We subconsciously decided we would confront death together. Almost delirious on the verge of spiritual revelation, we forced ourselves on.

A dropped ice axe, an essential climbing tool, and jammed rope made things more difficult. We had to cut and jettison the rope. It was too dangerous to climb back to try and free it, leaving just one 50m rope, making an abseil descent impossible. We now had no alternative but to go up and over the summit.

Somehow we endured hell for four more days, struggling over the summit and descending the south-west flank, which was in a dangerously unstable avalanche-prone state with fresh snow. Eventually we reached the meagre food cache we'd stashed at the foot of the route a week earlier – enough for a brew and a snack. Then we staggered like two skeletons to base camp. It was empty – no tents, no food. We had been abandoned!

The two other climbers and our Indian liaison officer had left, assuming we had perished on the mountain. The road head was two more days away, and we had to push on, exhausted and suffering from dehydration, starvation and constipation, wearing only the clothes we'd come off the mountain in. We arrived at the road head stripped of our usual Western affluence, like beggars in India, with no money or passports. A Sikh temple fed us rice, dahl, lime pickle, chapattis and tea, then a Hindu temple and a Hindu pilgrim lent us the necessary money to reach New Delhi. At the British High Commission we discovered we had been reported missing, presumed dead – but we were very much alive, if rather thin, dirty and smelly!

This was a salutary lesson, but in retrospect we reminisce on this epic as a good time! It was such an intense death-embracing experience to pull through. To survive it is beyond description – for me it's certainly a better inner feeling than scoring a goal in the World Cup or winning the Wimbledon tennis championship.

An incident that happened to me in the Lake District reminds me that epics and tragedies can occur all too easily even in the British hills. They should never be underestimated, especially in winter. Even the smallest snowslide (which is essentially an avalanche) in the Lake District fells can kill. It does not take an enormous spectacular Himalayan avalanche. Most British avalanche victims are killed by being swept into boulders or over crags, rather than being buried. The only permanently inhabited dwelling to be hit by an avalanche in Britain was not in the Scottish Highlands, but in Kent. A pub called the 'Snowdrop' more recently occupied the site, and it is now an antiques shop.

It is when we go out in winter determined to have 'fun' that we put ourselves at real risk. The recently set up Scottish Avalanche Information Service issues guidelines on the avalanche risk on a scale of one to five, to help climbers, walkers and skiers assess the danger of going on the hill. Experienced climbers should be aware of the risk factor anyway, but that still doesn't stop them being avalanched.

One winter in early March, I was involved in an avalanche on Great End, a 2500ft (760m) hill in the Lake District. The three Gullies on Great End's North Face – South-east, Central and Custs – offer classic winter climbing. I'd climbed all of them many years before and knew of many previous avalanche incidents, particularly in Central Gully.

Seathwaite, at the head of Borrowdale, is the wettest recorded place in England. Here it was raining, and together with my climbing partner Andrea Stimson, I set off up Grains Gill in the 'Ming', an affectionate way of describing the mist, drizzle and sleet! Further up the valley on Great End it was snowing, with a strong wind and thick hill fog. The north-facing gullies of Great End hold snow and ice longer than most in the Lake District, even in March, and I knew there would be plenty in Central Gully (grade II/III).

The fresh, wet snow was lying 18in (45cm) deep, and we ploughed on up the soggy, white covering. I knew there was a high avalanche risk and that the new snow could easily slide on the hard, slippery surface of the old snow underneath. Nevertheless, we were determined to have a go at the gully. Such determination can often be a fatal mistake.

A roped pair were already in the gully and we quickly climbed up over the lower ice pitch to where they were, about 260ft (80m) higher. We climbed unroped, as the route was well within our capabilities. The roped pair took the right fork and we decided to escape out of the left fork.

I was getting a little scared by now, well aware of the avalanche risk, as we stomped steps up to our knees into the snowfield. Here, almost 2ft (0.5m) of fresh, wet snow was lying over a hard, old layer. It could slide at any moment and we were perforating the slope with our footsteps, weakening it like sheets of toilet paper ready to snap off for a wipe-out.

I'd just reached the bottom of an ice pitch, when I heard the rumble and a whoosh of what I thought was another spindrift avalanche, and then the snow engulfed me.

It was like having a lorry-load of wet sand tipped on to me. I was immediately overpowered and overwhelmed. Instinctively I fought and tried to 'swim' to the side of the gully wall about 10ft (3m) to my right. I could hardly move in the dense, suffocating mass of snow, but somehow I hit the gully wall, bruising my arm, which slowed me down as the avalanche swept and accelerated over me.

The avalanche from above had also overloaded and triggered the slope we were on, and the gully was swept bare, back to the old, hard layer of snow (névé).

Andrea and the two roped climbers had gone. I had escaped after being swept down about 32ft (10m), and was now alone in the gully. Shaken and shocked, I climbed down expecting the worst – buried and battered bodies. I was relieved to see all three on the surface, though they had been taken about 400ft (120m).

Andrea had escaped with a bruised back and a few cuts to her face, but the roped pair had fared worse. The leader had been bumped over rocks, and had a broken pelvis, broken back and head injuries.

There was little we could do, as any attempt to move him might have paralysed him. The weather turned worse, the wind picked up and hypothermia became another problem for the casualty. It was three hours before the Keswick Mountain Rescue Team could evacuate him by stretcher to a Sea King helicopter which had flown from the RAF base at Boulmer in Northumberland. It was too dangerous for the chopper to do a winch in the mist and wind, and it had to wait on a flat area at the top of Grains Gill. The casualty was taken directly to hospital as the rest of us walked back down into the rain at Seathwaite.

The hills can never be totally safe, and this accident in Seathwaite brought me to reflect on what causes many of the accidents on our hills. There are many more accidents on our roads than on the hills, but unless it is a multiple motorway pile-up, a single hill fatality usually gets much more publicity.

There's much done to try and prevent accidents on the roads, for example, seat belts must be worn by law and a test must be passed before you can go out alone. You don't have to pass any tests before you can go into the hills and I hope that such draconian measures are never introduced. The hills are about freedom.

Accidents happen for many reasons. Perhaps bad weather and poor equipment contribute, but in particular, a lack of navigation skills is a major factor. Hill walkers straying off route and then slipping over a cliff is an all too frequent scenario.

There is no substitute for serving a good 'apprenticeship' in the hills and learning the skills, particularly of navigation, in all weather conditions. It's easy to navigate on a fine summer day, but entirely different when bad weather 'socks in'.

When I started hill walking on the North Yorkshire Moors, I learned to navigate over the featureless moor tops in thick cloud and at night – a skill on which I still often have to rely. Being a mountain climber makes me feel privileged. I have been in situations 'close to the edge', but I love life. I do not climb to die, I climb to live.

Useful addresses

British Mountaineering Council,
Crawford House,
Precinct Centre,
Booth Street East,
Manchester, M13 9RZ.
061-273 5835.

Countryside Commission,
John Dower House,
Crescent Place,
Cheltenham,
Gloucestershire, GL50 3RA.
(0242) 521381.

Expedition Advisory Centre,
1 Kensington Gore,
London, SW7 2AR.
071-581 2057.

Forestry Commission,
231 Corstorphine Road,
Edinburgh, EH12 7AT.
031-334 0303.

Glenmore Lodge,
(offers mountain safety courses)
Aviemore,
Inverness-shire, PH22 1QU.
(047986) 256.

Input Nutrition Consultants,
19 Craigton Court,
Aberdeen, AB1 7PF.
(0224) 316814.

Medical Advisory Service for Travellers Abroad (MASTA),
c/o The London School of Hygiene
and Tropical Medicine,
Keppel Street,
London, WC1E 7HT.
071-636 8636.

Mountain Medicine Data Centre,
c/o The Department of Neurological
Sciences,
St. Bartholomews Hospital,
38 Little Britain,
London, EC1A 7BE.
071-600 9000.

National Trust,
36 Queen Anne's Gate,
London, SW1H 0AS.
071-222 9251.

Nomad Travel Pharmacy,
3–4 Turnpike Lane,
London, N8 0PX.
081-889 7014.

Ordnance Survey of Northern Ireland,
Colby House,
Stranmillis Court,
Belfast, BT9 5BJ.
(0232) 661244.

Ordnance Survey,
Romsey Road,
Maybush,
Southampton, SO9 4DH.
(0703) 792749.

Plas y Brenin,
(offers mountain safety courses)
Capel Curig,
Gwynedd, LL24 0ET.
(06904) 208.

Ramblers Association,
1–5 Wandsworth Road,
London, SW8 2XX.
071-582 6878.

Royal Geographical Society,
1 Kensington Gore,
London, SW7 2AR.
071-589 5466.

Scottish Youth Hostels Association,
7 Glebe Crescent,
Stirling, FK8 2JA.
(0786) 2821.

Sierra Club,
730 Polk Street,
San Francisco, CA94109,
USA.

The Camping and Caravanning Club Ltd.,
Greenfields House,
Westwood Way,
Coventry, CV4 8JH.
(0203) 694995.

Trail Walker,
EMAP Pursuit Publishing Ltd.,
Bretton Court,
Bretton,
Peterborough, PE3 8DZ.
(0733) 264666.

Youth Hostels Association,
Trevelyan House,
8 St Stephen's Hill,
St Albans,
Hertfordshire, AL1 2DY.
(0727) 855215.

Publishers/Booksellers specializing in walking/travel

Cicerone Press,
2 Police Square,
Milnthorpe,
Cumbria, LA7 7PY.
(05395) 62069.

Cordee Books and Maps,
3a De Montfort Street,
Leicester, LE1 7HD.
(0533) 543579.

Edward Stanford Ltd,
12 Long Acre,
London, WC2E 9LP.
071-836 1321.

McCarta Ltd.,
122 Kings Cross Road,
London, WC1X 9DX.

Rand McNally Map Store,
10 East 53rd Street,
New York, NY,
USA.

The Map Shop,
15 High Street,
Upton-on-Severn,
Worcestershire, WR8 0HJ.
(0684) 593146.

Equipment Repairs

Shoecare Ltd,
Unit 4,
Yarrow Mill,
Yarrow Road,
Chorley,
Lancashire, PR6 0LP.
(0257) 232333.

Fennell Turner and Taylor Ltd,
Southway House,
South Way,
Cirencester,
Gloucestershire, GL7 1HL.

Fogg Travel Insurance,
Crow Hill Drive,
Mansfield,
Nottinghamshire, NG19 7AE.
(0623) 631331.

Snowcard Insurance Services Ltd,
Lower Boddington,
Daventry,
Northamptonshire, NN11 6XZ.
(0327) 62805.

West Mercia Insurance Services,
High Street,
Wombourne,
Wolverton,
West Midlands, WV5 9DN.

Walking and Trekking Holiday Companies

Accessible Isolation: *(0730) 812535*
Adventure Trekking for Women: *031-661 1959*
Africa Explored: *(0633) 222250*
Alfred Gregory: *(0742) 729428*
All-Ways Pacific: *(0494) 766766*
Alternative Travel Group: *(0865) 310399*
American Adventures: *(0892) 511894*
Andes Expeditions: *(0557) 31747*
Arctic Experience: *(0737) 362321*
Ariadne: *(0379) 852945*
Ascent Travel: *(0383) 880432*
Bespoke Holidays: *(0732) 366130*
Capricorn Adventure: *(0492) 549733*
CHA: *061-225 1000*
Chandertal Tours: *(0323) 646604*
Classic Nepal: *(0773) 873497*

Countrywide Holidays: *061-225 1000*
David Halford Travel: *(0223) 327412*
David Oswin Expeditions: *(0228) 75518*
DGI: *(06904) 344*
Dick Phillips: *(0434) 381440*
Eclipse Wilderness Discovery: *(05394) 44033*
Encounter Overland: *071-370 6845*
Exodus Expeditions: *081-675 5550*
ExplorAsia: *071-630 7102*
Explore Worldwide: *(0252) 319448*
Footprint Adventures: *(0522) 690852*
Ganbie Tours: *081-659 8217*
Greyhound World Travel: *(0342) 317317*
Headwater Holidays: *(0606) 48699*
HF Holidays Ltd: *081-905 9556*
High Adventure: *(0203) 395422*
High Places: *(0742) 822333*
Himalaya: *081-995 3642*
Himalayan Kingdoms Ltd: *(0272) 237163*
Himalayan Travel Ltd: *(0981) 550246*
Journey Latin America: *081-747 8315*
Karakoram Experience: *(07687) 73966*
Lam Rim Travel Ltd: *(0772) 743693*
Local Lands: *031-554 1634*
Moswin Tours: *(0533) 714982*
Mountain Trek: *(0942) 676650*
Nature Trek: *(0962) 733051*
Nepal Trekking: *(0482) 703135*
Nepal Treks: *(0272) 656966*
New Zealand Travel: *081-748 4455*
North West Frontiers: *(0854) 612571*
Okavango: *081-341 9442*
Out There Trekking: *(0742) 588508*
Peak International: *(0296) 624225*
Promotion Nepal Europe Ltd: *071-229 3528*
Ramblers Holidays: *(0707) 331133*
Roama Travel: *(0258) 860298*
Russell Hafter: *(0786) 824515*
Sherpa Expeditions: *081-577 1717*
Silver Fern Holidays: *(0602) 401111*
Simply Travel: *081-747 1011*
Sobek Travel: *010 90 483 32117*

Spantrek: *(0457) 836250*
SVP France: *(0243) 377862*
Swiss Experience Holidays: *(0922) 410170*
Swiss Holidays: *(0903) 743193*
Tempo Travel: *081-361 1131*
Thamserku Trekking: *(0686) 688244*
Tracks: *071-937 3028*
Trek America Ltd: *(0869) 38777*
Trek Force: *071-498 0855*
Trek Travel UK: *021-742 5420*
Twickers Worldwide: *081-892 7606*
Waymark Holidays: *(0753) 516477*
World Expeditions: *(0628) 74174*
Worldsaway Ltd: *(0373) 858956*
Worldwide Journeys and Expeditions: *071-381 8638*

UK Tourist Boards

England
Cumbria Tourist Board
(covering the county of Cumbria),
Ashleigh, Holly Road,
Windermere,
Cumbria LA23 2AQ.
(05394) 44444.

East Anglia Tourist Board
(covering the counties of
Cambridgeshire, Essex, Norfolk
and Suffolk),
Toppesfield Hall,
Hadleigh,
Suffolk, IP7 5DN.
(0473) 822922.

East Midlands Tourist Board
(covering the counties of
Derbyshire, Leicestershire,
Lincolnshire, Northamptonshire
and Nottinghamshire),
Exchequergate,
Lincoln,
Lincolnshire, LN2 1PZ.
(0522) 531521/3.

Heart of England Tourist Board
(covering the counties of
Gloucestershire, Hereford &
Worcester, Shropshire,
Staffordshire, Warwickshire and
West Midlands),
Woodside,
Larkhill Road,
Worcester,
Worcestershire, WR5 2EF.
(0905) 763436.

Northumbria Tourist Board
(covering the counties of Cleveland,
Durham, Northumberland, and
Tyne and Wear),
Aykley Heads,
Durham, DH1 5UX.
091-384 6905.

North West Tourist Board
(covering the counties of Cheshire,
Greater Manchester, Lancashire,
Merseyside and the High Peak
District of Derbyshire),
Swan House,
Swan Meadow Road,
Wigan Pier,
Wigan,
Lancashire, WN3 5BB.
(0942) 821222.

**South East England Tourist
Board**
(covering the counties of East and
West Sussex, Kent and Surrey),
The Old Brew House,
Warwick Park,
Tunbridge Wells,
Kent, TN2 5TU.
(0892) 540766.

Southern Tourist Board
(covering the counties of Eastern
and Northern Dorset, Hampshire
and Isle of Wight),
40 Chamberlayne Road,
Eastleigh,
Hampshire, SO5 5JH.
(0703) 620006.

West Country Tourist Board
(covering the counties of Avon,
Cornwall, Devon, Dorset [parts
of], Somerset, Wiltshire and Isles
of Scilly),
60 St David's Hill,
Exeter,
Devon, EX4 4SY.
(0392) 76351.

**Yorkshire and Humberside
Tourist Board**
(covering the counties of
Humberside, North Yorkshire,
South Yorkshire and West
Yorkshire),
312 Tadcaster Road,
York, YO2 2HF.
(0904) 707961.

Wales
The Wales Tourist Board,
Brunel House,
2 Fitzalan Road,
Cardiff, CF2 1UY.
(0222) 499909.

Scotland
The Scottish Tourist Board,
23 Ravelston Terrace,
Edinburgh, EH4 3EU.
031-332 2433.

Northern Ireland
Northern Ireland Tourist Board,
St. Anne's Court,
59 North Street,
Belfast, BT1 1NB.
(0232) 231221.

Channel Isles
Jersey Tourism,
Liberation Square,
St. Helier,
Jersey,
Channel Islands.
(0534) 500700.

**States of Guernsey Tourist
Board,**
PO Box 23,
White Rock,
St. Peter Port,
Guernsey,
Channel Islands.
(0481) 726611.

Overseas Tourist Boards

Anguilla Tourist Office,
3 Epirus Road,
London, SW6 7UJ.
071-937 7725.

**Antigua and Barbuda Tourist
Office,**
Antigua House,
15 Thayer Street,
London, WIM 5LD.
071-486 7073.

Australian Tourist Commission,
Gemini House,
10–18 Putney Hill,
London, SW15 6AA.
081-780 2227.

**Queensland Tourist & Travel
Corporation,**
Queensland House,
392–3 Strand,
London, WC2R 0LZ.
071-836 7242.

**Austrian National Tourist
Office,**
30 St. George Street,
London, W1R 0AL.
071-629 0461.

Bahamas Tourist Office,
10 Chesterfield Street,
London, W1X 8AH.
071-629 5238.

Barbados Board of Tourism,
263 Tottenham Court Road,
London, W1P 9AA.
071-636 9448.

Belgian Tourist Office,
Premier House,
2 Gayton Road,
Harrow,
Middlesex, HA1 2XU.
081-861 3300.

Bermuda Tourism,
1 Battersea Church Road,
London, SW11 3LY.
071-734 8813.

**British Virgin Islands Tourist
Board,**
110 St. Martin's Lane,
London, WC2N 4DY.
071-240 4259.

**Bulgarian National Tourist
Office,**
18 Princes Street,
London, W1R 7RE.
071-499 6988.

Canadian High Commission,
Canada House,
Trafalgar Square,
London, SW1Y 5BJ.
071-629 9492.

Travel Alberta,
Alberta House,
1 Mount Street,
London, W1Y 5AA.
071-491 3430.

Tourism British Columbia,
British Columbia Government
House,
1 Regent Street,
London, SW1Y 4NS.
071-930 6857.

Ontario Tourism,
21 Knightsbridge,
London, SW1X 7LY.
071-245 1222.

Quebec Tourism,
Quebec Government Office,
59 Pall Mall,
London, SW1Y 5JH.
071-930 8314.

**Cayman Islands Dept. of
Tourism,**
Trevor House,
100 Brompton Road,
London, SW3 1EX.
071-581 9960.

China National Tourist Office,
4 Glentworth Street,
London, NW1 5PG.
071-935 9427.

**Commonwealth of
Independent States –
Intourist,**
Intourist House,
219 Marsh Wall,
London, E14 9FJ.
071-538 08600.

Cyprus Tourism Organisation,
213 Regent Street,
London, W1R 8DA.
071-734 9822.

**Czechoslovak Tourist Office
Cedok (London) Ltd,**
17–18 Old Bond Street,
London, W1X 4RB.
071-629 6058.

Denmark Tourist Board,
Sceptre House,
169–173 Regent Street,
London, W1R 8PY.
071-734 2637.

Dominica Tourist Office,
1 Collingham Gardens,
London, SW5 0HW.
071-835 1937.

**Dubai Commerce and Tourism
Promotion Board,**
34 Buckingham Palace Road,
London, SW1W 0RE.
071-828 5961.

Egypt Tourist Office,
168 Piccadilly,
London, W1V 9DE.
071-493 5282.

Falkland Islands Tourist Board,
Falkland House,
14 Broadway,
London, SW1H 0BH.
071-222 2542.

Finnish Tourist Board,
66–68 Haymarket,
London, SW1Y 4RF.
071-839 4048.

**French Government Tourist
Office,**
178 Piccadilly,
London, W1V 0AL.
071-491 7622.

Western Loire Tourist Board,
375 Upper Richmond Road West,
London, SW14 7NX.
071-392 1580.

Gambia National Tourist Office,
Gambia High Commission Building,
57 Kensington Court,
London, W8 5DG.
071-937 9618–9.

German National Tourist Office,
Nightingale House,
65 Curzon Street,
London, W1Y 7PE.
071-495 3990.

Gibraltar Information Bureau,
179 Strand,
London, WC2R 1EH.
071-836 0777–8.

**Greek National Tourist
Organisation,**
4 Conduit Street,
London, W1R 0DJ.
071-734 5997.

Grenada Board of Tourism,
1 Collingham Gardens,
Earls Court,
London, SW5 0HW.
071-370 5164-5.

Hong Kong Tourist Association,
4th Floor,
125 Pall Mall,
London, SW1Y 5EA.
071-930 4775.

Hungarian Tourist Office,
6 Conduit Street,
London, W1R 9TG.
071-091 3588.

**Iceland Tourist Information
Bureau,**
Icelandair,
172 Tottenham Court Road,
London, W1P 9LG.
071-388 5346.

**Government of India Tourist
Office,**
7 Cork Street,
London, W1X 1PB.
071-437 3677–8.

Irish Tourist Board,
Ireland House,
150–151 New Bond Street,
London, W1Y 0AQ.
071-493 3201.

**Israel Government Tourist
Office,**
18 Great Marlborough Street,
London, W1V 1AF.
071-434 3651.

**Italian State Tourist Board
(ENIT),**
1 Princess Street,
London, W1R 8AY.
071-408 1254.

Jamaica Tourist Board,
1–2 Prince Consort Road,
London, SW7 2BZ.
071-224 0505.

**Japan National Tourist
Organisation,**
167 Regent Street,
London, W1R 7FD.
071-734 9638.

Jersey Tourism,
35 Albermarle Street,
London, W1X 3FB.
071-493 5278.

Jordan Tourist Office,
211 Regent Street,
London, W1R 7DD.
071-437 9465.

Kenya National Tourist Office,
25 Brook's Mews,
off Davies Street,
London, W1Y 1LG.
071-355 3144.

**Korea National Tourism
  Corporation,**
2nd Floor,
Vogue House,
1 Hanover Square,
London, W1R 9RD.
071-409 2100.

Luxembourg Tourist Office,
122 Regent Street,
London, W1R 5FE.
071-434 2800.

**Macau Tourist Information
  Bureau,**
6 Sherlock Mews,
off Paddington Street,
London, W1M 3RH.
071-224 3390.

**Malaysia Tourism Promotion
  Board,**
Malaysia House,
57 Trafalgar Square,
London, WC2N 5DU.
071-930 7932.

Malta National Tourist Office,
Suite 300,
Mappins House,
4 Winsley Street,
London, W1N 7AR.
071-323 0506.

**Mauritius Government Tourist
  Office,**
32–33 Elvaston Place,
London, SW7 5NW.
071-584 3666.

Mexican Ministry of Tourism,
60–61 Trafalgar Square,
London, WC2N 5DS.
071-839 3177.

**Monaco Government Tourist
  and Convention Office,**
3–113 Chelsea Garden Market,
Chelsea Harbour,
London, SW10 0XE.
071-352 9962.

**Moroccan National Tourist
  Office,**
205 Regent Street,
London, W1R 7DE.
071-437 0073.

Nassau,
Cable Beach,
Island Promotion Board,
306 Upper Richmond Road West,
East Sheen,
London, SW14 7JG.
(081 878 5569.

Netherlands Board of Tourism,
25–28 Buckingham Gate,
London, SW1E 6LD.
071-630 0451.

New Zealand Tourism Board,
New Zealand House,
Haymarket,
London, SW1Y 4TQ.
071-973 0360.

Northern Ireland Tourist Board,
11 Berkeley Street,
London, W1X 5AD.
071-493 0601.

Norwegian Tourist Board,
Charles House,
5 Lower Regent Street,
London, SW1Y 4LR.
071-839 6255.

Peru Tourist Board,
72 Sloane Street,
London, SW1 9SP.
071-235 2747.

**Philippine Department of
  Tourism,**
17 Albemarle Street,
London, W1X 7HA.
071-499 5443.

**Polish National Tourist Office
  'ORBIS',**
82 Mortimer Street,
London, W1N 7DE.
071-636 2217.

**Portuguese National Tourist
  Office,**
22–25a Sackville Street,
London, W1X 1DE.
071-494 1441.

Puerto Rico Tourism Company,
67–69 Whitfield Street,
London, W1P 5RL.
071-636 6558.

Seychelles Tourist Office,
111 Baker Street,
London, W1M 1FE.
071-224 1670.

**National Tourist Board of Sierra
  Leone,**
375 Upper Richmond Road West,
London, SW14 7NX.
081-392 9188.

**Singapore Tourist Promotion
  Board,**
First Floor,
Carrington House,
126-130 Regent Street,
London, W1R 5FE.
071-437 0033.

South Africa Tourism Board,
5-6 Alt Grove,
Wimbledon, SW19 4DZ.
081-944 6646.

Spanish Tourist Office,
57–58 St. James's Street,
London, SW1A 1LD.
071-499 0901.

**Sri Lanka (Ceylon) Tourist
  Board,**
13 Hyde Park Gardens,
London, W2 2LU.
071-262 5009.

**St. Kitts & Nevis Tourism
  Board,**
10 Kensington Court,
London, W8 5DL.
071-376 0881.

St. Lucia Tourist Board,
10 Kensington Court,
London, W8 5DL.
071-937 1969.

**St. Vincent and The Grenadines
  Tourist Office,**
10 Kensington Court,
London, W8 5DL.
071-937 6570.

Swedish Tourist Office,
29-31 Oxford Street,
London, W1R 1RE.
071-437 5816/7/8.

Swiss National Tourist Office,
Swiss Centre,
Swiss Court,
London, W1V 8EE.
071-734 1921.

Tanzania Trade Centre,
Tanzania High Commission,
78-80 Borough High Street,
London, SE1 1LL.
071-407 0566.

Tourism Authority of Thailand,
49 Albemarle Street,
London, W1X 3FE.
071-499 7679.

**Trinidad and Tobago Tourist
    Office,**
8a Hammersmith Broadway,
London, W6 7AL.
(081 741 4466.

**Tunisian National Tourist
    Board,**
77a Wigmore Street,
London, W1H 9LJ.
071-224 5561.

**Turkish Embassy Information
    Counsellor's Office,**
First Floor,
170–173 Piccadilly,
London, W1V 9DD.
071-073 8681.

**United States Travel & Tourism
    Administration,**
PO Box 1EN,
London, W1A 1EN.
071-495 4466.

**Californian Marketing Services
    Limited,**
Suite 433,
High Holborn,
52–54 High Holborn,
London, WC1V 6RB.
071-242 3131.

Florida Division of Tourism,
18–24 Westbourne Grove,
London, W2 5RH.
071-727 8854.

Hawaii Visitors Bureau,
14 The Green,
Richmond,
Surrey, TW9 1PX.
081-332 6969.

**New York State Division of
    Tourism,**
2 Cinnamon Row,
Plantation Wharf,
York Place,
London, SW11 3TW.
071-978 5275.

US Virgin Islands Tourist Office,
2 Cinnamon Row,
Plantation Wharf,
York Place,
London, SW11 3TW.
071-978 5262.

**Washington DC Convention and
    Visitors Association,**
375 Upper Richmond Road West,
London, SW14 7NX.
081-392 9187.

**Washington State Tourist
    Office,**
2 Cinnamon Row,
Plantation Wharf,
York Place,
London, SW11 3TW.
071-978 5233.

Zambia National Tourist Board,
2 Palace Gate,
Kensington,
London, W8 5NG.
071-589 6343–4.

Zimbabwe Tourist Office,
Zimbabwe House,
429 The Strand,
London, WC2R 0QE.
071-836 7755.

**National Parks in England and
Wales**

Brecon Beacons National Park,
7 Glamorgan Street,
Brecon,
Powys, LD3 7DP.
(0874) 624437.

Broads Authority,
18 Colegate,
Norwich,
Norfolk, NR3 1BQ.
(0603) 61073.

**Dartmoor National Park
    Authority,**
'Parke',
Haytor Road,
Bovey Tracey,
Devon, TQ13 9JQ.
(0626) 832093.

Exmoor National Park,
Exmoor House,
Dulverton,
Somerset, TA22 9HL.
(0398) 23665.

Lake District National Park,
Brockhole National Park Centre,
Windermere,
Cumbria, LA23 1LG.
(05394) 46601.

Northumberland National Park,
Eastburn,
South Park,
Hexham,
Northumberland, NE46 1BS.
(0434) 605555.

**North York Moors National
    Park,**
The Old Vicarage,
Bondgate,
Helmsley,
York, YO6 5BP.
(0439) 70657.

Peak National Park,
Aldern House,
Baslow Road,
Bakewell,
Derbyshire, DE4 1AE.
(0629) 814321.

**Pembrokeshire Coast National
    Park,**
County Offices,
Haverfordwest,
Dyfed, SA61 1QZ.
(0437) 764591.

Snowdonia National Park,
Penrhyndeudraeth,
Gwynedd, LL48 6LS.
(0766) 770274.

Yorkshire Dales National Park,
'Colvend',
Hebden Road,
Grassington,
Skipton,
Yorkshire, BD23 5LB.
(0756) 752748.

Council for National Parks,
246 Lavender Hill,
London, SW11 1LJ.
071-924 4077.

**Equipment Manufacturers/
Distributors**

Key
R Rucksacks
T Tents
B Sleeping bags
S Accessories including stoves
W Waterproof clothing
M Midwear and base layer clothing
F Footwear

Abris Ltd,
Howard Town Mills,
Mill Street,
Glossop,
Derbyshire,
SK13 8PT.
(0457) 863966.
R T B S W M F

Adidas (UK) Ltd,
PO Box 1,
First Avenue,
Cheshire,
SK12 1UT.
(0625) 876406.
F

Alpina-Euroski Ltd,
Dolphin House,
67a North Road,
Brighton,
BN1 1YD.
(0273) 688258.
R W M

Asolo,
Ventura,
Hall House,
New Hutton,
nr. Kendal,
Cumbria,
LA8 0AH.
(0539) 728386.
F

Aztec,
Burton McCall Group Ltd,
163 Parker Drive,
Leicester,
LE4 0JP.
(0533) 340800.
R B M

BCB International Ltd,
Clydesmuir Road
Industrial Estate,
Tremorfa,
Cardiff,
CF2 2QS.
(0222) 464463.
R T B S W M F

Baggins,
Unit T4,
Keighley Business Centre,
Knowle Mills,
South Street,
Keighley.
(0535) 605684.
R M

Berghaus Ltd,
17-19 Brindley Road,
Hertburn Industrial Estate,
District 11,
Washington,
Tyne and Wear,
NE37 2SF.
091-415 0200.
R W M F

Big Pack,
Ardblair Sports Importers Ltd,
Rivendell,
Main Street,
Follifoot,
Yorkshire,
HG3 1DZ.
(0250) 873863.
R T B W M

Blacks Camping and Leisure,
Unit 3,
Stevenson Industrial Estate,
Washington,
Tyne and Wear,
NE37 3HR.
091-417 8800.
R T B S W M F

Blue Hills,
Unit T4,
Keighley Business Centre,
Knowle Mills,
South Street,
Keighley.
(0535) 605684.
R

Bradsport Ltd,
Camroyd Street,
Dewsbury,
West Yorkshire,
WF13 1PG.
(0924) 467510.
W M

The Brasher Boot Company,
White Cross,
Lancaster,
LA1.
(0524) 841000.
F

Bridgedale,
Burton McCall Group Ltd,
163 Parker Drive,
Leicester,
LE4 0JP.
(0533) 340800.
M F

Buffalo,
Meersbrook Works,
19 Valley Road,
Sheffield,
S8 9FT.
(0742) 588481.
B W M

Camp,
Allcord Ltd,
Ilford Road,
Newcastle upon Tyne,
NE2 3NX.
091-284 8444.
R T B S W M

Camping Gaz Ltd,
9 Albert Street,
Slough,
SL1 2SH.
(0753) 692707.
S

Calange Outdoor Clothing Ltd,
PO Box 61,
Stockport,
Cheshire,
SK3 0AP.
061-474 7097.
W M

Caravan,
Snuggledown of Norway (UK) Ltd,
39 Burners Lane,
Kiln Farm,
Milton Keynes,
MK11 3HJ.
(0908) 563101.
R T B W M

Cascade Designs Ltd,
Dwyer Road,
Midleton,
County Cork,
Ireland.
010 353 12 632399.
S

Cassin,
Orion Equipment,
261 Sauchiehall Street,
Glasgow,
G2 3EZ.
041-332 7513.
S

Cima,
Vango (Scotland) Ltd,
70 East Hamilton Street,
Ladyburn,
Greenock,
Renfrewshire,
PA15 2UB.
(0475) 44122.
F

Cobmaster,
Cobles,
74 Back Church Lane,
London,
E1 1LX.
081-481 1503.
R T B S W M

Coleman UK PLC,
Parish Wharf Estate,
Harbour Road,
Portishead,
Bristol,
BS20 9DA.
(0275) 845024.
R T B S

Columbia Sportswear Company,
Dyehouse Lane,
Glastonbury,
Somerset,
BA6 9LZ.
(0458) 834019.
W M

Conquest Tents,
13 Quay Lane,
Gosport,
Hampshire,
PO12 4LT.
(0705) 528711.
T

Craghoppers Ltd,
Bradford Road,
Birstall,
Batley,
West Yorkshire,
WF17 9DH.
(0924) 478481.
W M

Cresta Alloway Sports Ltd,
Blandford Forum,
Dorset,
DT11 7TE.
(0258) 454666.
F

Crewsaver Ltd,
Mumby Road,
Gosport,
Hampshire,
PO12 1AQ.
(0708) 528621.
S

Dachstein,
Jag Sports Equipment Ltd,
The Street,
Horton Kirby,
Kent,
DA4 9BY.
(0322) 864273.
F

Daimor,
David Moore & Co,
Belgrave Mill,
Keswick Avenue,
Oldham,
Lancashire,
OL8 2LZ.
061-626 6225.
B

Daisy Roots,
Third Avenue,
Westfield Trading Estate,
Midsomer Norton,
Bath,
BA3 4XD.
(0761) 417777.
F

Dalesman International Ltd,
Dalesman House,
Marathon Place,
Moss Side Industrial Estate,
Leyland,
Lancashire,
PR5 3QN.
(0772) 453918.
R T B S W M F

Danner Boots Ltd,
Old Hall Farm,
Higham,
South Yorkshire,
S75 1PF.
(0226) 388460.
F

Demon,
DA Enterprises,
Ransom Business Park,
Southwell Road,
Mansfield,
Nottinghamshire,
NG21 0EP.
(0623) 29521.
F

Design Mats Ltd,
Unit 6,
Llantrisant Business Park,
Llantrisant,
Mid Glamorgan,
CF7 8LF.
(0443) 238345.
S

db Mountainsport Ltd,
10 Kent Street,
Kendal,
Cumbria,
LA9 4AU.
(0539) 733842.
F

Duofold,
Dawson Consumer Products Ltd,
Wakefield Road,
Huddersfield,
West Yorkshire,
HD5 8PT.
(0484) 538181.
M

Epigas (Taymar Ltd.),
Wear Mill,
King Street West,
Stockport,
Cheshire,
SK3 0AJ.
061-477 4141.
S

Eppik,
Feanor House,
2 Fitzmaurice Court,
Rackheath Industrial Estate,
Norwich,
Norfolk,
NR13 6PY.
(0603) 721583.
M

Edelrid,
Outdoor Pursuit Services,
Derbyshire
Level,
Glossop,
SK13 9PT.
(0457) 853247.
S

Faces Designs on Mountains,
Old Englishe Road,
Matlock,
Derbyshire,
DE4 3LT.
(0629) 57670.
S

Field & Trek PLC,
Unit 3,
Wates Way,
Brentwood,
Essex,
CM15 9TB.
(0227) 233122.
R T B S W M F

Gold-Eck,
Adventures Extraordinaires (UK)
  Ltd,
The Coach House,
Cross Lanes,
Hebden Bridge,
West Yorkshire,
HX7 7EW.
(0422) 845891.
B

Gronell,
Nordic Imports,
Aviemore,
Inverness-shire,
PH22 1QH.
(0479) 811153.
F

Hi-Tec Sports PLC,
Hi-Tec House,
Aviation Way,
Southend on Sea,
Essex.
(0702) 541741.
F

G. T. Hawkins Ltd,
Overstone Road,
Northampton,
NN1 3JJ.
(0604) 32293.
F

Helly-Hansen (UK) Ltd,
College Street,
Kempston,
Bedford,
MK42 8NA.
(0234) 266966.
W M

High Country,
Giffard Newton & Sons Ltd,
71 Townsend Road,
Chesham,
Buckinghamshire,
HP5 2AD.
(0494) 782388.
F

**Jack Wolfskin Adventure
  Equipment,**
12a
Kingstown Broadway,
Carlisle,
CA3 0HA.
(0228) 27624.
R T B W M

Javlin International Ltd,
Javlin House,
3/11 Edgedale Road,
Sheffield,
S7 2BQ.
(0742) 585782.
W M

Karrimor International Ltd,
Petre Road,
Clayton-le-Moors,
Accrington,
BB5 5JP.
(0254) 385911.
R B S W M F

Kathmandu Trekking,
5 Crabtree Lane,
Great Bookham,
Leatherhead,
Surrey,
KT23 4PG.
(0372) 454773.
R T B S W M

Keela International Ltd,
Nasmyth Road,
Southfield Industrial Estate,
Glenrothes,
Fyfe,
KY6 2SD.
(0592) 771241.
W

Khyam Design,
Willenhall Lane,
Bloxwich,
Walsall,
WS3 2XR.
(0922) 711243.
T

Kidderminster Footwear,
Main Warehouse,
New Road,
Kidderminster,
DY10 1AL.
(0562) 744022.
F

Lichfield,
John James Hawley Ltd,
Lichfield Road,
Walsall,
West Midlands,
WS4 2HX.
(0922) 25641.
T

Line 7 International,
Modular Business Park,
Units 12-14,
Aspley Close,
Four Ashes,
Wolverhampton,
WV10 7DE.
(0902) 791166.
W M F

Llewelyn Wynne,
Business Park,
8 Barnett Wood Lane,
Leatherhead,
Surrey,
KT22 7DG.
(0372) 377713.
R T B S W M F

Loveson Footwear,
Thomas H. Loveday Ltd,
Station Road,
Irthlingborough,
Wellingborough,
Northamptonshire,
NN9 5QE.
(0933) 652652.
F

Lowe Alpine,
Europa Sport,
Ann Street,
Kendal,
Cumbria,
LA9 6AB.
(0539) 724740.
R W M

Lyon Equipment,
Rise Hill Mill,
Dent,
Sedbergh,
Cumbria,
LA10 5QL.
(05875) 370.
B S

Mascot,
Mascot House,
401 Old Road,
Clacton-on-Sea,
Essex,
CO15 3RL.
(0255) 432773.
W M

Medik C. I. Ltd,
3 Trafalgar Terrace,
New St. John's Road,
St. Helier,
Jersey,
Channel Islands,
JE2 3LE.
(0534) 24010.
S

MSR,
Outdoor Pursuit Services,
Derbyshire
Level,
Glossop,
SK13 9PT.
(0457) 853247.
S

Macpac UK Ltd,
PO Box 61,
Stockport,
Cheshire,
SK3 0AP.
061-474 7097.
R T B W M

Mephisto Shoes,
1 The Tanyard,
Street,
Somerset,
BA16 0HD.
(0458) 46599.
F

Merrell (Europe) Ltd,
CCS Centre,
Vale Lane,
Bedminster,
Bristol,
BS3 5RU.
(0272) 636363.
F

Mileta Sports Ltd,
Spen Vale Mills,
Station Lane,
Heckmondwike,
West Yorkshire,
WF16 0NQ.
(0924) 409311.
W M

Millets,
Mansard Close,
Westgate,
Northampton,
NN5 5DL.
(0604) 758232.
R T B S W M F

Mont-Bell (UK) Ltd,
The Mill,
Glasshouses,
Pateley Bridge,
Harrogate,
North Yorkshire,
HG3 5QH.
(0423) 711624.
W M

Mountain Equipment Ltd,
Peaco House,
Hyde,
Cheshire,
SK14 1RD.
061-366 5020.
B W M

Mountain Range,
PO Box 1,
Alston,
Cumbria,
CA9 3TS.
(0434) 381742.
W M

Mountaincraft,
YHA Adventure Shops PLC,
19
High Street,
Staines,
Middlesex,
TW18 4QX.
(0784) 458625.
R T B S W M F

Mountain Technology (Glencoe) Ltd,
Old Ferry Road,
Onich,
Inverness-shire,
PH33 6SA.
(08553) 222.
S

Musto Ltd,
1 Armstrong Road,
Benfleet,
Essex,
SS7 4QE.
(0268) 759466.
W M

NeeBee Ltd,
Britannia House,
Station Road,
Kettering,
Northamptonshire,
NN15 7HJ.
(0536) 411736.
F

Neuwald,
Europa Sport,
Ann Street,
Kendal,
Cumbria,
LA9 6AB.
(0539) 724740.
F

New Balance Athletic Shoes (UK) Ltd,
16
Chesford Grange,
Woolston,
Warrington,
Cheshire,
WA1 4RQ.
(0925) 821182.
F

Nikwax Waterproofing,
Unit F,
Durgates Industrial Estate,
Wadhurst,
East Sussex,
TN5 6DF.
(0892) 783855.
S

North Cape (Scotland) Ltd,
Springkerse Industrial Estate,
Stirling,
FK7 7SW.
(0786) 63983.
W M

The North Face,
PO Box 16,
Industrial Estate,
Port Glasgow,
PA14 5XL.
(0475) 41344.
R T B W M

Olympic,
Danner Boots Ltd,
Old Hall Farm,
Higham,
South Yorkshire,
S75 1PF.
(0226) 388460.
F

Optimus Division,
Camping Gaz GB Ltd,
Holcot Lane,
Sywell,
nr. Northampton,
NN6 0BE.
(0604) 790303.
S

Outbound,
Cobles,
74 Back Church Lane,
London,
E1 1LX.
081-481 1503.
R T B S W M

Outdoor Leisure Ltd,
Moac House,
Demmings Road Industrial Estate,
Demmings Road,
Cheadle,
Cheshire,
SK8 2PE.
061-428 1178.
W M F

Paramo,
Unit F,
Durgates Industrial Estate,
Wadhurst,
East Sussex,
TN5 6DF.
(0892) 883855.
W

Patagonia,
The Granary,
113 Lavender Walk,
London,
SW11 1JS.
071-924 2155.
W M

Peak 1,
Coleman UK,
Parish Wharf Estate,
Harbour Road,
Portishead,
Bristol,
BS20 9DA.
(0275) 845024.
R T B S

Peter Storm Ltd,
14 High Pavement,
Nottingham,
NG1 1HP.
(0602) 506911.
W M

Phoenix Mountaineering Ltd,
Coquetdale
Trading Estate,
Amble,
Morpeth,
Northumberland,
NE65 0PE.
(0665) 710934.
T W M

Pod Sacs,
Unit 1,
5 Osberton Place,
Sheffield,
S11 8XL.
(0742) 684569.
R

Polaris,
L Block,
Bolsover Enterprise Park,
Station Road,
Bolsover,
S44 6BH.
(0246) 240218.
W M

Polywarm Products Ltd,
Cambuslang Road,
Farme Cross,
Rutherglen,
Glasgow,
G73 1RS.
041-647 2392.
B

Primus Ltd,
Stephenson Way,
Formby,
Merseyside,
L37 8EQ.
(0704) 878614.
S

Rab Down Equipment,
32 Edward Street,
Sheffield,
S3 7GB.
(0742) 757544.
B M

Reebok UK Ltd,
Moor Lane Mills,
Moor Lane,
Lancaster,
LA1 1GF.
(0524) 580100.
F

Regatta,
Risol Ltd,
Risol House,
Mercury Way,
Urmston,
Manchester,
M31 2LT.
061-747 5899.
W M

Relum Ltd,
Carlton Park Industrial Estate,
Kelsale,
Saxmundham,
Suffolk,
IP17 2NL.
(0728) 603271.
R T W M

Rohan Designs,
30 Maryland Road,
Tongwell,
Milton Keynes,
Buckinghamshire,
MK15 8HN.
(0908) 618888.
W M

Ronhill Sports Ltd,
PO Box 11,
Hyde,
Cheshire,
SK14 1RD.
061-368 6894.
M

Sanmarco,
Allcord Ltd,
Ilford Road,
Newcastle upon Tyne,
NE2 3NX.
091-284 8444.
F

**Robert Saunders (Chigwell)
    Ltd,**
Five Oaks Lane,
Chigwell,
Essex,
IG7 4QP.
081-500 2447.
T M

Scarpa,
Berghaus Ltd,
17-19 Brindley Road,
Hertburn Industrial Estate,
District 11,
Washington,
Tyne and Wear,
NE37 2SF.
091-415 0200.
F

Scottish Mountain Gear,
The Old Stables,
Station Road,
Musselburgh,
EH21 7PE.
031-665 6512.
R

Scout Shops,
Camping and Outdoor Centre,
Churchill Industrial Estate,
Lancing,
West
Sussex,
BN15 8UG.
(0903) 755352.
R T B S W M F

Silking Ltd,
5 Lancer House,
Hussar Court,
Westside View,
Waterlooville,
Hampshire,
PO7 7SE.
(0705) 268880.
M

Silva (UK) Ltd,
Unit 10,
Sky Business Park,
Thorpe Industrial Park,
Egham,
Surrey,
TW20 8RF.
(0784) 471721.
S

Snowsled Ltd,
Street Farm Workshops,
Doughton,
Tetbury,
Gloucestershire,
GL8 8TP.
(0666) 504002.
W M

Snuggledown of Norway (UK) Ltd,
39 Burners Lane,
Kiln Farm,
Milton Keynes,
MK11 3HJ.
(0908) 563101.
B

Snugpak,
Brett Harris Ltd,
Waterloo Mills,
Howden Road,
Silsden,
West Yorkshire,
BD20 0HA.
(0535) 654479.
B M

Sorbothane,
Leyland & Birmingham Rubber Co.
Ltd,
Golden Hill Lane,
Leyland,
nr. Preston,
Lancashire,
PR5 1UB.
(0772) 421434.
S

Spenco Medical (UK) Ltd,
Burrell Road,
Haywards Heath,
West Sussex,
RH16 1TW.
(0444) 415171.
S

Sprayway Ltd,
16 Chester Street,
Manchester,
M1 5GE.
061-236 4239.
W M

I. & M. Steiner Ltd,
Reynard Mills Trading
Estate,
Windmill Road,
Brentford,
Middlesex,
TW8 9LY.
081-847 4422.
R T B S W M F

Stubai,
Trailwise,
5 Harold Avenue,
Dukinfield,
Cheshire,
SK16 5NH.
061-339 2781.
S

Sub Zero Technology Ltd,
35 Churchill Way,
Saddington Road,
Fleckney,
Leicester,
LE8 0UD.
(0533) 402634.
M

Tenson,
Plymouth House,
The Square,
Sawbridgeworth,
Hertfordshire,
CM21 9AN.
(0279) 600618.
W M

Terrain,
Third Avenue,
Westfield Trading Estate,
Midsomer Norton,
Bath,
BA3 4XD.
(0761) 417777.
F

Tilley International PLC,
30–32 High Street,
Frimley,
Surrey,
GU16 5JF.
(0276) 691996.
S

Timberland,
Unit 5,
St. Anthony's Way,
Feltham,
Middlesex,
TW14 0NH.
081-890 6116.
F

Tog 24,
Mileta Sports Ltd,
Spen Vale Mills,
Station Lane,
Heckmondwike,
West Yorkshire,
WF16 0NQ.
(0924) 409311.
W M

Trangia,
Karrimor International Ltd,
Petre Road,
Clayton-le-Moors,
Accrington,
BB5 5JP.
(0254) 385911.
S

Trezeta,
Burton McCall Group Ltd,
163 Parker Drive,
Leicester, LE4 0JP.
(0533) 340800.
F

Troll Safety Equipment,
Spring Mill,
Spring Street,
Uppermill,
Saddleworth, OL3 6AA.
(0457) 878822.
S M

Vander Ltd,
Cloudbase,
Brunel Road,
Newton Abbot,
Devon, TQ12 4YQ.
(0626) 333666.
W M

Vango (Scotland) Ltd,
70 East Hamilton Street,
Ladyburn,
Greenock,
Renfrewshire, PA15 2UB.
(0475) 44122.
R T B W M

Vaude (UK) Ltd,
Unit DC72/5,
Haltwhistle Industrial Estate,
Haltwhistle,
Northumberland, NE49 9HA.
(0434) 320744.
R T B W M

Viking Optical Ltd,
Blyth Road,
Halesworth,
Suffolk, IP19 8EN.
(0986) 875315.
S

Walkabout Leisurewear Ltd,
Unit 8,
Lockwood Way,
Blackhorse Lane,
Walthamstow,
London, E17 5RB.
081-527 5252.
W

Walrus Waterproofs Ltd,
Mersey Street,
Bulwell,
Nottingham, NG6 8JA.
(0602) 277736.
W

Wild Country Ltd,
Meverill Road,
Tideswell,
Buxton,
Derbyshire, SK17 8PY.
(0298) 871010.
R T W M

Wolverine Wilderness,
1–3 The Wheelwrights,
Temple Farm Industrial Estate,
Southend,
Essex, SS2 5RD.
(0702) 603366.
F

Wynnster,
Llewelyn Wynne,
Business Park,
8 Barnett Wood Lane,
Leatherhead,
Surrey, KT22 7DG.
(0372) 377713.
R T B S W M F

Yoredale Weatherwear Ltd,
Yoredale House,
1-3 Well Lane,
Batley,
West Yorkshire, WF17 5HQ.
(0924) 420305.
W M

Zamberlan,
Europa Sport,
Ann Street,
Kendal,
Cumbria, LA9 6AB.
(0539) 724740.
F

Typical Kit List for Backpacking

Rucksack
Tent
Sleeping bag
Sleeping mat
Stove
Fuel
Food
Water container
Water purifying tablets or filter

Waterproofs
Boots
Warm underwear
Shorts
T-shirt
Lightweight trousers or breeches

Socks (at least 2 pairs)
Hat
Gloves
Underpants,
2 pairs
Pullover,
fleece or fibre-pile top
Extra warm clothing, depending on
    conditions

Compass
Maps and map case
Pocket knife

Note pad and pens

First-aid kit
Wash kit (should contain
    biodegradable soap)
Toilet paper (unbleached)
Lighter (cheap, disposable model,
use for burning toilet paper)
Insect repellent
Sun cream
Handkerchief

Optional
Camera/binoculars in pouch
Film
A good book
Teddy bear